Gendered Fields

Rural Studies Series

Gendered Fields

Rural Women, Agriculture, and Environment

Carolyn E. Sachs

WestviewPress

A Division of HarperCollins*Publishers*

Rural Studies Series, Sponsored by the Rural Sociological Society

All photographs by Carolyn E. Sachs except where noted

Published in 1996 in the United States of America by Westview Press, Inc., 5500 Central Avenue, Boulder, Colorado 80301-2877, and in the United Kingdom by Westview Press, 12 Hid's Copse Road, Cumnor Hill, Oxford OX2 9JJ

Library of Congress Cataloging-in-Publication Data
Sachs, Carolyn E., 1950–
  Gendered fields : rural women, agriculture, and environment/
Carolyn E. Sachs
    p. cm. —(Rural studies series)
  Includes bibliographical references (p.) and index.
  ISBN 0-8133-2519-6 (hc). — ISBN 0-8133-2520-X (pb)
    1. Women in rural development. 2. Rural women. 3. Women in
agriculture. 4. Agriculture—Environmental aspects. I. Title.
II. Series: Rural studies series of the Rural Sociological Society.
HQ1240.S28 1996
338.9'0082—dc20   95-43943
                                                                      CIP

The paper used in this publication meets the requirements of the American National Standard for Permanence of Paper for Printed Library Materials Z39.48-1984.

10   9   8   7   6   5   4   3   2   1

Contents

Tables and Photographs

Acknowledgments

In many respects this book resulted from the assistance, encouragement, and hard work of other people and organizations. Most important, I would like to thank the rural women who spent their precious time talking with me, answering questions, and inspiring me to continue this work.

The Rockefeller Foundation provided a yearlong fellowship on feminist issues and rural women at the University of Iowa that enabled me to write this book. I am grateful to Margery Wolf for initiating the program on rural women at the University of Iowa and supporting me during my time in Iowa. Laurel Zastro worked diligently as my research assistant and helped shape this work. I would like to thank my colleagues and friends in Iowa City who provided intellectual, administrative, and emotional support, including Martha Chamallas, Geeta Patel, Deb Fink, Mary Whalen, Kathy Janz, Nancy Reinke, Susan Birrell, Sally Kenney, and Florence Babb.

Much of the later work occurred at Penn State University, and I benefited greatly from conversations with and critical readings by friends and colleagues there. Robin Becker's close reading and comments on several chapters improved my writing substantially, and her encouragement pushed me to attempt new approaches. Lyn Garling lived with me and the book and contributed many insights that affected my way of thinking about agriculture and other issues discussed herein as well. Sara Postelwaite's reading and comments on the manuscript prompted me to significantly alter the text. Lumane Claude worked as a graduate assistant, researching data and bibliographic information. Ongoing collaborations and conversations with Patricia Allen on sustainable agriculture and with Dorothy Blair on ecofeminism and deep ecology challenged me to consider different approaches. I would also like to thank my colleagues in rural sociology and women's studies at Penn State.

Andy Deseran and Bo Beaulieu assisted and encouraged me from their positions as Rural Studies Series editors at Westview Press. The extremely helpful comments by Dee Ann Wenk on an earlier draft substantially improved the book. Thanks go as well to Kellie Masterson, Julia Joun, and Laurie Milford, my editors at Westview, for their encouragement, helpful comments, and support.

I am grateful for Robbie Swanger's secretarial assistance on the many drafts of the book.

Finally, I dedicate this book to my parents and sister, who made it possible for me to move down this path.

Carolyn E. Sachs

1

Situating Rural Women
in Theory and Practice

Portrayals and perceptions of rural women's lives range widely from romanticized harmonious images of women working with nature in bucolic settings, as portrayed by Sue Hubbell in *A Country Year* to representations of overworked, strong women grinding out their daily existence, as represented in Alice Walker's *Everyday Use* and Tsitsi Dangarembga's *Nervous Conditions*. Literature, theater, and other forms of cultural production generate particular portraits serving specific interests.

Sue Hubbell presents her life in the Ozark Mountains in the United States:

> My share of the Ozarks is unusual and striking. My farm lies two hundred and fifty feet above a swift, showy river to the north and a small creek to the south, its run broken by waterfalls. Creek and river join just to the east, so I live on a peninsula of land. The back fifty acres are covered with second-growth timber, and I take my firewood there. Last summer when I was cutting firewood, I came across a magnificent black walnut, tall and straight, with no jutting branches to mar its value as a timber tree. I don't expect to sell it, although even a single walnut so straight and unblemished would fetch a good price, but I cut some trees near it to give it room. The botanic name for black walnut is *Juglans nigra*—"Black Nut Tree of God," a suitable name for a tree of such dignity, and I wanted to give it space. Over the past twelve years I have learned that a tree needs space to grow, that coyotes sing down by the creek in January, that I can drive a nail into oak only when it is green, that bees know more about making honey than I do, that love can become sadness, and that there are more questions than answers. (1983:xiii)

By contrast, Alice Walker describes an older African-American rural woman:

In real life I am a large, big-boned woman with rough, man-working hands. In the winter I wear flannel nightgowns to bed and overalls during the day. I can kill and clean a hog as mercilessly as a man. My fat keeps me hot in zero weather. I can work outside all day, breaking ice to get water for washing; I can eat pork liver cooked over the open fire minutes after it comes steaming from the hog. One winter I knocked a bull calf straight in the brain between the eyes with a sledge hammer and had the meat hung up to chill before nightfall. (1986:1462)

Also portraying the difficult work of rural women, Dangarembga describes the efforts of an eight-year-old girl to earn school fees in Rhodesia in the 1960s:

More often than not I woke up before dawn, the first lifting of the darkness occurring while I was sweeping the yard. Before it was fully light I would be on my way to the river and then returning along the foot path through the trees and past other homesteads, where the women were just waking, my water-drum balanced on my head-pad of leaves and green twigs, and the drum not quite full because when it was full it was too heavy for me to lift on to my head without help. While the cocks were crowing and the hens were shaking the sleep out of their feathers, I made the fire, swept the kitchen and boiled water for washing and for tea. By the time the sun rose I was in my field, in the first days hoeing and clearing; then digging holes thirty inches apart, with a single swing of the hoe, as we had been taught in our garden periods at school; then dropping the seeds into them, two or three at a time, and covering them with one or two sweeps of my foot; then waiting for the seeds to germinate and cultivating and waiting for the weeds to grow and cultivating again. At about ten o'clock, which I judge by the height and heat of the sun, I would go to the family fields to work with my mother, sometimes my father and, in the afternoons after school, my brother. (1988:20)

Although we might understand that Hubbell, Walker, and Dangarembga present particular versions of rural women, we may not know how to evaluate and compare these representations with each other or with reality. All of these images contain kernels of truth, but they only begin to capture the diversity, complexity, and contradictions evident in rural women's lives—in which work, knowledge, and empowerment strategies grow directly from a place distinct from that of urban women.

What is it about rural areas that provides distinct contexts for women and gender relations, and how are these contexts shifting? Theories of rural society provide clues to answer these questions. High levels of poverty in the countryside are often ignored because of the dominance of urban places. Environmental degradation creates new sources of stress for rural people and places, and agricultural intensification changes work and livelihood strategies. Global restructuring brings new employment to rural places. All of these factors set the stage for particular forms of social and gender relations in rural localities. However, for the most part, rural social theories inadequately conceptualize gender relations. Urban-based feminist theory and practice also inadequately address the context of rural women's lives. A major project of feminist thinking involves "decentering," that is, altering the concept that Western, white, urban, middle-class women universally represent women. As feminist theorists and practitioners struggle to address critiques of racism, classism, westernism, northernism, colonialism, and heterosexism, new versions of feminism emerge that acknowledge the diversity of women's experiences. Rural women constitute yet another category of women that theorists have not thoroughly considered.

Although rural women's lives differ from those of their urban counterparts, we must not view rural women as homogeneous, as they differ by race, class, ethnicity, and sexuality; in short, there is no universal rural woman. Women have lived and worked in rural areas as farmers, farmers' wives, slaves, landowners, agricultural workers, mothers, and healers. In many parts of the world, rural women work harder, suffer greater material deprivation, and have less access to income-earning and employment opportunities than urban or rural men, or urban women. Although sometimes oppressed and exploited, rural women also create and shape rural life.

This book fits within the broader effort of feminist scholarship to decenter the experiences of white, Western, upper-middle-class, urban women by expanding the field to include the experiences and understandings of groups of women outside these conventional categories. I use feminist theory to explore the commonalities and differences in rural women's experiences while infusing feminist and rural social theories with rural women's understandings and strategies for coping, surviving, shaping, and changing their daily lives. The overarching purpose of this book is to expand feminist theory to include the study of rural women and to provide a theoretical basis for understanding and transforming the institutional subordination of rural women.

What Is Rural?

Changes in rural areas and in scholarly work on rural life raise the question of how to define "rural." Drawing boundaries between rural and urban people's lives poses problems for scholars and policymakers. Theories on society traditionally present dichotomous distinctions between rural and urban places and people. This oppositional approach characterizes much social theory, which assigns such polar traits as gemeinschaft/gesellschaft, organic/mechanical, traditional/modern, and folk/urban to various societies. These dichotomous distinctions tend to disregard site-specific differences and to view rural areas as homogeneous and unchanging. They neglect the continuous movement of people between urban and rural locations and assume a linear progression toward urban social relations. Recent theoretical work on uneven development between urban and rural places (Harvey, 1989; Lyson and Falk, 1993) and the impact of global economic restructuring force a reassessment of the value of these categories.

We typically see rural life as synonymous with agriculture and farm communities; however, demographic shifts, capitalization of agriculture, and global economic restructuring drastically alter rural people's daily lives and challenge us to reconsider the nature of rural life. Recognizing that only a small proportion of people living in rural areas in advanced industrial economies work in agriculture, rural sociologists, geographers, and others struggle to redefine rurality. At one extreme is Howard Newby, a leading British scholar of rural life. Newby argues for the abandonment of the concept "rural" as theoretically untenable in light of the declining importance of agriculture in rural areas. As Whatmore describes Newby's approach, "Cast adrift from its agricultural 'anchor' the category 'rural' effectively became theoretically abandoned" (Whatmore, 1993:605). In the United States, William Friedland (1982) also notes increasing homogeneity between rural and urban places. He contends that agricultural relations no longer characterize rural society and that a gemeinschaft-like "rural society" is essentially nonexistent. However, these conceptual rejections of the rural category do not sit well with some other rural theorists who challenge the theoretical extinction of the term "rurality." For Sarah Whatmore, the significance of rurality is "centered on the forcefulness of the idea and experience of rurality in social and political struggles over identity and environment rather than on a territorial definition of rural as a category of social space" (1993:607).

In developing regions, the rural category seems less problematic because a large proportion of people continue to live and work in rural spaces and engage in agriculture. However, in all regions of the world, fewer rural households practice agriculture, and many of them depend on both nonagricultural and agricultural activities for their survival. Consequently, fewer people throughout the world depend on agriculture as their sole means of survival. According to Whatmore and others, rurality does not need to be defined solely in terms of reliance on agriculture.

Following Whatmore, I argue that both the idea and the experience of rurality impact the lives of women and men in many localities. Rural identity, not necessarily bound to agriculture, may actually transcend rural localities. Men and women alike move between rural and urban spaces, carrying their experiences and identities with them. Scholars theorizing about the connection between space and social relations face challenges as rural areas continue to shift away from reliance on agriculture. Examining this shift is crucial to understanding rural and urban women's lives because it holds the potential to change the balance of gender relations. To further this effort, I draw herein on the experiences of rural women in the United States, Africa, Asia, and Latin America to contrast and compare the differences, similarities, and complexities in rural women's lives.

Theorizing About Rural Women

Scholarly work on rural women's lives in particular locations and time periods has flourished in recent years, yet theories of rural society and feminist scholarship incorporate only fragments of this work. Feminist theorists have moved beyond liberal, radical, and Marxist categories of analysis, to develop new feminist epistemologies and methodologies. In this book, I draw on several recent breakthroughs and debates in feminist theory, including (1) feminist epistemologies and women's standpoint, (2) an understanding of race, class, ethnic, and sexuality differences in women's lives, and (3) women's strategies of resistance to counter various forms of oppression as they attempt to shape and change their lives.

Throughout the book, I explicate the way current debates in feminist theory relate to the lives of rural women. In addition, I illustrate how observing rural women's lives can illuminate feminist debates. I assume that rural women's experiences and perspectives are distinct from those of urban women and are of consequence to feminist theory and practice. To that end, I explore four questions that are particularly important for feminist theory and understanding rural women's lives:

- what are women's relationships to the natural environment?
- what are the forms of patriarchal relations in the countryside?
- how does global economic restructuring affect rural women?
- what strategies do rural women utilize for shaping their lives?

Women and the Environment

Some feminists argue that Western science and capitalist development strategies devalue women's vast knowledge and experience of the natural world. Many rural women work in agricultural production as their major life activity and interact heavily with the natural world in their efforts for subsistence needs for water, fuel, and housing. While everyone must depend on the natural world for subsistence, Western or urbanized people are often remote from the sources of their needs. In contrast, Third

World women often spend their daily lives gathering fuelwood from forests, collecting drinking water from streams, and raising plants and animals for their families' food. Structural shifts in global and local economies alter rural people's connection to the natural world, encourage rural-to-urban migration, change work and livelihood strategies in the countryside, and alter women's strategies for survival.

Rural women thoroughly know and interact with their local environments. For example, because they often supply water for their families and also make sanitary arrangements, they know how to locate water sources and assess water quality and can compensate for seasonal fluctuations in water availability (Rodda, 1991). Feminist critics of science point to women's knowledge as providing alternative angles of vision, and they question the legitimacy of Western science as the sole source of authority. Scientists breed hybrid seeds with little recognition that rural women farmers not only know about a diverse array of seeds but understand how to adapt them to particular ecological conditions. The global ecological crisis compels those involved in environmental movements to question received ideas about resources, land use, and public policy. Consequently, Western science may now be complicated by the knowledge that indigenous populations, of course including women, bring to these issues. The ecofeminist movement, in fact, emphasizes the explicit connections between women and the environment.

Rural women's connections to the natural world can inform feminist theory. Their knowledge and experiences offer a materialist base for ecofeminism and suggest practical strategies for solving ecological crises. Throughout this book, I emphasize the depth and value of women's knowledge. Furthermore, I illustrate the ways in which scientists, agricultural policymakers, and patriarchal family structures devalue women's knowledge.

Patriarchal Relations in Agriculture

Although women do the majority of work in agriculture at the global level, elder men, for the most part, still own the land, control women's labor, and make agricultural decisions in patriarchal social systems. In most areas of the world, the family remains the primary unit of production in agriculture. State policies in the United States, Latin America, and Africa often explicitly support these patriarchal family farms through extension programs, government loans, and marketing policies. It is thus timely to reexamine gender relations when the continual demise of family farms and growth of agro-industries are disrupting traditional patriarchal systems.

Although patriarchal family structures and cultural traditions tend to confine rural women, their subordination remains incomplete. Such women are by no means powerless, as is revealed by their ability to cope, survive, work together, change their lives, and, as Joan Jensen (1986) puts it, "loosen the bonds." Structural changes in agricultural production throughout the world that undermine the viability of many family farms alter gender divisions of labor in families, thus setting the stage for shifts in the form of patriarchal control over women's lives. Although elaborate debates and discussions on the demise or persistence of family farms have ensued, rural scholars' failure to direct attention to the centrality of gender relations in maintaining and changing family farms limits their understanding of these shifts.

Scholarly work on women in agriculture during the past decade has focused primarily on documenting the variety and extent of women's contributions in particular localities. Such studies suggest that women do the majority of work in agriculture at the global level (Blumberg, 1981; Poats, Schmink, and Spring, 1988). Despite these documentation efforts, few state policies, such as provision of credit or agricultural training, have been established to improve farm women's lives. Thus, there is a need for scholars to reconceptualize women's work and rethink strategies for improving women's lives on farms.

Agrarian and domestic discourses concerning rural families bolster patriarchal relations. Societies continue to legitimize the subordination of women through romanticized narratives that misinterpret rural women's lives. These discourses take various forms in different regions and localities. For example, in Europe and the United States agrarian ideologies romanticize and celebrate rural life and families, often covering or veiling women's situations in these communities and families. In many Asian countries, colonial discourses advocating female domestication and the "housewifization" of women reinforce or reconstruct patriarchal relations in rural places.

As an increasing proportion of the world's food and agricultural production shifts to large-scale, nonfamily-managed farms, women do not necessarily benefit. Increased export crop production and the incursion of agro-industries into rural areas increases women's wage employment in agriculture and alters women's subordination to patriarchal authority within the family. However, these changes may or may not expand women's options. For example, in the United States, the transition from family to large-scale farms has not significantly improved women's position in rural areas. Women on family farms seldom gain economic power as agricultural enterprises expand; likewise, few women hold positions of power in agro-industries. Rather, such systems tend to exacerbate class, ethnic, and racial differences and privileges in rural areas and often rely heavily on the cheap labor of working-class people, especially racial and ethnic minorities. In the past, women working in large-scale agricultural enterprises not owned by their families frequently suffered, and they continue to suffer exploitative working conditions today. Black women worked in cotton fields under slavery in the United States from the 1500s to 1862. Latinas today work under difficult conditions for low pay in the fields owned by large agribusiness firms in California. Female Tamil tea pickers on plantations in Sri Lanka live in substandard housing and receive low wages. Gender, race, and class identities are important factors in agricultural systems. Frequently, certain groups of women—often racial and ethnic minorities—perform hard physical labor that would be considered men's work and unsuitable for women whose families own farms. Women of racial and ethnic minorities claim that they experience forms of exploitation unknown to women in the dominant culture. Nowhere are such claims as obvious as in agriculture.

Global Restructuring

Global economic restructuring is characterized by the ascendance of finance capital, industrial reorganization, and labor market shifts. Such massive economic restructuring depends heavily on an increase in the workload of women in formal, informal, and household economies in both rural and urban areas. Shifts in rural women's daily lives and their abilities to resist patriarchal forms cannot be separated from the continual growth and expansion of capitalism and international political struggles for power. Rural people and places enter the global system on unfavorable terms. For example, debt crises in the 1980s and early 1990s forced Third World governments to stabilize their recessionary economies by producing exports for foreign exchange, limiting spending for health, education, and welfare, and reducing public sector employment. These government policies place increasing burdens on rural households and often demand more work from women in the informal economy and in their households.

To be sure, the economic crisis of the 1980s and 1990s in the Third World is not an anomaly. Rather, it is the legacy of the resistance to capitalism and colonialism by generations of long-suffering Third World men and women (Acosta-Belen and Bose, 1990). Nonetheless, the current shifts in global and national economies are so rapid and dramatic that we need to rethink the context of women's lives. Understanding rural women's lives in relation to global restructuring is a complicated undertaking that involves uncovering multiple layers of relationships. First, I explore how global restructuring differentially affects rural and urban people and places. These effects also vary by gender, race, ethnicity, class, and sexuality. Then I focus on several shifts in the global economy that have particular significance for rural people: restructuring of agriculture, agro-industrial development, reorganization of employment in mining and logging, movement of manufacturing away from urban centers in the West, and the growth of the service economy.

Women's Resistance Efforts

The vast majority of feminist movements are centered in urban areas. In comparison to urban women, rural women remain reluctant to form feminist organizations that focus specifically on actively challenging male authority and privilege. For example, in the United States, rural women tend to join political organizations that support their families or farm organizations rather than participating in organizations related specifically to women's empowerment. However, some rural women actively promote women's rights. For example, rural women in Zimbabwe who participated in resistance struggles demanded rights under the new political regime. However, unfortunately, for them, it was primarily elite urban women under the new regime who led the movement for women's rights and benefited from policy changes. Although rural women have not been at the forefront of feminist movements, they take steps to significantly shape their lives. We can see the work of grass-roots organizations in cooperatives, rotating credit schemes, resistance to environmental destruction, and women's land movements to see women taking action. Reconsidering what constitutes resistance allows a broader understanding of how rural women struggle to shape their lives and the rural places they inhabit.

Writers of fiction, such as Charlotte Perkins Gilman (*Herland*, 1979) and Sally Gearheart (*The Wanderground*, 1978), chose to situate their feminist utopias in rural areas. Feminist utopianists and ecofeminists alike envision rural areas as the context for a thriving feminist culture and society in opposition to patriarchal culture. Given the urban roots of feminist movements, how do we account for the persistence of the rural utopia? I examine here why rural women remain less likely than urban women to form organizations challenging the patriarchal structures that dominate their lives. I then explore the types of resistance strategies adopted by rural women, including contemporary radical or visionary projects by rural women and the possibilities they hold for challenging patriarchal forms of organization. Throughout, I emphasize how class, ethnicity, race, and nationality determine women's forms of resistance.

A Note on Perspectives, Methods, and Data

This book draws on my research on and documentation of the experiences of rural women from different regions of the world. Although I focus on contemporary rural women's lives, I also use historical accounts to provide a context for contemporary situations. My major sources of information include studies of rural women, rural women's writings, and interviews with rural women conducted both by myself and other researchers. I have collected data through in-depth interviews in multiple studies of rural women's lives. In the course of different research projects,

I have interviewed many women including women farmers in the United States, women working in cropping systems in Swaziland, women in the sustainable agriculture movement, farm and nonfarm women in rural Pennsylvania, women farmers and cooperative members in Zimbabwe, and U.S. rural women involved in the women's land movement. Throughout the book, I use the voices of rural women.

My interest in rural women's lives, especially rural women's involvement in agriculture, evolved from my early experiences and academic interests. I spent my early childhood in white upper-middle-class suburbs, with weekend forays into the countryside to visit relatives or go on vacation. Later as a young woman, I lived or visited for various periods of time in small towns or the countryside in Michigan, California, and Kentucky. While I enjoyed many of the activities that rural life affords, the lack of diversity in rural society felt stifling as I moved back and forth between those very different settings.

My first adult foray into agriculture was as a fruit picker in Wenatchee, Washington. I had just bicycled across the country and had arrived on the West Coast with little money. Other cyclists said it was easy to make money picking apples. A friend and I rode over the Cascades to investigate this, hoping to earn some quick money to continue our bicycle tour. Physically strong and adapted to living outside with minimal material provisions, we began picking apples, undaunted by the prospect of sleeping in the orchard and doing hard physical labor. However, as white middle-class young women, we were unprepared for the unsanitary living conditions, withheld pay, low wages, dangers from chemicals, mistreatment by employers, disrespect from government workers, and disdain of local people. When my friend and I left the orchards two months later, we did not have much more money than when we arrived. We carried a range of experiences away with us, and as a feminist and sociologist, I came away with many unanswered questions about our agricultural system. Since that time, I have studied the sociology of agriculture and conducted research on women in agriculture, sustainable agriculture, agriculture science, and the food system. I have visited farms and rural areas and spoken with rural women in the United States, Zimbabwe, Swaziland, Cameroon, Egypt, Sri Lanka, and Vietnam. I have repeatedly discovered similarities in the problems women agriculturalists face, as well as differences in their ways of coping, surviving, and changing their situations.

2

Feminist Theory and Rural Women

Despite limited attention to rural women's lives, in recent years feminist theory has matured, developed, and become ever more inclusive. Moving beyond the attempts of the early important work of various feminisms—liberal, socialist, and radical—to categorize women's lives and experiences in terms of established theoretical frameworks, feminist theorists have broken new ground. New feminist theories have been created in the search to understand women's daily lives, their angles of vision, and differences among women. Much of this new theoretical work, still to be incorporated into studies of rural women's lives, offers possibilities and new avenues for studying rural women.

For the most part, scholarly studies on rural women document rural women's work but have often remained in "feminist empiricism" in Sandra Harding's (1986) term, meaning that the studies document the efforts of women that remain invisible from the male-dominant perspective. Studies of rural women—few and far between until the late 1970s—flourished with the rise of feminist scholarship and contributed substantially to our understanding of rural women's lives; their authors advocated change in rural social theories (Whatmore, 1991; Flora, 1985; Tickameyer and Bokemeier, 1988; Fink, 1992). Despite the excellent scholarship on rural women since the 1970s, rural social theories largely fail to incorporate insights from feminist work. Feminist theorists as well as rural social theorists remain inattentive to rural women's concerns; their urban-focused, theoretical work inadequately addresses the context of rural women's lives.

Essential first steps for research on rural women included documenting the extent of women's work, creating an adequate definition of work, and pointing out changes in farm and rural women's work. For example, studies of farm women in the United States revealed that women participate in farming activities to a greater extent than typically assumed; they do the abundance of both household labor and subsistence production, and they often keep their family's farm financially afloat through their off-farm work (Fink, 1986; Sachs, 1983; Rosenfeld, 1985). Studies of rural women in many regions of the world focus on the importance and inter-section of women's productive and reproductive labor (Beneria and Sen, 1981). For example, studies on sub-Saharan Africa report that women produce approximately 80 percent of the food, in addition to collecting fire-wood, providing water, and performing innumerable other activities to satisfy the subsistence needs of their families (Blumberg, 1992: 1).

However, merely documenting women's work proved insufficient for providing strategies for women to alter gender relations and enhance their lives. Strategies put forward as a result of these studies included providing women with credit, increasing their access to land, and educating them in agriculture. For the most part, governments moved slowly to adopt these strategies; some nations implemented policies, but in most nations women generally lack access to these resources. Perhaps major theoretical breakthroughs in feminist theory may provide new insights and strategies for changing rural social relations to improve women's lives.

In the passages that follow I consider to what extent three significant theoretical breakthroughs and ongoing debates in feminist theory seem relevant and responsive to the study of rural women's lives, including (1) feminist epistemology, (2) awareness of difference, and (3) women's resis-tance. Moreover, advances in feminist thought go well beyond these three breakthroughs, and further on other strands of feminist theorizing are brought into play, introducing ecofeminism, feminist critiques of science, critiques of patriarchy, feminist critiques of global restructuring, and new conceptualizations of women's work. I use these theoretical insights as points of departure to address specific aspects of rural women's lives— their relationships to nature, patriarchal families, global restructuring, and strategies for change.

Feminist Epistemologies: From Women's Standpoint to Situated Knowledge

The mind of the man and the mind of the woman is the same but this business of liv-ing makes women use their minds in ways that men don't even have to think about.
— **Ruth Shay, quoted in Collins, 1990**

The building of feminist theories of knowledge, or epistemology, con-stitutes one of the major achievements and ongoing efforts in feminist scholarship. Women's standpoint, a central concept in feminist theories of knowledge, provides the basis of feminist standpoint theory. This theoretical orientation emphasizes that women's shared common set of social experiences—such as subordination to men, or responsibility for house-work and child care, or fewer opportunities in the labor market—pro-vides them with ways of seeing and understanding that differ from those of men. As Bettina Aptheker succinctly explains, "Women have a con-sciousness of social reality that is distinct from that put forth by men" (1989:7). Women's consciousness, or standpoint, is not necessarily eman-cipatory. However, feminism can transform women's understandings into a feminist standpoint that some argue provides truer understanding of social life than is possible from the male perspective (Harding, 1986).

The concept of women's standpoint remains the subject of much debate and discussion among feminist scholars. Most standpoint theorists agree that women's consciousness is socially constructed, deriving from their common set of social experiences, or in the words of the black inner-city resident quoted previously, Ruth Shay, from "this business of living." They also generally agree that women's consciousness does not derive from their biology and actively reject or shy away from postulating about an "essential" woman. But controversy remains concerning what exactly composes the everyday life experiences that provide women with differ-ent ways of viewing the world. Several troubling questions raised in the conceptualization of women's and feminist standpoints include: What exactly is this different kind of knowledge that women possess? Where does the knowledge come from? What is the relationship between wom-en's standpoint and feminist standpoints? Is this knowledge privileged? How does this knowledge contribute to possibilities for changing gender relations and the world?

Different answers to these questions emerge from two distinctly differ-ent versions of feminist standpoint theory associated with socialist femi-nist and radical feminist perspectives. Within each of these schools of thought, multiple turns and reinterpretations led only to deeper questions. Finally, Donna Haraway's (1991) incisive perceptions resulted in radical rethinking and the possibility that feminists should reject the very notion of a privileged feminist standpoint. In this regards it is worth discussing the various debates within socialist feminist and radical feminist traditions related to the women's or feminist standpoint, following Haraway's argu-ment in calling for a focus on women's situated knowledge.

Women's Ways of Knowing

Harding's (1986) work on feminist epistemologies stands at the forefront of conceptualizing women's ways of knowing. In her excellent book on feminism and science, she examines how earlier feminist critiques of sci-ence evolved into theories of feminist ways of knowing. She outlines the evolution of feminist standpoint epistemologies, especially the socialist feminist approach, and delineates the different arguments used to explain women's particular and privileged viewpoint. The theoretical basis for the socialist feminist approach is grounded in the Marxist argument that all knowledge is socially constructed, that the dominant social ideology emerges from the ideology of the dominant class, and that oppressed classes hold the most advantageous standpoint (Jaggar, 1983). Using this perspective, the socialist feminist philosophy holds that women's consciousness, or standpoint, emerges from the social context of their lives, specifically from the sexual division of labor and from women's subordination to men. Following Marx's line of argument that the proletariat, due to its subordinate position, holds the most advantageous position for interpreting and overthrowing capitalism, socialist feminists anchor women's privileged standpoint in their subordinate position. Like the advantaged consciousness of the proletariat vis-à-vis the bourgeoisie, women's standpoint, which is preferred and less distorted than men's, results from women's common oppression and offers the possibility for comprehending and transforming patriarchal relations.

Within the socialist feminist tradition, scholars such as Hillary Rose, Nancy Hartsock, and Dorothy Smith differ about the everyday life experiences that provide women with particular standpoints. Rose (1983) views women's work activities as characterized by the unity of hand, brain, and heart. In contrast to men's activities, which typically separate mental and manual labor and often lack emotional labor, women's activities provide a different and fuller basis of knowledge. For Hartsock (1983), women's standpoint comes from their immersion in subsistence and child care-activities, which place them in a more sensuous, concrete, and relational world than men typically inhabit. Thus, in studying farm women, for example, we might expect that their responsibility for emotional labor provides them with a different perspective than men concerning family farms. Smith (1987), a sociologist who long advocated the existence of a feminist standpoint, also sees women's standpoint as deriving from their work activities, but goes further and argues that women's work also shapes men's consciousness. Because women take care of men's bodies and their immediate surroundings, men remain free to dwell in the world of the abstract. Thus, the particular character of women's activities enables men to inhabit a different world and to interpret the world in a distorted fashion. Smith contends that the more successfully women perform their work the more invisible such work becomes to men—thus women's work seems natural, instinctual, or emotional. For example, an African woman describes her husband's inability to see the multiple tasks she performs: "I sometimes wonder if this man sees what I do. I have just returned from the garden, and I am having a cup of tea while the baby suckles and I prepare food. He wants me to cut his hair right away. After that he will want to bathe and I have not fetched the water" (Obbo, 1990:213). Another woman in the United States, Rosa Wakefield, a black domestic worker, sums up how the invisibility of black women's work allows others to dwell in the abstract and distorts the consciousness of those not engaged in such work: "If you eats these dinners and don't cook'em, if you wears these clothes and don't buy or iron them, then you might start thinking that the good fairy or some spirit did all that. . . . Black folks don't have no time to be thinking like that. . . . But when you don't have anything else to do, you can think like that. It's bad for your mind, though" (as quoted in Collins, 1990:26). Based on Marxist understanding of consciousness, the oppressed classes (black women in this case) hold a privileged position for interpreting reality and also have an interest in changing reality.

In her review of the feminist standpoint position, Harding delineates the proposed rationale for the privileged feminist standpoint, claiming to cover the entire spectrum of feminist epistemologies. Jacqueline Zita (1989) and Liz Stanley (1990) correctly point out that Harding thoroughly covers the socialist feminist position but barely acknowledges radical feminists' conception of the feminist standpoint.

Radical feminists propose that women's standpoint emerges primarily from the sexual exploitation of women by men: Sexual domination therefore determines women's consciousness and is what must be overcome. They criticize socialist feminists' focus on analyzing and changing the division of labor between women and men, while apparently overlooking how rape, sexual abuse, pornography, and prostitution exploit and denigrate women. As Zita suggests, "gender must be seen as more strenuously and additionally created through the deployment of power in the codes of sexual violence and sexual practice" (1989:162–163). Radical feminists, who are criticized for posing ideological solutions in the form of an alternative women's culture, in fact also see women's subordination deriving from material reality—in this case, from the sexual division of the erotic as well as the sexual division of labor.

Alison Jaggar (1983) credits radical feminists for the insights that women's perceptions of reality are different from those of men and that male interpretations are often misinterpretations that distort reality. However, she identifies several problems that underlie the radical feminist standpoint. First, radical feminists posit that women's innate faculties of perception, or ways of knowing, are unavailable to men. Jaggar sees no evidence that women possess innate faculties of perception that men lack. Instead, she suggests that, due to their subordination, women have developed particular sensitivity to behavioral cues. Second, radical feminists emphasize women's sensitivity, based on emotions, to information men fail to notice—information both different and more dependable than the type men can notice. While concurring about the importance of feelings in identifying questions, Jaggar seems less sure that feelings provide systematic answers to problems. We must remember as well that feelings and emotions come from social constructions; they do not derive out of thin air. Thus, radical and socialist feminists generally agree that women's standpoints derive from their experiences of domination, but feminists disagree about what exactly constitutes these experiences, and how and why this knowledge is privileged remains problematic, particularly since it may have something to do with why many women reject feminism.

Why Women Reject Feminism

Socialist and radical feminist theorists face problems explaining why women's standpoint is not always a feminist standpoint and why the majority of women actually reject feminism. We see a distinction between women's standpoint and a feminist standpoint: A feminist viewpoint does not immediately derive from women's experiences. Following Marx, socialist feminists explain how the antifeminist consciousness of many women derives from their daily lives: "The daily experience of oppressed groups provides them with an immediate awareness of their own suffering but they do not perceive immediately the underlying causes of this suffering nor even necessarily perceive it as oppression" (Jaggar, 1983:382). As Dorothy Smith (1987) puts it, women's experience of their own labor remains incomprehensible within men's conceptual schemes. Because men's abstract concepts define the world, women remain unable to comprehend or express their experiences in an undistorted form. Only through developing a feminist consciousness (in a similar manner to Marx's argument for the development of working-class consciousness) can women come to understand their oppressed position and be empowered to come together to change their situation. Radical feminists explain women's rejection of feminism as the result of the dominance of patriarchal culture. Alison Jaggar (1983) and Rita Felski (1989), among others, criticize this approach as overly deterministic since it conceives of patriarchal ideology as homogeneous and uniformly repressive.

Situated Knowledge—Moving Beyond Standpoints

Pushed by women's rejection of feminism in tandem with feminists' inability to agree on which feminist values constitute a feminist standpoint, several theorists have moved beyond the concept of standpoint. Donna Haraway states, "There is no single feminist standpoint because our maps require too many dimensions for that metaphor to ground our visions" (1991:96). Rather than arguing for any one privileged feminist standpoint, Haraway sees knowledge as situated and embodied and calls for "politics and epistemologies of location, positioning and situating, where partiality and not universality is the condition of being heard to make rational knowledge claims. These are claims on people's lives; the view from a body, always a complex, contradictory, structuring and struc- tured body, versus the view from above, from nowhere, from simplicity" (1991:195). She warns feminists against following in the footsteps of pow- erful, dominant groups in claiming to see from above, from nowhere, from unlocatable positions. Rather, she insists that all knowledge is par- tial and embodied; feminists do not need to claim universality to make rational knowledge claims.

But recognition that knowledge claims are partial threatens to under- mine the very basis of feminism. What of the standpoints of the subju- gated? Are they preferred over the partial perspectives of dominant groups? Haraway acknowledges that there are good reasons for trusting the vantage points of the subjugated, but she also recognizes the dangers in romanticizing and uncritically accepting the views of the less powerful.

> The standpoints of the subjugated are not 'innocent' positions. On the con- trary, they are preferred because in principle they are least likely to allow denial of the critical and interpretive core of all knowledge. They are savvy to modes of denial through repression, forgetting, and disappearing acts— ways of being nowhere while claiming to see comprehensively. . . 'Subjugated' standpoints are preferred because they promise more adequate, sustained, objective, transforming accounts of the world. But how to see from below is a problem. (1991:191)

Haraway's concept of situated knowledge proves particularly helpful in grappling with questions relating to rural women: What knowledge do rural women possess? Is rural women's knowledge privileged? Has rural women's standpoint been transformed into a feminist epistemology? To what extent do rural women's standpoints provide a basis for changing gender relations? Rural women's knowledge is situated in their particular localities and daily activities. In most cultural settings, rural women's sit- uated perspectives come from their connections to the environment, from their work in subsistence, reproductive, and productive realms, and from the patriarchal nature of rural families. These experiences provide partic- ular angles of vision or partial perspectives that offer the possibility of seeing differently than from dominant perspectives. For example, using the concept of situated knowledge, we might explore what knowledge

Vietnamese women farmers possess concerning cropping systems or how African women farmers experience the effects of patriarchal authority on their families. The concept of women's situated knowledge offers particular promise for exploring rural women's connections to the natural environment. Examining rural women's situated knowledge offers possibilities for ecofeminists, who draw on the special connection between women's lives and the natural world to build a social and political movement (King, 1989; Diamond and Orenstein, 1990). With the exception of the works of Carolyn Merchant (1989), Vandana Shiva (1988), and Bina Agarwal (1991), ecofeminist analysis rarely explores the connections between rural women's daily lives and the natural environment. For the most part, women's connection to the natural world is described in metaphors associating women with nature or in the search for past matrilineal cultures that both granted relatively high status to women and had harmonious relations with the natural world. Understanding the daily lives of rural women and their situated knowledge may well lay the groundwork for developing a feminist standpoint with a materialist as well as an ideological justification for ecofeminist theory and practice.

Multiple rural women's standpoints exist. Rural women's standpoints may be preferable because such women are "subjugated"—they experience extremely oppressive conditions as a result of the gender divisions of labor in rural areas and the patriarchal conditions that pervades rural life; nevertheless, their standpoint remain only partial. Rural women's subjugated and situated knowledge offers these women possibilities for different and possibly emancipatory knowledge and social action. However, as a result of their subjugated positions, they remain plagued by the problem of how to "see from below." Rural women's knowledge and experience only rarely results in feminist politics and activism. Due to the particular patriarchal relations that characterize social relations in rural areas, rural women in Vietnam, Zimbabwe, and the United States resist but seldom directly challenge patriarchal dominance.

Thus, Haraway's insistence on partial and situated knowledge resolves the problem for feminists attempting to define the feminist standpoint position and sets the stage for the development of a postmodern feminism. For our purposes here, postmodernism is defined as philosophical skepticism, more precisely as the deconstruction of ideas concerning truth, knowledge, power, self, and language that have characterized Western thinking since the Enlightenment (Flax, 1990).

Postmodernism, with its focus on situated or partial knowledge, also addresses questions and controversies surrounding the notion that there is a universal woman and therefore, a woman's, or feminist, standpoint. Recognition of the multiple forms of oppression experienced by women in various racial, class, ethnic, and sexuality groups raises serious questions about the existence of a feminist standpoint, or common basis of solidarity for women. Black feminists, lesbian feminists, feminists from Asia, Africa, and Latin America criticize the notion of a universal feminist position for defining women's existence in terms of Western, white, heterosexual, middle-class women's experiences and for failing to include multiple voices and experiences. Harding (1991) argues that standpoint theory is not necessarily essentialist and is not overtly racist or class biased; rather, the emphasis on beginning research and scholarship with the realities of women's lives can be equally helpful for understanding the lives of women in oppressed classes, races, and cultures.

Postmodern theory argues that we speak with a multitude of voices and subjectivities in which no particular vantage point can be more privileged than another. Perhaps as Jane Parpart (1993) suggests, postmodernism offers lessons for women and development theory and practice. Questioning the assumption that Third World development means westernization or modernization, postmodernists recognize the need to look to local, subjugated knowledge for guidance. Looking to the reality of the daily lives and experiences of Third World women, recognizing differences between women, and not privileging white, western feminists are ways to provide new possibilities for challenging "development discourse that represents Third World women as the vulnerable other" (1993:456). The turn toward postmodernism and the notion of fractured identities, increasingly embraced by some feminist theorists, leaves others skeptical of joining the largely male-dominated postmodern discourse, because it seems to pull the rug out from under feminist and socialist struggles (Zita, 1989). Some feminists criticize this position, arguing that the multitude of subjectivities seems to end in total relativism precluding political action.

From my perspective, the greatest political danger of postmodernism comes with an emphasis on difference and diversity devoid of analysis of power and oppression or political agendas. The postmodern turn in scholarship oozes into our work and increasingly enters academic and political dialogue. Work by feminist theorists struggling with issues of diversity and difference leads the way in overcoming the depoliticizing possibilities of postmodernism via grounded and political analyses of difference.

Difference—Race, Class, Ethnicity, Nationality, and Sexuality

The strength of women lies in recognizing differences between us as creative, and in standing to those distortions which we inherited without blame, but which are now ours to alter. The angers of women can transform differences through insight into power. For anger between peers births change, not destruction, and the discomfort and sense of loss it often causes is not fatal, but a sign of growth.

—Audre Lorde, 1982

Early feminist theories and practices assumed the existence of a "universal woman"—and the experiences of white, upper-middle-class, heterosexual, Western women represented all women. Now feminist analysts and practitioners generally recognize the imperative of taking into account differences between women according to race, class, ethnicity, nationality, and sexuality. Rather than preoccupying ourselves with decentering male experiences, situations, power, and interests, feminists must also come to terms with decentering the universal woman in feminist thought (Harding, 1991). New versions of feminism acknowledge the diversity of women's experiences. Ongoing struggles with these differences in women's studies and the women's movement raise questions about whether it is possible or desirable to have a unified women's movement.

Most agree that women's experiences differ by race, class, ethnicity, nationality, and sexuality, that the form of women's oppression varies. However, the question for feminist theory and practice remains whether women share experiences that can result in common actions or strategies of resistance to patriarchal practices and ideologies. Aptheker (1989) argues that the diversity of women's experience does not negate the pervasiveness of institutionalized subordination of women as the commonality underlying women's experience. Thus, she insists that constructing a feminist vision remains possible through seeking commonality to be arrived at by seriously considering women's diversity. Women's diverse experiences need not be a source of division and weakness in the women's movement; we can learn to use these differences as sources of strength (Jaggar, 1983).

Others are not so sure. Numerous writers view the differences among women as a factor that creates varying needs, movements, and theoretical traditions. Teresa Amott and Julie Matthaei (1991) argue that no common experience of gender exists across race, ethnicity, and class lines, nor do women share a common experience of gender oppression. Nevertheless, they see that the possibility for dialogue exists. Liz Stanley acknowledges that women share experiences of oppression, but not the same experiences: "The social contexts within which different kinds of women live, work, struggle, and make sense of their lives differ widely across the world and between different groupings of women" (1990:22). Janet Momsen and Janet Townsend (1987) see a more complicated picture and argue that worldwide continuity of the subordination of women coexists with regional and local diversity.

Women of color express particular concern with the tendency of white feminists to equivocate concerning the importance of "difference." Feminist theorists tend to recognize and discuss difference but then submerge difference in the rhetoric of commonality of oppression. Gloria Anzaldúa (1990) points out that diversity and difference are ambiguous terms, defined differently by white feminists and women of color. As she states, "Often white feminists want to minimize racial difference by taking comfort in the fact that we are all women. . . . They are usually annoyed with the actuality (though not the concept) of 'differences,' want to blur racial difference, want to smooth things out" (1990:xxi). For women of color or others who live in multiple worlds with multiple identities, difference and multiplicity compose the context of their understandings. Writings by African-American, Third World, and lesbian feminists recenter feminist theory and move the debate on difference forward.

African-American Women

Patricia Hill Collins's (1990) excellent book thoroughly describes the contours of black feminist thought. Collins's analysis emphasizes that race, class, and gender oppression are not additive but are interconnected and part of a historically created system. Black women's particular angle of vision or standpoint emerges from their legacy of struggle. They share the experience of being black women in a society that denigrates women of African descent, and they are unable to separate the experience of being female from being black. Collins cautions against portraying black women solely as victims of oppression or as heroic resisters. She attempts to ground a black feminist standpoint in an epistemological position that avoids the pitfalls of Marxist positivism or the relativism of postmodernism. Drawing on Haraway, she describes black feminist thought as situated, subjugated knowledge embedded in communities where African-American women live and work. She neither claims that a black feminist standpoint is "the one true interpretation of reality" or that competing knowledge claims are equal. Black women's standpoint offers one angle of vision—a partial perspective. Collins suggests that different groups, such as African-American men, Latina lesbians, or Asian-American women, validate certain ideas as true, but each group's standpoint or truth remains partial and unfinished. Dialogue, she feels, offers the possibility of resolving these truth claims, but the crucial effort is to decenter the dominant group—a feat unlikely to occur without struggle.

Recognizing differences in rural women's lives provides more complicated pictures of rural women. Much of the scholarship on rural women focuses on farm women or farmwives, or on comparing farm and nonfarm women, and fails to delve deeply into other differences in rural women's lives. Just as feminist scholars focus on middle-class white women, scholars studying women in rural areas in the United States tend to focus their attention on white, privileged farm women. Studies of rural places and of rural women tend to gloss over differences and until recently essentially ignored the situations of rural African Americans, Mexican Americans, and Native Americans, who have the highest poverty rates in the United States. In 1989, the rural poverty rate was 40 percent for African-Americans percent, 38 percent for Mexican Americans, and 30 percent for Native Americans (Rural Sociology Society Task Force on Persistent Rural Poverty, 1993:176). Scholars of rural women in the United States face a major challenge with the need to incorporate African-American, Latina, and Native American women into their work and to move these studies from the margin to the center of their theories.

Colonizing Third World Women

African-American and Third World feminists agree that Western feminism misrepresents women of color. Chandra Mohanty critiques Western feminism for portraying "Third World women as a homogeneous, undifferentiated group leading truncated lives, victimized by the combined weight of 'their' traditions, cultures, and beliefs and 'our' (Eurocentric) history" (1989–1990:180). Such portrayals inadvertently define Western women as subjects of struggle, whereas Third World women appear as inarticulate victims whose lives can be improved if they embrace a universal sisterhood that includes all women across racial and national lines. "Assumptions of privilege and ethnocentric universality on the one hand, and inadequate self-consciousness about the effect of Western scholarship on the 'third world' in the context of a world system dominated by the West on the other, characterize a sizable extent of Western feminist work on women in the third world" (Mohanty, 1991:53). Mohanty warns against Western feminist analysts' ignorance of global power relations and homogenization of Third World women into a category defined as "religious (read 'not progressive'), family oriented (read 'traditional'), legal minors (read 'they are not conscious-of-their-rights'), illiterate (read 'ignorant'), domestic (read 'backward'), and sometimes revolutionary (read 'their-country-is-in-a-state-of-war; they-must-fight!')"(1991:53). Such representations fail to acknowledge material and cultural specificity and erase resistance. Mohanty argues that Western feminists colonize the voices of Third World women; Third World women must speak as subjects participating in struggles.

   In discussing the contributions and problems of feminist analysis of African societies, Patricia Stamp applauds feminists' efforts to demonstrate the centrality of gender relations in production, and to point out the crucial economic contribution of women. Stamp highlights the problems encountered in using neo-classical and Marxist economic categories to understand African economy and society. However, she contends that much of this work fails to break through assumptions of Western feminism, for example, by favoring the economic realm over other aspects of human social relations, by assuming that family and household hold the same meaning and take the same form as in the West, and by resorting to a vague, ahistorical explanation of women's problems as related to male domination (Stamp, 1990).

As Stamp implies, discussions of rural women might easily fall into Mohanty's trap of "homogenizing" rural women and defining their lives in contrast to the more liberated lives of urban women in any given culture. In fact, scholars often consider rural women more religious, family oriented and traditional than urban women. Because sites of centers of scientific knowledge production and feminist movements are centered in urban areas, this marginalizes rural women's experiences and voices. One challenge faced by scholars involves how to avoid colonizing the voices of rural women, and how instead to seriously face and understand the different contexts of rural women's lives, not falling into the trap of portraying the universal rural woman as a white, farmwife or as a Third World woman of color who appears as the ultimate victim of patriarchy and capitalism. Feminist theorists, such as Mohanty or Collins or me, remain caught in a bind. We call for marginalized groups of women to add their perspectives to feminist discourse and practice in order to enable subjects to speak for themselves, but we realize that the academic and literary worlds are closed or alien to many of these women.

Sexuality

> *Being women together was not enough. We were different. Being gay girls together was not enough. We were different. Being black together was not enough. We were different. Being black women together was not enough. We were different. Being black dykes together was not enough. We were different.*
>
> —Audre Lorde, 1982

Lesbian feminist theory, on the cutting edge of thinking concerning sexuality and gender, challenges heterosexist assumptions of feminist theory. Lesbian theorists criticize feminist theory for excluding lesbians and construct theory more inclusive of lesbian experience (Allen, 1990; Fuss, 1991; Frye, 1983). Further, lesbian and gay theorists challenge the compulsory status of heterosexuality and point to the precarious and terrifying boundaries between heterosexuality and homosexuality, questioning dichotomous conceptualizations of gender and sexuality. In fact, Judith Butler (1990) argues that gender categories are not set but are performances that are acted on daily. Diana Fuss reveals how dichotomous distinctions between heterosexuality and homosexuality reinforce and maintain heterosexual identity: Heterosexuality "secures its self-identity and shores up its ontological boundaries by protecting itself from what it sees as the continual predatory encroachment of its contaminated other, homosexuality" (Fuss, 1991). Until recently, feminist theorists and activists, responding to accusations of fostering homosexuality, struggled with these terrifying boundaries privately, constraining their theorizing and thinking about gender and sexuality. In fact, theorists focusing on rural women or gender in rural areas seldom directly address issues of sexuality, often explicitly and implicitly erasing lesbian experience. Lesbians in rural places remain invisible to scholars, to other rural people, and to the urban gay and lesbian culture.

In thinking about lesbians and gays in rural areas, it is helpful to turn to theorists who argue against lesbian essentialism. Lesbians are not homogeneous: "The error made in lesbian essentialism, in forging unity, sameness and coherency, where there exists difference, discontinuity, and contradictory heterogeneity, is in taking the dominant cultural view too seriously, as if the social/clinical category of 'lesbian' designated a homogeneous kind" (Zita, 1990:340–341). Zita uses the autobiographies of three women to explore how the problem of reductive lesbian essentialism subordinates race, class, ethnicity, and even erotic difference to the primacy of lesbian as the central category for defining the self. She suggests that the commonality between lesbians is sexual desire, a desire outlawed by dominant culture. Sexual desire between women occurs across multiple social locations of race, class, language, and social relations (Zita, 1990). One of these social locations that remains unexplored concerns women who reside in rural areas.

Ann Ferguson (1990) agrees with Zita on dismissing the existence of a singular lesbian identity. However, she sees differences in sexual formations that occur within different countries and regions as well as within different races, ethnicities, and classes within cultures. These include different senses of self-identification associated with lesbian sexual practices. Any attempt to build an international lesbian political movement must accommodate these differences, resisting domination by the cultural imperialism of Western lesbians.

What happens to rural women who experience sexual desire for other women? Lesbians in rural areas live quite removed from the centers of lesbian and gay culture, that is, large metropolitan areas. Due to the pressure to conform to heterosexuality in rural areas, many lesbians and gays flock to cities in an effort to find gay and lesbian spaces and communities.

However, compulsory heterosexuality in rural areas remains incomplete—not all lesbians leave rural areas; in fact, as I discuss later, some lesbians are moving into rural areas. As Ferguson (1990) suggests, these women may not publicly or privately identify themselves as lesbians. Rural areas support few, if any, gay- or lesbian-designated spaces where homosexuals can safely express their identity. Studies of rural women rarely raise the issue of sexual identity, often overlooking or negating possibilities other than heterosexuality. This suggests the need to look more closely at sexuality and, by not automatically assuming that the patriarchal character of rural families is completely pervasive, to recognize that compulsory heterosexuality remains incomplete.

Arguments against essentialism suggest that in understanding the lives of rural women we must consider relations of power and privileges based on race, class, nationality, ethnicity, and sexuality. In recognizing differences, we need not negate connections among women and common strategies of action for women. As Aptheker (1989) explains, the diversity of women's experiences does not negate the pervasiveness of institutionalized subordination of women as the commonality underlying women's experience. It remains possible to construct feminist visions that seek commonality through diversity, but we must take differences among women seriously.

Women's Resistance

Feminists recognize the vantage points of different groups of women. The next step involves acknowledging that women not only experience different forms of oppression, but that women's oppression in any given case remains incomplete; they resist. In emphasizing the subordination and oppression of women, feminist theorists err in viewing women exclusively or primarily as victims, missing the obvious fact that women often are survivors and creators (Aptheker, 1989); only rarely are women completely powerless (Stanley and Wise, 1990). For example, Collins cautions that "portraying Black women solely as passive, unfortunate recipients of racial and sexual abuse stifles notions that Black women can actively work to change our circumstances and bring about changes in our lives" (1990:237). Similarly, Third World women warn against interpreting their lives as filled with pure drudgery and oppression (Shiva, 1988; Mohanty, 1991). Rather than seeing women as helpless victims of an all-powerful, patriarchal ideology, we must account for women's potential for creativity and agency within a context of limited options. Social structures not only constrain, they also enable; thus, social structures serve not simply as barriers to action but also as preconditions for the possibility of meaningful choices (Felski, 1989).

One way to reconfigure women's potential is to note that resistance is more than organized struggle. The daily activities of their lives shape many women's opportunities for resistance. Women's acts of resistance against oppression take many forms, often unseen or underappreciated for their cumulative effects. Understanding women's strategies of resistance involves redefining what counts as resistance to include acts typically considered outside the political realm (Aptheker, 1989). Politics, normally contrasted with economics or personal issues, shields economic and personal issues from political contestation (Fraser, 1989). Thus, many of women's private and market concerns are viewed as only marginally legitimate political issues. Women must contest the boundaries of what is considered political because their oppression often remains rooted in personal conditions resulting from the concerns of family, marriage, sexuality, and motherhood. Traditional understandings of resistance as social rather than individual, political rather than personal, and inclusive of large numbers of people in conscious alliance working toward a common goal often inaccurately define women's activities as outside the political realm, assume that women accept their subordinate position, and situate women as ultimate victims.

One type of resistance frequently engaged in by women involves creating the conditions necessary for life. In societies where these conditions are continuously undermined, women's struggles for survival and connection with their families constitute acts of resistance. Caroline Moser (1989) distinguishes between women's organizing for practical and strategic issues. Practical needs, such as providing food, clothing, and shelter for their families often guide women's organizing activities. Organizing around these needs does not challenge traditional gender divisions of labor or women's subordinate positions in society. For example, black women slaves' attempts to care for their own families offered a mode of resisting the white slaveowners' control over their lives. More recently, for many African-American women, the constraints of racism, sexism, and poverty work against their participation in organized political action; however, these black women struggle against multiple oppressions in their attempts to merely raise their children (Collins, 1990). In many regions of Latin America, women's efforts revolve around such practical issues as creating food kitchens or groups that demand release and information about political prisoners. Although concern about women's equity and strategic gender issues remain peripheral to many of these efforts, demands for women's rights often emerge as women become empowered through their organizational experiences.

The most recognizable type of resistance engaged in by women is their struggle against the oppression that results from misogynist, class, racial, or homophobic attitudes. This type of women's resistance, long acknowledged as political, frequently takes on a different form than does male political activism. Women's marginalization or exclusion from traditional institutional centers of power such as trade unions, farm organizations, political parties, social movements, and the armed forces pushes them to turn to alternative forms of resistance. For example, women in agriculture, excluded from leadership in traditional farm organizations, form organizations that address the needs of only farm women. Women environmentalists who are concerned about the health and ecological conditions in their communities organize at the grass-roots level rather than relying on national environmental organizations to solve their problems.

Several common themes emerge in women's resistance against oppression. Women's acts forge connections, which in turn often create networks or community associations. Also, women in organizations frequently take responsibility for facilitating group dynamics and interactions. Their efforts to connect also spill over into women's representation of themselves in public arenas. Rather than putting forth their concerns as isolated individuals, women often represent themselves as members of households and communities. Women, who are strongly rooted in class, ethnic, and cultural communities, work hard at maintaining networks and relationships that give life to communities (Ackelsburg, 1988). Their efforts to form connections based on appeals to preserve cultural heritage provide multiple outcomes and motivations for privileged, as compared to disadvantaged, groups. Whereas identity politics for Chicanos, African Americans, Native Americans, blacks in South Africa, or other subordinated groups derive from progressive foundations, similar appeals to identity, community, relatedness, and connection by privileged groups often reinforce racism, xenophobia, and heterosexism. Many women internalize the perception of their position as subordinates; they may be resigned or reactionary in their political positions. Thus, women's groups may not necessarily improve women's position; such groups may, in fact, reinforce and maintain inequitable gender relations.

Patriarchal forms and traditional values prevail and organized feminist struggles remain relatively rare in rural areas. Rural women shy away from widely embracing feminism, but this by no means suggests that these women do not resist domination. Many rural women's activities, which occur in women's (not necessarily feminist) organizations as well as in male-dominated organizations, are geared toward forging connections between their families and communities; they do not participate simply to improve their individual situations. Women's resistance strategies take a variety of forms, as with women's participation in the environmental movement, in struggles to preserve the family farm, and in women's attempts to acquire land. Although they sometimes are empowering to individual women, these activities serve more broadly to improve the conditions of life. Women's activism does not always make the participants conscious of what they share as women; at times women participate in movements that reinforce rather than challenge their place of subordination. As discussed earlier, subjugated perspectives are not always emancipatory.

In discussing rural women and rural social relations in this book, I begin with rural women who have some connection to the land, while recognizing that many rural women no longer depend exclusively on agriculture or the land for their livelihoods. I situate rural women's lives in the context of global shifts, at the same time addressing local, racial, ethnic, class, and sexuality differences.

3

Rural Women and Nature

Perhaps like no other group, rural women live close to the natural world. Raising plants and animals for their families' food, producing agricultural goods for the market, gathering fuelwood for cooking, and collecting water from streams and local wells set the rhythm for rural women's activities in many localities. In their daily contact with plants, animals, land, and water, women are knowledgeable about and utilize local species and environments. Yet Western science and capitalist development agendas often devalue, disregard, or usurp rural women's knowledge of the natural world. At the same time, Western science and capitalist interests use the symbolic association of women with nature to devalue and dominate both women and nature. In this chapter, I argue that women living in rural areas with close direct relations to the natural world may provide unique insights into human interactions with the environment and into feminist theorizing and political action.

The demands and changes of global and national economies are rapidly undermining rural women's connections to the natural world. In many areas of the world, women are losing access to and knowledge of local environments. Specific changes in the lives of rural women vary by region and locality and depend on local forms of capitalist penetration and social relations. Nevertheless, several common factors affect rural women in a wide variety of localities: increasing commercialization of agriculture, declining ability of small-scale producers to support their families, and the destruction of forests. In certain regions, such as Latin America and the United States, the commercialization of agriculture has caused rural women to lose access to land and a means of survival, which pushes them to migrate to cities. In other areas of the world, especially in southern and eastern Africa, where a high proportion of men migrate in search of wage employment, women remain in rural areas to farm the land and provide for the subsistence needs of their families. Destruction of forests by commercial logging operations in many regions of India,

Latin America, and Southeast Asia undermines women's ability to provide food, fodder, and other basic necessities for their households.

As the connections between rural women and their local environments
are uncoupling, ecofeminists are celebrating women's connection to nature
as a key to ending environmental destruction. Arguing that the domination of women and the domination of nature are intimately connected,
ecofeminists look to women to solve global environmental problems.
Although ecofeminism emerged largely as an urban-based intellectual and
political movement of women with limited ties or involvement with rural
life, ecofeminist writers have recently begun to explore the connections
between rural women and the natural world and are providing insights
into how rural women's knowledge might provide a key for resolving
environmental problems (Shiva, 1988; Merchant, 1989; Agarwal, 1992).

Theorizing Women's Connection to Nature

Human relations with the environment are distinctly gendered and take
multiple forms in different contexts. Various cultures invoke particular
connections between women and nature, in some cases these connections
provide the rationale to dominate women, and in others, to celebrate
women. There are five different ways in which women's relationships
with nature is presented that are of interest here. First, many cultures
symbolically associate women with nature, and using the metaphor
Mother Earth appears to be the most common sort of association.
Associating women with nature in this way often contributes to the
exploitation and domination of both women and nature. Second, feminist
critics of science reveal the way in which science uses the symbolic association of women and nature—not to celebrate this connection but to
legitimate the domination of both (Griffin, 1978; Keller, 1983; Merchant,
1980). Third, feminist animal rights activists point out how women and
animals are dominated and mistreated by patriarchal societies. Fourth,
ecofeminists, who agree with feminist critics of science that there are intimate links between the domination of nature and women, propose
reclaiming women's association with nature. They propose that through
embracing, celebrating, and redefining women's relations with nature
these connections can offer potential emancipation for both women and
nature. Fifth, a final approach, most directly applicable to understanding
rural women's connection to nature, calls for a materialist understanding
of women's relationship with nature, as suggested by Agarwal (1992).
Rather than following the predominant ecofeminist approach focusing on
women's symbolic association with nature, Agarwal suggests that the
daily activities of rural women's lives form the basis of feminist environmentalism as an alternate strategy for tackling environmental problems. I

"Buds." Photograph by Abby Lynn Bogomolny. Used by permission.

begin with the most familiar and pervasive perspective, the symbolic association between women and land, because that theme seems to run through all the others.

Mother Nature: Symbolic Association Between Women and the Land

Many cultures have adopted the concept of the nurturing mother as a guiding metaphor (Merchant, 1980). The images of earth as mother and nature as female extend across cultures and time, not necessarily boding well for either earth or nature. These images portray Mother Earth as the provider of sustenance for humans in the same way that mothers provide sustenance to their young. This nurturing image of nature as female contrasts sharply with the image of female and nature as wild and uncontrollable (Merchant, 1980). In Western Europe in the 1500s and 1600s, these images existed simultaneously. However, the metaphor of the earth as the nurturing, benevolent mother gradually disappeared as Western science chose to replace it with another: nature as the wild, uncontrollable female in need of domination. Thus, rather than opting for working in harmony with a benevolent mother nature, science emphasized power over nature.

Certain Native American tribes also viewed the earth as mother and interpreted European exploitation of the land as an outrage against Mother Earth. In the late 1800s, Smohallo, a Nez Percé leader, expressed outrage at the Europeans' attempts to encourage his tribe to engage in agriculture, finding it a sacrilege against Mother Earth: "You ask me to plow the ground. Shall I take a knife and tear my mother's bosom? . . . You ask me to cut grass and make hay and sell it and be rich like white men. But how dare I cut off my mother's hair?" (as quoted in Janiewski, 1988:39). Andean peoples worshiped the fertility of Mother Earth: "All adored the earth, which they called Pachamama, which means Earth Mother; and it was common for them to place a long stone, like an altar or statue, in the middle of their fields, in honor of this goddess, in order, in that spot, to offer her prayers and invoke her, asking her to watch over and fertilize their fields; and when certain plots of land were found to be more fertile, so much greater was their respect for her" (as quoted in Silverblatt, 1987:24).

On the other side of the globe in South Asia, in Indian (Hindu) cosmology, "Nature is symbolized as the embodiment of the feminine principle" (Shiva, 1988:38) and is characterized by creativity, activity, productivity, diversity, connectedness of all beings, continuity between humans and nature, and sanctity of life. Indian cosmology refrains from viewing the feminine principle in opposition to the masculine principle but rather sees the relationship as a duality in unity. Vandana Shiva reminds us that the feminine principle, not exclusively embodied in women, represents activity and creativity in nature and in men, as well as in women. Thus, she suggests that "the revolutionary and liberational potential of the recovery of the feminine principle consists in its challenging the concepts, categories and processes which have created the threat to life, and in providing oppositional categories that create and enlarge the spaces for maintaining and enriching all life in nature and society" (Shiva, 1988:46). She continues, "The feminine principle becomes a category of challenge which locates nature and women as the source of life and wealth, and as such active subjects, maintaining and creating life-processes" (Shiva, 1988:46). However, these appeals to the symbolic association between women, nature, and earth often stand in stark contrast to women's actual relation with the land, which is where feminist critiques of science come in.

Feminist Critiques of Science

And he has devised ways to separate himself from her. He sends machines to do his labor. His working has become as effortless as hers. He accomplishes days of labor with a small motion of his hand. His efforts are more astonishing than hers. No longer praying, no longer imploring, he pronounces words from a distance and his orders are carried out. Even with his back turned to her, she yields to him. And in his mind, he imagines that he can conceive without her. In his mind, he develops the means to supplant her miracles with his own. In his mind, he no longer relies on her. What he possesses, he says, is his to use and to abandon.

—Susan Griffin, 1978

For some thinkers, science altered the association of women and nature from one of respect to one of domination. Evelyn Fox Keller (1985), for example, argues that underlying metaphors in Western epistemology have legitimized the domination of both women and nature. Dualistic gender metaphors associate women with nature, subjectivity, and emotion, and men with culture, objectivity, and reason. These metaphors provide rationales for the exploitation and control of both women and nature. For evidence, we need only look to Keller, who vividly describes Sir Francis Bacon's (1561–1626) reliance on sexual imagery to exemplify the view that science could dominate and master nature. For example, in extolling the benefits of science and associated technologies, Bacon claimed that scientists do not "merely exert a gentle guidance over nature's course; they have the power to conquer and subdue her, to shake her to her foundations" (as quoted in Keller, 1985:36). The association of nature with women allowed men of science to dissociate themselves from nature, perceiving themselves as superior to nature. In unveiling Bacon's metaphor of the birth of science, Keller carefully notes the complexities and subtleties of Bacon's vision. Male sexual aggressiveness and virility form the driving force of science, but underneath this male virility lies the recognition that some form of marriage between mind and nature must occur for science to be born. Bacon imagines the male scientist fathering future scientific geniuses, thereby appropriating and denying the maternal and further denying the feminine as subject. Fear of women's sexuality reached its height in late seventeenth-century Europe, but science offered men an antidote: "In the ideological system that emerged and prevailed, science was a purely male and chaste venture, seeking dominion over, rather than commingling with, a female nature; it promised, and indeed helped promote, the simultaneous vanquishing of nature and of female voracity" (Keller, 1985:61).

Keller (1985) also argues that ideologies of gender, nature, and science that emerged after the seventeenth century in Europe provided support for the polarization of gender required by industrial capitalism. Scientific ideology responded to the growing split between men and women, between public and private, and between work and home with dualistic distinctions between mind and nature, between objective and subjective, and between reason and feeling, and a mechanized, desexualized science defined in opposition to everything female was promoted.

Today, dualistic gender metaphors remain at the heart of the values of the scientific enterprise. Science associates objectivity, reason, and mind with males; and subjectivity, feeling, and nature are the realm of women. As Harding (1986) explains, these dualistic gender metaphors are applied to perceived dichotomies that rarely have anything to do with sex differences. Such metaphorical associations not only lack grounding in actual gender differences but serve to legitimate the domination of both women and nature.

Armed with science's "objective" view of nature as external to man and as a force to be dominated, Western epistemology tenaciously attempts to control nature and women. Fortunately, complete domination remains unattainable. The so-called environmental crisis and the continual efforts of the feminist movement reveal the incompleteness of this project of male domination in Western society, as both nature and women resist domination. Feminists, joined by other critics of science, call for an end to dualistic, reductionist approaches in science and challenge women's exclusion from science.

The exclusion and marginalization of women in science represents another focus point for feminist critics of science. Harding (1986) reveals that questioning the exclusion of women from science led to more serious questioning of the epistemological grounding of science, specifically to inquiry about the notion of objectivity and about what and whose knowledge is legitimate. Feminist critics of science now ask what a feminist standpoint can contribute to science. Can a feminist standpoint transform science, and if so, what would such a successor science be? Most agree that a feminist successor science must question the notion of objectivity, that is, the notion that the scientist as subject must be separate from the object of investigation. The claim of objectivity acts in the service of hierarchy and positivism to legitimate what is considered to be knowledge (Haraway, 1991). Rejecting objectivity as the basis for science renders privileged knowledge obsolete and raises the fundamental question: What counts as legitimate knowledge? Coming to terms with the concept of objectivity remains problematic for feminist critics of science. Haraway (1991) describes feminists as simultaneously rejecting objectivity, and claiming a privileged way of knowing—actually another form of objectivity. This gives rise to another question: Is it possible to create a science that is not symbolically or empirically male-centered but still capable of some claim to truth? Haraway suggests the need for some form of knowledge that "gives some enforceable, reliable accounts of things not reducible to power moves and agnostic, high-status games of rhetoric or to scientistic, positivist arrogance" (1991:188). From her perspective, feminist objectivity means situated knowledge—the realization that "objectivity is about limited location and situated knowledge, not about transcendence and splitting of subject and object" (1991:190). Haraway argues for partial perspectives as the key to feminist objectivity, arguing that truth claims do not depend on universality; but rather on situated knowledge claims. In a somewhat different mode, Harding (1991), while critical of the notion of value-free objectivity, expresses reluctance to abandon the concept of objectivity altogether. Rather, she proposes "strong objectivity." She suggests that feminist standpoint epistemology calls for strengthened notions of objectivity, rather than forcing a choice between value-free objectivity and judgmental relativism. Strong objectivity requires that all knowledge claims be socially situated and that the cultural, historical, and sociological relativism inherent in all human beliefs be recognized. Thus, these theorists, while not completely rejecting science, call for evaluation of different claims to knowledge. From Harding's perspective, the knowledge claims of science must be subjected to the same scrutiny as other claims to knowledge.

Feminist scrutiny of agricultural science is rare, but recently Jack Kloppenburg suggested that feminist analysis of science, especially Haraway's vision of partial realities, may help to reconstruct an alternative agricultural science. Different forms of knowledge in agriculture already exist, as local knowledge, farmers' knowledge, and scientific knowledge, each of which has different and partial perspectives. As Kloppenburg suggests, "farmers know something that agricultural scientists do not know and cannot completely know; and vice versa. Articulations between these different ways of knowing need to be established not in order to combine the knowledges, and not to translate the knowledges, but to permit mutually beneficial dialogue" (1991:540). Thus, agricultural science could be revolutionized through attention to articulations of different ways of knowing and through decentering of science as the privileged way of knowing.

Feminism and Animal Rights

A different group of feminists has expressed concern with societal treatment of animals. Early feminists such as Margaret Fuller, Charlotte Perkins Gilman, Emma Goldman, Mary Wollstonecraft, Susan B. Anthony, Elizabeth Cady Stanton, and others protested the inhumane treatment of animals by advocating that vegetarianism and animal welfare reform be included on the feminist agenda (Donovan, 1990). For example, writing in 1845, Margaret Fuller anticipated that improvement of women's status and integration of women into public life would result in " 'plant-like gentleness'; a harmonic, peaceful rule; an end to violence of all kinds [including, she specifies, the slaughter of animals for food] and the institution of vegetarianism [substituting, she urges, 'pulse (beans) for animal food']" (Donovan, 1990:359). Women's rights advocates argued for better treatment for animals, called for vegetarianism, and joined in associating women's nature to that of plants. More recently Josephine Donovan (1990) outlined a feminist ethic of animal rights that rejects carnivorism; killing of live animals for clothing; hunting; trapping of wildlife for fur; rodeos; circuses; animal testing for beauty and cleaning products; and factory farming. From her perspective, a feminist ethic of animal rights adds to the broader animal rights movement through the attention given to the emotional and spiritual connection between humans and animals.

Recognition of connections between men's violation of the rights of animals and the rights of women underlies the feminist ethic of animal rights. In *Rape of the Wild*, Andrée Collard (1988) decries the similarities in male violence against animals, nature, and women. Some feminists, such as Carol Adams (1990), perceive raising and killing animals for food as the ultimate violation of animal rights. Adams insists that feminist theory and practice must include vegetarianism because "eating animals acts as a mirror and representation of patriarchal values" (1990:187). She claims that feminist theory must be informed by vegetarian insights and, similarly, that animal rights theory should incorporate feminist understandings. Focusing on the symbolic associations between male control of meat and women in Western patriarchal cultures, she writes that "meat is a symbol for what is not seen but is always there—patriarchal control of animals" (Adams, 1990:16). Adams's compelling analyses of texts highlights the association between male sexuality, power, and meat eating. She demonstrates that killing, butchering, and eating animals symbolize the virile male. As long as feminists take part in eating meat, they support a patriarchal culture that violates, objectifies, fragments, and "consumes" both animals and women. She asks: "How do we overthrow patriarchal power while eating its symbol?" (Adams, 1990:188).

In her essay "Why Did the Balinese Chicken Cross the Road?" Alice Walker (1991) struggles with her relationship with animals and vegetarianism. She describes her encounter with a chicken in Bali:

> This then is about a chicken I knew in Bali. I do not know her name or that of her parents and grandparents. I do not know where she was from originally. Suddenly on a day whose morning had been rainy, there she was, on the path in front of us (my own family, on our way back to our temporary shelter), trying to look for worms, trying to point out other possible food items to her three chicks, and trying at the same time to get herself and her young ones across the road. . . . It was one of those moments that will be engraved on my brain forever. For I really saw her. (1991:207)

Remembering her encounter with the chicken on her return from Bali, Alice Walker attempted to give up meat, but reflects that she may never be a pure vegetarian: "I console myself by recognizing that this diet, in which ninety percent of what I eat is nonmeat and nondairy, though not pristinely vegetarian, is still completely different from and less barbarous than the one I was raised on—in which meat was a mainstay—and that perhaps if they knew or cared (and somehow I know they know and care), my chicken and fish sister/fellow travelers on the planet might give me credit for effort" (1991:208–209).

In a later chapter, I take closer look at women's daily involvement with animals to enhance feminist theorizing about the connection between women and animals and formulation of a feminist ethic of animal rights. Violence against animals ranges from raising animals in inhumane environments to killing animals for sport or survival to raising animals for subsistence. Walker's fascinating reflections on her encounter with the Balinese chicken and her Western diet omit the relationship of the chicken to women in Bali. A feminist analysis decrying violence against both women and animals should not blind us to women's as well as men's participation in killing animals for both subsistence and sport. Further on, I examine rural women's relationship with animals to reveal how women benefit from their association with animals, how daily work with animals is gendered, as well as the ways in which symbolic and economic control of animals reinforces patriarchal culture. But here I turn to ecofeminism, a broader view of women's relationship to nature.

Ecofeminism

Ecofeminism represents an emerging perspective dealing with women's relationships with nature by articulating women's different ways of knowing the natural world. Ecofeminism, a new social movement that emerged in the 1980s as an outgrowth of the environmental and women's movements, explores, redefines, and politicizes the connections between women and nature. During the 1980s, feminists within the environmental movement worried about the lack of attention to women's issues and began to promote the connection between the domination of women and the domination of nature (Salleh, 1984; King, 1990). From an epistemological standpoint, ecofeminists build on the work of feminist critics of science by recognizing the connection between the domination of women and the domination of nature. However, ecofeminists say the connection between women and nature has emancipatory potential. Ynestra King (1990), one of the first and leading advocates for ecofeminism, argues that Western patriarchal societies' views of women as "closer" to nature than men legitimizes the subjugation of women and nature. In dualistic epistemologies, nature and culture, mind and body, and male and female are separated. Women are associated with nature and body; men, with culture and mind. Males appear as above nature, body, and women. King recognizes that the nature-culture dualism is a function of culture but suggests that ecofeminists "consciously choose not to sever the woman-nature connection by joining male culture. Rather, we can use it as a vantage point for creating a different kind of culture and politics that would integrate intuitive, spiritual, and rational forms of knowledge, embracing both science and magic insofar as they enable us to transform the nature-culture distinction and to envision and create a free, ecological society" (1989:23). Ecofeminism encompasses insights and perspectives from liberal, cultural, social, and socialist feminism to address relationships between people and the environment (Merchant, 1992). For example, cultural ecofeminists recast these relationships in more than economic terms. Val Plumwood (1991) recognizes that Western rationalism's rejection of emotionality, sensuality, and relatedness as aspects of humanity incorrectly positions humans as over, above, and opposed to nature and to anything female. Socialist ecofeminists object to patriarchal and capitalist domination of women and nature and advocate a total restructuring of the market economy (Merchant, 1992).

Combining various aspects of ecofeminism, Vandana Shiva (1988), another leading thinker in ecofeminism, approaches the philosophy from the standpoint of Third World women, particularly Indian women. She agrees with other feminist critics of Western science in her reproach of dominant modes of perception such as reductionism, duality, and linearity, which emanate from Western, male-oriented science and society. Rejecting the epistemological positions of Western science, she calls for the recovery of the feminine principle defined by Indian cosmology as the key to transforming the destructive forces of Western patriarchy, science, and capitalism. Shiva is particularly critical of the dichotomization ontology characteristic of Western science and thought that leads to domination over nature and people. She argues that Third World women have privileged access to a life-sustaining principle through their links to nature as they obtain food, water, fuel, shelter, and other basic necessities. As the above suggests, ecofeminists such as King and Shiva turn the women-nature association on its head and retheorize women's symbolic association with the natural environment to suggest ways in which the association has emancipatory possibilities. Because of their association with nature and the subordination of both, women have a high stake in ending and challenging the domination of both nature and women. These authors recognize that solutions to ecological problems must be tied to social and gender transformations.

Rethinking Ecofeminism

The diverse social perspectives of ecofeminism, ranging from socialist feminism to green politics to goddess-based spirituality, subject the movement to criticism from feminists and ecologists alike. As a relatively new social movement, ecofeminism contains theoretical and philosophical underpinnings that are continually being redefined. By rethinking ecofeminism, theorists may hope to bring several key issues to light, including those I discuss here: reliance on the symbolic association of women with nature; classification and definition of both women and nature as biologically essential rather than socially constructed entities; and neglect of the concrete realities of women's daily existence (Agarwal, 1992).

Symbols, values, and metaphors provide the ideological justification for domination of women and nature, but ecofeminist attempts to claim and celebrate the symbolic connection between women and nature do not address the global ecological crisis. Janet Biehl (1991) complains that ecofeminism carries the woman-nature metaphor too far. Her scathing critique suggests that ecofeminism rejects rationalism, essentializes women, and moves in nonprogressive directions. Appeals to the neolithic age and to goddess worship suggest to her that ecofeminism embraces irrationalism; she expresses concern that rejecting reason can produce reactionary results. Although Biehl raises important questions concerning the epistemological grounding of ecofeminism, the severe tone of her critique cuts off dialogue rather than facilitating thoughtfulness.

Agarwal's (1992) less inflammatory and more enlightening critique of ecofeminism focuses on the failure of ecofeminism to move beyond the symbolic and ideological associations between women and nature. She suggests that women's and men's relations with the environment must be understood as rooted in their concrete, material realities. Using the example of rural Indian women, she suggests that women are victims of the destruction of nature. However, as a consequence of their daily lives, they possess specific knowledge about the environment. Rather than rejecting the connection between women and environment, she argues that women's perspectives on the environment may provide alternative visions for human relations with the environment based on material realities rather than symbolic connections.

The assumption that women are "closer" to nature than men raises problems for ecofeminists. Those who examine women's connections to nature have been hampered by problematic definitions of both "women" and "nature" as essential categories. It is necessary to recognize that both women and nature are socially defined. Postulating a unique association between women and nature requires that we explain what it is about women across diverse experiences and understandings that results in a unique connection to nature. We meet with the danger of resorting to biological determinism, that is, implying that women's closeness to nature derives from their ability to give birth, breast-feed, and menstruate. Feminists have battled long and hard to overcome arguments proclaiming women's biological inferiority to men; biology-as-destiny arguments often result in the domination of women (Mellor, 1992). Thus, ecofeminists who wander into this territory and celebrate women's biology might inadvertently foster biological essentialism. Such privileging of women's biology accepts centuries of claims that men are removed from and above nature and gives credence to a mind-body duality for men but not for women. Although there are indeed biological differences between women and men, we must be skeptical of privileging women's bodies as "closer to nature."

In fact, the very notion of closeness to nature entails viewing nature as an essential category. We must be cautious in reifying nature when, in fact, nature is also a socially constructed category, perceived differently by people across time and space (Fitzsimmons, 1989). Ideas about what constitutes nature and its physical transformations are not static but are defined differently across societies (Stamp, 1990). The present global concern over nature and the environment often results in advocacy of preserving a timeless nature rather than more appropriately rethinking the relationship of humans with nature. Distancing Western and Third World urban elites from contact with "nature" facilitates both the conservationists' abstract conception of pristine nature (the scenic view perspective) and the view that nature can be dominated (the control perspective). Women, feminist or not, are certainly not exempt from taking either the scenic view or the control perspective.

Another problem of ecofeminism, that is closely related to essentializing women involves presenting women as a unitary category. In positing the connection between women and nature, ecofeminists often fail to note the differences among women by class, race, ethnicity, and nationality (Agarwal, 1992). Women's complex relations with the natural world differ widely by their class, racial, ethnic, and national identities.

A more fruitful approach for comprehending women's distinct relations to the natural world focuses on women's daily activities and understandings rather than on women's symbolic or essential connections to the environment. Women of different classes, races, localities, ethnicities, and nationalities have numerous and varied interactions with nature. I am reminded of discussions with a group of women farmers adjacent to the forest surrounding Mt. Kenya, who see elephants' destruction of their crops as their major problem. These women perceive of elephants as dangerous animals that pose a threat to their livelihoods, in contrast to the European tourists in the nearby lodge (including me), who view these animals as exotic and inspiring. Women's relations with "nature"—elephants in this case—vary enormously by their race, class, and nationality. Rural women's work, such as gathering fuel, fodder, and water and cultivating food for their families' subsistence, places them in a particular relationship with the natural environment. In addition, responsibility for daily physical care of adults, children, and infants typically falls to women. Because of this, Agarwal suggests that women are "likely to be affected adversely in quite specific ways by environmental degradation. At the same time, in the course of their everyday interactions with nature, they acquire a special knowledge of species varieties and the processes of natural regeneration" (1992:126). To take advantage of this special knowledge, Agarwal (1992) poses the term "feminist environmentalism" as an alternative to ecofeminism, in an attempt to move beyond the symbolic connections between women and nature. In her view, women must struggle with resources as well as meanings. Feminist environmentalism offers possibilities and challenges for both feminism and environmentalism. Agarwal recommends that on the feminist front, there would be a need to challenge and transform notions about gender as well as the actual division of work and resources between the genders. On the environmental front, there would be a need to challenge and transform not only notions about the relationship between people and nature but also the actual methods of appropriation of nature's resources by the privileged (Agarwal, 1992:127).

By focusing on the material relations of women with the environment, it would be increasingly difficult to romanticize women's connection to the natural world. When ecofeminists romanticize women's connections to nature, they fail to recognize that these connections often entail arduous physical labor, struggles for survival, and environmental degradation.

Most important, women's connections to nature have a material grounding based on their daily activities. The notion that women may provide alternative perspectives and strategies for dealing with environmental problems coincides with recent scholarship on feminist epistemologies. Here, Haraway's (1991) concept of situated knowledge helps us to view women's relationship with nature. Haraway's insistence that all knowledge claims are partial and situated suggests that women's daily relations with their localities may provide them with partial perspectives that differ from men's perspectives. Valuing of situated knowledge complements Agarwal's insistence that we understand rural women's particular connections to the environment in terms of their daily lives in specific localities.

Women's Work with Nature

Rural women's work with nature varies across space and time, but it is safe to say that in the late twentieth century, the penetration of capitalism, state interventions, and the needs of the changing global economy has transformed women's work in most rural localities. Extraction of natural resources from rural areas for the needs of an increasingly urbanized population fuels development of capitalist centers. Rural people, although not innocent pawns, seldom represent the major beneficiaries of capitalist development. They depend on employment related to the use and extraction of natural resources to earn income and they rely on nature for their subsistence needs as well. In both their subsistence and income-earning activities, rural people disrupt and change the natural world. Agriculture—hardly "natural"—involves total disruption and transformation of natural ecosystems. Deborah Fink cautions against blindly accepting romanticized agrarian images of rural people as being closer to nature and more moral than others. In describing how farmers on North American plains removed the natural vegetation and wild animals and replaced them with livestock and crop production systems designed to serve human interests, she reminds us that "farming represented a different kind of tampering with the natural environment than that which occurred in the city, but it was no more natural" (1992:194).

Romanticizing the connection between rural people and nature, especially in the third world, also skims over the difficulties and struggles in rural people's lives. For example, Shiva (1988) finds similarities between women's work and nature's work and suggests that both involve renewal, the creation of sustenance, and are often decentered, local, and in harmony with the prevalent ecosystem. She argues that capitalist society devalues the quiet work and invisible wealth created by nature and women in contrast to the value and visibility given to men's work, which frequently disrupts the natural world. Brinda Rao (1991) agrees with Shiva that women and tribal people have had harmonious relationships with nature; however, she warns against romanticizing and idealizing the relationship of indigenous people and rural women with nature. As she points out, their lives include deprivation and hard physical labor. Further, although indigenous practices may disrupt the environment less than commodity-driven, capital-intensive practices, indigenous people also alter natural systems. For example, people in the Peruvian Andes plant indigenous crops such as potatoes, quinoa, and oca, but in the process, they disrupt the natural local ecosystem. Thus, rural women are connected to nature through their daily activities, but they are not connected to a pristine nature. Instead, they transform the natural world to provide for human needs.

Diverse theoretical underpinnings characterize ecofeminist politics. Recent advances, such as materialist perspectives on the connections between women's daily lives and the environment now complement symbolic perspectives. In chapters 4, 5, and 6, I discuss rural women's work with land, plants, and animals to illustrate the variations in women's daily activities in their connection to nature, suggesting how women's situated knowledge and practices might provide keys to global sustainability.

4

Rural Women's Connections to the Land

Despite the symbolic association between women and the land and the widespread cultural perception of earth as mother, at best estimate, women own only 1 percent of the world's land (Dankelman and Davidson, 1988). Land, which is of course extremely significant in the social relations of farming, is usually a farmer's principal asset. Women produce the majority of the world's food, but they share limited control over, ownership of, and access to land. Although obviously necessary for production, land also provides collateral for access to credit and other forms of capital. Thus, women's exclusion from landownership limits their access to credit, capital, and other resources (Whatmore, 1991).

Most countries lack actual data on women's titles to land; few countries disaggregate landownership data by gender of the landowner. In the United States, which does have data on women's landownership, women were sole owners of 39 million acres of farmland in 1987, approximately 4 percent of all farmland (U.S.D.A., 1987). Although few women hold legal titles to land, rural women are not equally landless, and they do not all have the same relationship to the land. Women's access to land varies by marital status, class position, race, and ethnicity. Socioeconomic factors and state land policies affect women's land access and ownership as well.

As in so many areas of their lives, women's limited access to land is usually defined by their relationships to men, specifically by their husbands' or fathers' ownership or access to land. Rural women from upper-class and privileged racial and ethnic groups, although not always individually holding legal title to land, often gain access to income through land owned by their husbands or fathers. Many women own land jointly with their husbands or other family members. Assessing the extent of this joint ownership remains difficult, because quantitative data on women's joint ownership exists for few countries. In England, for example, women's ownership of land usually takes the form of joint ownership with their husbands. Farm families often initiate joint ownership to avoid tax liabilities in case

45

of the husband's death and to insure transfer of the farm to the next male heir. In these cases, women hold title to the land but rarely consider that the farm belongs to them for their own use (Whatmore, 1991). In other regions of the world, many women possess use rights to land owned by their families, cooperatives, or the state. However, other rural women have little or no access to land either through formal title or use rights.

Women from subjugated racial and ethnic groups often work land that they rarely own or control. With global changes in the agricultural system, an increasing number of landless women in many localities work on the land as hired agricultural workers. At the global level, women's access to productive land is decreasing with privatization, with concentration and fragmentation of land holdings, and with degradation. Land consolidation disenfranchises men as well as women from their land, but when land is consolidated, it usually becomes the property of fewer men, not of women. Public policies are thus critical in determining women's relationship to land. Land privatization, land reform and titling that does not specifically include women, and policies that encourage the separation of land owner-ship from management are all examples of exemplify land policies that decrease women's options in agricultural production (Flora, 1988).

The global trend in land policy leans towards privatization, although policies take multiple forms in different regions of the world. The breakup of socialist systems of land distribution in Eastern Europe, the former Soviet Union, Vietnam, and other countries further accelerates these trends. State policies also shape land distribution and the size of private landholdings. In Europe and North America state policies and capitalist agriculture set the stage for concentration of landownership and the pro-gressive displacement of people from the land. At the same time that landownership was consolidated in the United States, the breakup of colonialism in Asia, Africa, and Latin America fostered various types of land reform, including land resettlement schemes, the privatization of common lands, and the establishment of communal farms, which were usually developed to stifle peasant resistance movements. Unfortunately, land reforms that are initiated to put down peasant rebellions often end up limiting women's access to land. Here, I discuss how various colonial and state policies of privatization and land distribution limit women's access to land, after which I show how the failure of public policies to pre-vent land degradation affects rural women's lives.

Privatization and the Demise of Communal Land

Commercial agriculture alters land use and ownership patterns world wide. Alain de Janvry and E. Phillip LeVeen (1986) argue that it is essen-tially the privatization of land that forms capitalist social relations in agri-culture. Increased productivity provides the major justification for privatization. Colonial regimes and national governments in most regions of the world replaced traditional patterns of land use rights with privatization or state ownership of land, or a combination of the two. Throughout North America, South America, Africa, and many areas of Asia, colonial expansion privatized land by disrupting and usurping tribal rights to land. These often violent claims to land disenfranchised numerous indigenous ethnic groups in various regions of the world from their access to land.

Another justification for privatization of land or other natural resources derives from the "tragedy of the commons." G. Hardin's (1968) well respected but also much debated theory of the tragedy of the commons provides justification for increasing the privatization of natural resources, including land. Hardin argues that all resources owned in common will eventually be overexploited because individuals take as much as possible for personal use, given their lack of incentive for protecting common resources. Following Hardin, policymakers and scholars view privatization as the key to conserving resources, if people can be taught to internalize the costs and benefits of resource use, are rewarded for individual responsibility, and learn that rational use of the environment will benefit them.

Numerous problematic assumptions underlie the tragedy of the commons argument (McCay and Acheson, 1987). First, tragedy of the commons theorists make no distinction between open access and regulated access to common property; they assume open access with no formal or informal rules for regulating or monitoring use. Second, an individualistic, economic bias pervades the theory, as does the assumption that each individual will try to maximize short-term gains. Third, conceiving of common property from a Eurocentric perspective overlooks the specific contexts and multiple meanings that property holds for individuals and communities. Fourth, external authorities or privatization seems to offer solutions to natural resource problems to such theorists, whereas other possible solutions, such as local community management of resources, are ignored. Fifth, private owners do not necessarily protect natural resources for the long term. And finally, overexploitation problems, attributed to common property problems, often result from other factors, for example, the interests of capital.

N. S. Jodha offers a different view of common property resources. Using the dry regions of India as an example, he shows how state land policies privatizing common property resources disrupt traditional management systems and put additional pressure on the remaining common property. In the villages he studied, land area in common property declined from 31 to 22 percent between 1952 and 1982. These policy changes prompted villagers to give up traditional management practices that protected their land and resource base. In the dry regions of India, villages benefit enormously from common property. Poor households depend heavily on common property, especially for fuel and fodder, thus reducing rural income inequalities. These areas provide household income and employment during periods when other opportunities are virtually nonexistent. Jodha also discovered there was extensive interplay between common property and private farming systems, with 31 to 42 percent of nonpurchased farm inputs deriving from common property (Jodha, 1992:16). He suggests the tragedy of the commons becomes a self-fulfilling prophecy when common property converts from local management to open access. Policymakers devise misguided land-use policies based on inadequate comprehension of the social and environmental benefits of common property.

We need to add the perspective of gender to the problems of the tragedy of the commons theory discussed by Bonnie McCay and James Acheson (1987) and Jodha (1992). The decline in common property in the last thirty years means that women are hungrier, more isolated, and less able to provide for their families. First, women frequently lose their specified-use rights after privatization. Second, women and men follow different rules that control access to common property and resources (Rocheleau, 1988). Third, women often use resources at the margins of land use; they gather fodder, food, or fuel from common land not in agricultural or timber production. Fourth, women depend on the renewability and continued presence of natural resources to sustain their families' daily needs, thus they hold incentives to protect the land. Fifth, women often do their collecting in groups—the image of the individual herder or fisherman that typifies the tragedy of the commons argument omits the community interaction and interdependence of these women. Increasing privatization clearly specifies individual ownership of land—often to men—and forces women to either lose access to land use rights or to renegotiate these rights in their households and communities, which usually alters their resource conservation strategies.

The real tragedy is that colonial policies usurped women's rights to land and set the stage for the contemporary exclusion of women as landowners. In the following sections, I discuss how colonial and postcolonial policies in North America and Africa have excluded women from land.

Women's Access to Land in North America

Native Americans. In North America, British colonists and subsequently U.S. and Canadian governments disrupted Native American patterns of communal ownership that explicitly included women. Land transfers to individual European men favored family farms in the North and plantations in the South (Jensen, 1981).

Prior to the European presence, women produced the majority of agricultural goods in eastern North America. Although Native American women legally held no title to land, they gained access to land through their tribes and not only through their husbands' access to land. Many Native American agricultural societies were matrilineal with inheritance passed through female lines of descent. Maryann Oshana, a Chippewa, describes matrilineal tribes: "Women in these tribes owned houses, furnishings, fields, gardens, agricultural tools, art objects, livestock, and horses. Furthermore, these items were passed down through female lines. Regardless of marital status, women had the right to own and control property" (as quoted in Amott and Matthaei, 1990:35).

The Iroquois Great Law of Peace states that "women shall be considered the progenitors of the nation. They shall own the land and the soil. Men and women shall follow the status of their mothers. You are what your mother is: The ways in which you see the world and all things in it are through your mother's eyes" (as quoted in Amott and Matthaei, 1990:36).

By 1850, women Native Americans no longer composed the agriculturalists in the eastern United States. Almost all Native American tribes had been relocated or decimated, or had moved west of the Mississippi. Merchant (1989) discusses the ways in which disrupting Native American women's centrality in agriculture in New England set the stage both for women's continual displacement from agriculture in New England and for ecological depletion. Private ownership of land prevailed as European white men continued to be exclusive land owners. Several decades later in western North America, white settlers unsuccessfully encouraged Native American hunters and gatherers to adopt European methods of agriculture and views on gender relations. The governor of the Washington Territory informed a gathering of male Indian tribal leaders in 1855 of the U.S. government's vision for the Indians:

> Each man . . . will work to have his own land, his own horses, his own cattle, and his own home for himself and his children . . . We want your women to spin and weave and to make clothes . . . and [do] all the work of the house and lodges . . . We also want to provide you with tools for your farms, with ploughs and hoes, and shovels . . . and all the implements the white man has; we want in your houses plates and cups and brass and tin kettles, frying pans to cook your meat and bake ovens to bake your bread, like white people. (as quoted by Janiewski, 1988:38)

The U.S. government's attempt to alter the relations of Native Americans to the land and to change gender relations met with resistance. Native Americans disapproved of the attempts by missionaries and government officials to convince northwestern tribes that men should work in agriculture and that women's place was in the home. Sitting Bull, one of the leaders of the Oglala Teton Sioux tribe, in speaking to a white woman in the

1880s, revealed his concern about taking the land from women: "You are a woman, take pity on my women for they have no future. The young men can be like the white men, can till the soil, supply the food and clothing. They will take the work out of the hands of the women. And the women, to whom we have owed everything in the past, they will be stripped of all which gave them power and position among the people. Give my women a future!" (as quoted in Janiewski, 1988:41).

In his plea, Sitting Bull recognized that Native women's positions depended on their access to land. From the beginning, in fact, the U.S. government excluded European and African women as well as Native American women from landownership.

European Americans. In the United States, first law and then custom restricted white women from owning and controlling land. Laws and customs prevented married women from owning land, although women could legally inherit land upon the death of their parents or spouses. Under common law, married women lost their right to hold property. During the nineteenth century, women successfully achieved rights for married women to hold land in their own names. Nevertheless, men continued to control the vast majority of agricultural land (Jensen, 1991). As Wava Haney and Jane Knowles (1988) point out, this patriarchal organization of landownership and limited access to land as collateral set a precedent for excluding women from the capitalization of American agriculture in the twentieth century. Women's lack of capital severely constrained their ability to purchase land, as is evidenced by the fact that women who do own land are much more likely to have acquired it through inheritance or gift than are men. In 1978, 33 percent of farm women landowners acquired their land by inheritance or gift, as compared to only 11 percent of men. In addition, women, on average, own smaller farms than men; in 1978 farms operated by women averaged 112 acres compared to 131 acres for men (Geisler, Water, and Eadie, 1986:81).

Black Women. For other women in the United States, exclusion from access to land resulted not only because of their gender, but also because of their class and racial backgrounds. In the postbellum South, poor black and white women worked as sharecroppers with no legal title to land (Jones, 1985; Hagood, 1977; Sachs, 1983). Between 1865 and 1940, almost all rural black women and an increasing proportion of rural white women labored in agriculture under the tenancy system. Families depended on landlords for access to land, equipment, supplies, clothing, housing, and sometimes food (Jones, 1988). They were not on the proverbial agricultural ladder that would eventually result in landownership. As one tenant woman aptly described their condition, "We seem to move around in circles like the mule that pulls the syrup mill. We are never still, but we never get anywhere" (as quoted in Jones, 1988:17).

Jacqueline Jones argues convincingly that although southern rural black and white tenant women shared similar class positions in relation to land, the "legacy of slavery and the persistent exploitation of blacks as agricultural laborers produced histories of black and white women that were as separate as they were unequal" (1988:29). Both black and white women cared for their children, raised and cooked food, and did enormous amounts of work to support their families. But the meaning and consequences of this work differed for black and white women. Because many black women cared, cooked, and cleaned for white families, the time and energy they could devote to their own families was constrained. Taking care of their own children and raising and cooking for their own families had a different meaning for them; it was time spent not directly supporting white families.

As this brief history suggests, in the United States today, blacks have extremely limited access to land. Black access to agricultural land reached its height in 1920 and continually declined during the rest of the twentieth century. In 1920, blacks operated 746,717 farms in the United States and 1 in 7 farm operators was black. By 1987, the number of black-operated farms had declined to 22,954, with the ratio of black farm operators decreasing to 1 in 91. Concentration of farmland resulted in the loss of both black- and white-operated farms, but the decline for blacks was consistently higher. For example, in Maryland between 1982 and 1987, black-operated farms declined by 33 percent compared to 9 percent for whites (Demissie, 1992:23). Few, if any studies, focus specifically on black women's access to land, but clearly their access to land through their families is increasingly limited. Thus, the varied forms of women's historical exclusion from landownership in the United States essentially functioned to close any avenue of opportunity for women's future landownership.

Women's Land Movement. During the 1970s, a women's land movement emerged in the United States, organized to gain access to land for women. Recognizing that women's access to land was limited by combined class, race, and gender oppressions, numerous groups of women organized to establish areas of "women's land." Many, though not all, of these women were lesbians attempting to escape patriarchal culture and create safe, secure places for women to live and work. Between 1970 and 1990, women initiated at least 80 separate women's lands. Although the groups that support the effort vary in their politics, they agree on several common principles: resistance to individual ownership of land, nonhierarchal decisionmaking, commitment to care and nurturing of the land, and personal and spiritual growth. Long-term survival of these women's lands remains problematic due to lack of resources, isolation in remote areas with limited access to employment, transiency, and clashes in political and personal values. Nevertheless, many of these women's lands survive such travails, often by changing structures, or by expanding onto new women's lands.

In 1991 and 1992, Laurel Zastrow and I conducted interviews with over 30 women living on women's land in 15 states and provinces in the United States and Canada. These women freely offered their stories and provided us with information on the successes, problems, and continuing visions and realities in these women's lands. Many women's persistent efforts to build communities have continued over fifteen to twenty years' duration. With experience, these women quickly became aware of the limits of their skills and of their need to learn new skills. Those interviewed rated poverty and economic insecurity as their major problems. They counted their major successes as building houses, preserving the environment, and providing places for women to live. Many of these women articulated a radical vision of the countryside. Identifying themselves variously as lesbian-feminists, marxists, anarchists, and feminists, a good number of women viewed their efforts as attempts to create nonpatri-archal space and to preserve the earth. Some are separatists, focusing solely on building their own communities or other women's communities, whereas others actively participate in broader local and community politics related to environmental, sexuality, and gender issues. Although their impact on their local communities remains difficult to assess, they certainly bring different attitudes and perspectives into their areas. Many of the women hope to build stronger linkages with urban women's communities; few consider themselves closely connected to traditional rural culture. Lesbians without traditional ties to the land experience difficulties, but landownership comes no more easily to women in sub-Saharan Africa.

Colonial and Postcolonial Land Policies
in Sub-Saharan Africa

Using arguments amazingly similar to those used to convince Native Americans to transform their social relations, during the 1900s colonial officials and missionaries in southern and eastern Africa attempted to push men into farming. Like the British government in North America, colonial and postcolonial governments in southern and eastern Africa were successful in persuading Africans to consolidate land in men's names, with the goal of increasing cash crop production. In their overview of women and state policies in Africa, Jane Parpart and Kathleen Staudt (1989) claim that the most significant of all male gains in Africa has been land reform that places land in men's names. Traditional patterns of access to and control over land in most African societies showed unequal distribution between the sexes, with women's access to land usually being mediated by male family members—women's husbands, fathers, or adult sons (Lovett, 1990). Colonial and state land reform policies used these traditional systems to legitimize male landownership. In contrast to the situation in many other parts of the world, state policies and development strategies keep African women attached to the land, despite their limited direct or formal legal control over the land (Chazan, 1990).

In Kenya, for instance, colonial initiatives to privatize land in the 1950s and the government of Kenya's move to create individual ownership of land in 1963 undermined women's rights to land (Trenchard, 1987). Land tenure reform undermined customary land use in several ways. The government granted the most productive land to white settlers, whereas the more marginal land was designated as reserves for racial and ethnic groups. Policies for the reservation land then shifted, removing landownership from the traditional lineage pattern and investing individual household heads with land in order to stem African resistance to colonialism by creating a middle class African peasantry. Men were registered as landowners with the justification that "It is customary: Men own land and women do not own land" (as quoted in Lovett, 1990:38). For example, almost all the land in Luoland was registered by 1975, but only 6 percent of women had land registered in their names (Okeyo, 1980). Women's security on the land, previously protected under customary land rights, is now tenuous; women now farm their husbands' land as an obligation rather than as a right. Although women farm their husbands' land, their lack of ownership deprives them of collateral to obtain loans to acquire capital input for their agricultural enterprises.

In Zimbabwe as well, precolonial and colonial governing policies set the stage for women's limited access to land. Shona society, although patrilineal and strongly male-dominated, granted women use rights to land to grow their crops. Under colonial law, however, women were declared legal minors and often lost their customary rights to land (Jacobs, 1990). During the struggle for independence, women demanded that their interests be addressed by the postcolonial government and that land be allocated specifically to women. Control over land use represented the focal point of resistance against the Rhodesian government, in the guerrilla war waged mainly in the countryside. Women in villages actively supported the guerrilla movements, whereas the men, who lived in towns, were largely removed from the war in the countryside. As a result of women's direct involvement in the resistance, including their activities in forming the rhetoric of the liberation movements, the postcolonial Zimbabwe government passed legislation relating to women after coming to power. In 1982, the legal age of majority act, which was the major piece of legislation drawn up in direct response to women's involvement in the resistance, was passed. It conferred adult status on African women over eighteen years of age. However, such legislation proved more effective for addressing the needs of urban women (Pankhurst, 1989). Rural women seldom benefited from that legislation because it was in contradiction to traditional law and the authority of chiefs and headmen in rural areas. Rural women today express reluctance to use the courts because they perceive that when women do, they are generally unsuccessful, must pay court costs, and are also open to ridicule. Thus, D. Pankhurst (1989) suggests these laws fail to change rural women's lives substantially because women remain ill-informed about the degree to which the state could support them. Also, their deeply ingrained beliefs about marriage and inheritance, material poverty, and lack of education bar them from using legal channels.

For rural women, gaining access to land represents their major need: "Land itself is a great problem, we don't have enough of it. We are too crowded. Some of our sisters have no land at all. They want some land so that they can help themselves" (as quoted in Batezat and Mwalo, 1989:9). To address the problem of land access, the Zimbabwe government instituted land resettlement. Land resettlement programs, designed to improve the conditions of the peasantry, redistribute land taken from whites to black Africans. However, the effect of the resettlement program remains marginal, benefiting less than 5 percent of households in communal areas and composing only 16 percent of commercial farmland (Mumbengegwi, 1986). Resettlement schemes, not specifically designed to recognize of women's needs, grant women rights to land largely through their husbands. Rural women express anger at the major criterion for resettlement: Only men who were not working for wages are eligible. Women without husbands due to widowhood, divorce, or migration remain excluded from access to land.

Recognizing that land privatization seldom benefits African women, M. S. Muntemba, writing about Zambia, argues that socialized forms of land systems are preferable to privatization. "Land reforms and schemes resulting in privatization as the means of bolstering small-scale production must be challenged: They do not take women into consideration . . . instead, socialized forms of land systems in which all producers have usufructory rights must be fostered" (Muntemba, 1982). Despite these optimistic hopes, socialist land reform programs in many countries, such as in Ujamma in Tanzania, rarely brought gains for women. Clearly we will continue to see the expansion of privatization schemes in previously socialist countries. It is doubtful that concerns about women's access to land will guide public policies of land privatization. Perhaps more central and practical for the majority of rural women are polices relating to common property and land distribution.

Distribution of Land

Once private property governs access to land, the structural conditions are set for continued concentration and expropriation of land through market forces and state policies (de Janvry and LeVeen, 1986). These patterns of land tenure and distribution result in differential access of households to land. Land ownership is highly concentrated in most Third World countries, especially in Asia and Latin America. The majority of rural residents depend on agriculture for their survival and income. However, many work as tenants, sharecroppers, or as wage laborers on land that they do not own. In many areas of the world, concentration of the most productive land into large, commercial farms displaces many families from the land. Rural people continually migrate to urban areas to escape poverty and landlessness in the countryside; these migrants often form the core of the urban poor (Lipman-Blumen, 1986). Concentration of land squeezes peasants and smaller farmers onto smaller, often more marginal, plots of land, increasing poverty and land degradation.

Landless rural women compose the poorest of the poor. Because of severe inequities in land ownership, numerous rural women live in households with limited or no access to land. Landless and near-landless households constitute over 75 percent of rural households in many Asian and Latin American countries, including Bolivia, Guatemala, Indonesia, El Salvador, the Philippines, Sri Lanka, Bangladesh, Ecuador, and Peru (Dankelman and Davidson, 1988). Unable to depend on access to their families' land as a survival strategy, they seek access to income through informal activities or wage labor, often on large commercial farms or in agribusiness operations.

Various land reform programs designed to redistribute land to landless or near-landless households largely fail to benefit women directly. Policies of land reform in various Latin American countries target men as the principal direct beneficiaries. Carmen Diana Deere and Magdalena Leon's review of agrarian reform programs in thirteen Latin American countries found that despite variations in political motivations, extent of rural households effected, and organization of production, men were the primary beneficiaries. Even in Cuba and Nicaragua, socialist countries that specify rural women as beneficiaries, men were still favored. In Cuba, 25 percent of the beneficiaries were women, compared to 12 percent in Mexico, 6 percent in Nicaragua, and 4 percent in Honduras. Agrarian reform efforts excluded women as beneficiaries by designating household heads, usually men, as eligible for title to land. For example, in the Andean highlands, traditional land inheritance patterns were typically bilateral. Women's access to land ownership gave them power in agricultural decisionmaking and security, factors that kept them from being totally dependent on their spouses. Peruvian agrarian reform failed to benefit rural women because individual land titles went to male heads of household (Deere and Leon, 1987:122). As a consequence of limited opportunities, many young women leave rural areas to seek employment in urban areas. In various Latin American countries, landless and small peasant households send young women family members to urban areas; these women living in urban areas then send money to their rural households.

Land Degradation

Because you can die of overwork, because
you can die of the fire that melts
rock, because you can die of the poison
that kills the beetle and the slug,
we must come again to worship you
on our knees, the common living dirt.

—Marge Piercy, 1991

Major environmental problems that accompany agriculture include degradation of land through soil erosion, fertility decline due to overuse and poor production practices, and contamination of soil and water through use of chemical fertilizers and pesticides. These environmental problems may well have more far-reaching implications for women than their problems with either access to or ownership of land. What type of agriculture leads to land degradation? In what ways is land degradation a gendered process, that is to say, how are women implicated or affected differently than men?

Ecological systems are not only endangered by ecologically unwise agricultural practices, they are endangered by all agriculture (Redclift, 1987). Agriculture transforms natural ecosystems to serve human needs, replacing mature ecosystems characterized by high diversity, large biomass, and high stability with young systems, characterized by limited diversity, high productivity, and limited accumulation of biomass and organic material. Thus, as Michael Redclift explains, maximizing agricultural production inevitably leads to the removal of mature ecosystems or serves to slow their development. The costs involved include disruption of the natural mechanisms of ecosystem protection or resilience and the need to provide enormous amounts of energy not available from nature: "Fertilizers, fuels for machinery, irrigation technology, genetic selection of species and pest control are all facets of this attempt to renew immature ecological systems in a state of high productivity." The problem we face with our current ecologically harmful agricultural systems "is not simply how to compensate for the interruption of ecological succession, it is frequently how to ensure that production itself does not degrade resources beyond the point of renewal" (Redclift, 1987:18).

Soil loss and declining fertility, nutrient buildup and nitrogen contamination of soil and water, and pesticide contamination of soil and water head the list of the causes of land and water degradation. I briefly discuss each of these problems, elaborated elsewhere in detailed studies (Pimentel, et al., 1991; Blaikie, 1985), outlining their particular connection to or impact on women. I then discuss women's attempts to resolve these problems through their involvement in the sustainable agricultural movement.

Soil Loss and Fertility Decline

Loss of topsoil and fertility decline from agricultural practices create major problems in many regions of the world. Cultivation practices, decline of grazing lands, deforestation, salinization, and oversaturation of soils from irrigation cause soil loss and fertility decline. Large-scale, highly mechanized agricultural systems put intense pressure on soil. Interestingly, many of these agricultural methods that employ new technologies, such as the plow, that contribute to soil loss and declining soil quality are exactly those that have replaced women's agricultural methods. More than any other technology, plow cultivation causes soil erosion. As Ester Boserup (1970) argues, the use of plow cultivation distinguishes men's from women's cropping systems.

In the early 1900s, the use of tractors began to drastically transform agriculture in the United States. Tractors eased the physical burden of fieldwork and enabled fewer people to farm larger tracts of land. We cannot deny the beneficial aspects of tractors, but their introduction clearly altered the organization of work on farms and exacerbated soil erosion and compaction; the extent of the dust bowl of the 1930s in the United States illustrates the social and ecological consequences of overcultivation. On some farms, tractors replaced women's and children's family labor, whereas on other farms tractors displaced hired workers. Men, almost exclusively, design, own, and operate large-scale farm equipment such as tractors and harvesters. In the Midwest, the introduction of the tractor transformed gender relations on the farm (Jellison, 1993). Men owned and controlled mechanical equipment, and with few exceptions they operated mechanical equipment in the fields. One notable exception occurred during World War II, when a shortage of male labor on farms resulted in the establishment of the Women's Land Army and a call for women to become "tractorettes." Women drove tractors, but similar to their urban counterparts, the Rosie the Riveters, these women lost their places on tractors after the war.

In African regions relying on hoe cultivation, development agencies and national governments introduced the plow to men. Agriculture extension services trained men to use ox plows and drive tractors. Mechanical equipment other than hand tools for land preparation, whether tractors or plows, was viewed as men's domain. Women's limited use of heavy equipment did not derive from their desire to protect the soil; rather, men monopolized this equipment. These systems of production simultaneously marginalize women and damage the soil.

Numerous strategies minimize soil erosion, but recent efforts emphasize reduced tillage practices such as no-tillage, strip tillage, and ridge tillage which can significantly reduce soil erosion by 75 percent or more (National Research Council, 1989). To correct the problems associated with intensive mechanical cultivation, reversion to less intensive cultivation is now recommended. Recognizing these broader problems in U.S. grain-based production systems, Wes Jackson and Marty Bender (1984) propose perennial polycultures that do not depend on annual tillage in the plains as the solution to soil erosion and environmental degradation.

Continuous monoculture or short rotations make soils more susceptible to erosion and also contribute to a decline in soil organic matter and nutrients. For example, continuous cropping of corn and cotton, which have high nutrient needs, results in declining soil fertility and an increasing need to use fertilizers. In the tropics, shifting cultivation or fallow agriculture is the traditional strategy for maintaining soil fertility. The amount of land in shifting cultivation systems continues to decline, but as late as 1970 approximately one-third of the world's arable land was in shifting cultivation (Jones and O'Neill, 1993). Tropical soils rapidly lose fertility under cultivation and quickly show signs of nitrogen and potassium deficiency. Long fallow periods and burning traditionally solved problems of declining soil fertility. For example, the *chitemene* system of shifting cultivation in Zambia involves cutting and harvest of woody vegetation on a 1 to 5 hectare area and then piling and burning the wood for the entire area on a small plot about one-fifth that size (Rocheleau, 1988). High heat and ash concentrated from the woody biomass raise soil pH and soil fertility on the small cultivated plot. Crop rotation follows a six-year cycle with several years of lying fallow. Pressure to use land shortens fallow periods and reduces productivity.

Interestingly, many of the agricultural strategies historically used by women in various parts of world, such as limited tillage, intercropping, and fallow agriculture, are currently being introduced as sustainable agricultural practices. Women's marginalization or exclusion from capital intensive agriculture and large-scale landholding encouraged them to develop particular forms of labor-saving and land-intensive practices. These practices, often viewed as backward and a hindrance to agricultural development efforts, are now being reformulated as "new" approaches to agriculture, with only rare acknowledgment that many of these new approaches derive from women's traditional practices.

Nutrient Buildup and Nitrates in Groundwater

Heavy use of chemical fertilizer and concentration of feedlots and animal production cause major nitrogen contamination of groundwater in many regions of North America and Europe. When farmers increase the use of commercial fertilizer to raise nitrogen levels—the limiting nutrient in many soils—they are able to maintain and increase productivity. After 1945, the availability of cheap and easy-to-use anhydrous ammonia drastically transformed fertilizer use in agriculture. For example, U.S. nitrogen use increased from 62,000 tons in 1900 to 419,000 tons in 1940, then leaped to 1,847,000 in 1954 (Perkins and Holochuck, 1993:396). Fertilizer use continues to increase, and at present in the United States, high levels of nitrates in groundwater occur in intensive agricultural regions, especially in the Midwest and California. Several states promote strategies for decreasing groundwater contamination, but few major changes in agricultural production practices have been legislated (National Research Council, 1989). High levels of nitrates in water harm lactating women and infants particularly. In areas such as rural Iowa, health officials encourage women to purchase water for infants. Contaminated water puts additional pressure on women when they perform household tasks that use water, such as cooking, cleaning, and washing. Clearly, policies fail to consider women's perspectives.

Pesticide Contamination of Soil and Water

The global food system relies increasingly on pesticides as well as on chemical fertilizers. Systems of production based on monoculture, new plant varieties, and newly introduced crops often depend on the use of insecticides, fungicides, and herbicides. Since the 1950s, pesticide use has expanded rapidly both in terms of volume and market value. About 4.4 million tons of pesticides are applied annually, with a market value of $20 billion (Edwards, 1993:13). Developing countries use about 15 percent of the world's pesticides, a figure that includes 30 percent of world insecticide use (Bull, 1982:6). Pesticide use brings the benefits of health and increased production, and with that, problems of health effects, soil and water contamination, and pesticide resistance. Contamination of water by pesticides represents a growing problem throughout the world. In most regions of the world, the poorest people suffer most from pesticide poisonings, resulting from having to live near agricultural fields and their lack of options concerning access to safe water and health care. In many rural regions of the world, women supply water for their households, and the contamination of local water supplies adds extra hours to their day as they seek safe sources of water.

Problems with pesticide use for Asian rice farmers include direct exposure to pesticides, use of contaminated water for washing and watering livestock, and decline of the fish population in paddies. The following description illustrates the problems:

> In many ways, the rice farmers really live in the rice field environment. Their houses are surrounded by rice fields, they work barefooted in the fields, wash in the water spilling from the fields, their cattle drink it and their fowls peck in and around paddy fields ... There is no doubt that indiscriminate use of pesticides has an impact on the environment. There are reports of fish kills, particularly in the rice fields and irrigation canals, and there have been fatal cases of livestock poisoning (grazing on contaminated pastures) in plantations. (Bull, 1982:64)

For example, in the state of Karnataka in southwestern India, many poor laborers who worked in the rice fields contracted a crippling disease that was attributed to direct exposure to parathion and endrin in paddy fields and to eating crabs from the paddies that were also contaminated with pesticides (Bull, 1982). In most regions of Asia, women's work in rice production entails spending long hours in the paddies in knee-deep water transplanting and weeding. These women have developed high susceptibility to the effects of toxic chemicals.

Severe health effects from pesticide use are not limited to the Third World. It is estimated that approximately 313,000 U.S. farmworkers may suffer from pesticide-related illnesses annually. Risks for farmworkers increase geometrically when organophosphates, nonpersistent in the environment but acutely toxic, replaced persistent organochlorines such as DDT, which accumulated in soil, water, and animal tissue (Wasserstrom and Wiles, 1985:3). These new chemicals, fortunately, eliminate many of the environmental problems caused by DDT, but they pose greater hazards to the handlers of chemicals. U.S. farmworkers, many of whom are people of color, have high rates of both acute and chronic pesticide poisoning (Perfecto, 1992). Many farmworkers and their families, especially migrant workers, live and work in close proximity to pesticides and are exposed to far greater amounts of pesticides than typical consumers (National Research Council, 1989). For example, groundwater contamination by pesticides is especially acute in California vegetable- and fruit-producing regions such as the San Joaquin Valley. High proportions of Hispanic residents, many of whom are farmworkers, live in these regions, work in fields, and drink water from contaminated wells. Perhaps most disturbing of all, women and children are more vulnerable to the effects of pesticides than men, but U.S. government policy sets pesticide health standards based on the effects of pesticides on the healthy adult male (Gilbert, 1992). Even though pregnant women and their fetuses are particularly vulnerable to the effects of pesticides, the limited research that is conducted performs tests for the effects of specific pesticides only to determine rates of birth defects and miscarriage. People and organizations concerned about these environmental problems have coalesced to form a sustainable agriculture movement.

Women in the Sustainable Agriculture Movement

The sustainable agriculture movement emerged in the late 1970s to address problems associated with conventional agriculture, particularly pesticide use and the increasing power of agribusiness. The issues of sustainable agriculture and sustainable development were soon under discussion in mainstream agriculture and development policymaking institutions. Concepts of sustainable agriculture, originally intended as a challenge to conventional agriculture, are now regular subjects in policy discussions within the World Bank, the United States Department of Agriculture, and other national and international agricultural agencies. "Sustainability" has become a buzzword used by agriculture policymakers in the late 1980s and early 1990s, indicating concern with ecology and the environment. Patricia Allen and I argue that in these contexts the agenda for sustainable agriculture narrows considerably to technical approaches aimed to reduce the environmental impact of agricultural practices without questioning the inequitable class, race, and gender relations in agriculture (Allen and Sachs, 1992). How, in fact, does the sustainable agricultural movement relate to women?

To explore women's position and their experience in the sustainable agriculture movement, I conducted in-depth interviews with women farmers, activists, and academic leaders in the sustainable agriculture movement in California in 1990. I here supplement my findings with Grace Gershuny's (1991) interviews of women and men in the organic agricultural movement.

Women play key positions in the sustainable agriculture movement at the grass-roots level, often taking the lead by organizing local chapters, holding meetings, writing newsletters, and organizing conferences. As one of the state leaders affirmed, "Women are often working behind the scenes. All of my good volunteers that helped organize conferences and do mailings were women. Men have a way of getting into positions that are more glorious." Or, as a woman from Oregon explained, "It's interesting to note that most of the pesticide education work and environmental awareness on the local level is done by women. I've noticed that conferences seem to be attended by a lot of six-foot tall white men, but [the conferences] are all organized by women. The kind of work that has kept the organization stable has been done by women" (as quoted in Gershuny, 1991:8).

When interviewed, women organic farmers reported that they became involved in organic farming as a result of their concern over the toxic effects of pesticides, their desire to take care of land and preserve ecosystems, and their dissatisfaction with the organization of the food system. The respondents said they became involved with organic agriculture when it was a marginal occupation. They saw the evolution of organic agriculture into the mainstream as a mixed blessing, expressing concern that "large producers will squeeze out little people who are doing organic production because they believe in it" and that "bigger farmers want to put their land into organic production to make a profit, but for me it is a commitment." These women worried that many of the social values associated with organic farming would disappear as production increased.

Perhaps women approach organic farming differently than men. No consensus existed among the women I interviewed on whether women's approach to farming is unique. Many women said they approach farming differently than their husbands, but they also recognized differences among women, refuting an essentialist position. One woman explained the difference between women and men on organic farms: "My women friends know it's crazy to get on the production treadmill—we don't want our lives to be like that and want to hold on to family and social values as well as producing more. There is a tendency for male egos (and women with these egos) to get caught up in the money cycle and lose sight of why we are farming organically. This emphasis on production makes our lives insane and we need to think about slowing down a bit."

Grace Gershuny asked this question of the women and men she interviewed: "Have women served as the guardians of organic values, and can organic values be considered to be feminine values? How does this relate to feminism and to men in organic agriculture?" (1991:10). Some women responded that women's unique approach derives from their experience as mothers, although they insisted on a cultural rather than a biological basis for these experiences. Several of the women rejected the existence of "feminine values," noting that men in the organic agriculture movement tend to share caring and environmental values. Interestingly, the two men

Gershuny interviewed embraced the idea that feminist values offer opportunities for organic agriculture to transcend patriarchal systems.

Another question arises when considering values: Are these feminist values based on upper-class white women's values or do they include the values of women from different racial and ethnic groups? The U.S. sustainable agriculture movement remains predominantly white. The women leaders I interviewed were all white. However, many Latinas, for example, Dolores Huerta, take the lead in political protests against pesticide use, especially in conjunction with farmworker health issues. Dolores Huerta and Cesar Chavez organized the United Farm Workers (UFW) during the 1960s and 1970s. Their efforts resulted in increased pay and benefits, improved working conditions, and regulations related to pesticide use (Amott and Matthaei, 1990). The UFW employed innovative tactics such as hunger strikes and the grape boycott to achieve its aims. Issues were not framed as exclusively women's issues, but the concern with improved working and living conditions for workers and the reliance on consumer support in the boycott were clearly in the domain of women's concerns. Dolores Huerta (1992) remarks that the UFW was particularly concerned with the way misuse of pesticides affected farmworkers through contaminated wells, producing birth defects and cancer. She also describes companies that used pesticides for political control and in some incidents deliberately sprayed workers. Sustainable agriculture issues affect more than upper-middle-class white people. In fact many of the victims of pesticide-related illnesses and deaths are Hispanic and black farmworkers in the United States and farmworkers in Africa, Asia, and Latin America. Clearly issues of sustainability differ by class, race, and nationality; organic farmers are concerned with production and income, farmworkers are concerned with wages, living conditions, and worker safety; and consumers are concerned with food safety and cost. Outside the United States many women participate in sustainable agriculture organizations but possess limited representation in decisionmaking in the sustainable agriculture movement.

At the 1990 conference of the International Federation of Organic Agricultural Movements (IFOAM) in Budapest, women met to address their underrepresentation as speakers at the conference and as board members of IFOAM, which is an international federation of grass-roots, state, national, and continental organizations with representation from Africa, Asia, Europe, North America, South America, and Australia. Their complaints were based on the fact that women represent the majority of people involved in organic agricultural work worldwide. They called for a special workshop at the conference to discuss women's issues and presented a series of recommendations at the closing plenary session of the conference. These recommendations suggested establishing a special task force to address women's issues, incorporating more women on the board of IFOAM and in member organizations, and offering more sessions on women's involvement in organic farming in future conferences.

Although women pursue the practical aspect of issues and contribute to the success of the sustainable agriculture movement, rarely do they introduce feminist concerns as key issues. Men are assuming the leadership positions in the sustainable agriculture movement as it becomes institutionalized. At this juncture, women's voices may lead the way in calling for attention to be paid to deeper ecological and social questions (Allen, 1993)—despite the tendency of scientists and government officials to discredit women's knowledge and eclipse women's grass-roots activities.

Summary on Women and Land

Privatization, commercialization, and capitalization of agriculture contribute to women's declining control of and access to land. Patriarchal organization of rural households and patrilineal inheritance systems in combination with extant land policies erect major barriers to women's access to land. In agriculture, landownership provides the major source of collateral for obtaining access to other capital. Prevented from owning land, women lack the major source of collateral, which means they cannot get credit to buy equipment, more land, or more animals to succeed as modern farmers. In most regions of the world, women's exclusion from landownership limits their access to credit to purchase the required materials to succeed in an increasingly capital-intensive agricultural system. Although few women own land and even fewer exercise control over land, rural women's access to land varies by their class and ethnicity. Limited access to land and, consequently, capital historically situates women in a different relationship to capitalist agriculture than is enjoyed by men of their same class, racial group, and nationality. Concentration of landownership displaces many rural people from land; more poor people, especially in regions of Asia and Latin America, experience landlessness or near landlessness. Further, despite women's marginalization from control in the expansion of capitalist agriculture, women still provide the subsistence needs and the daily care for their children and families. Limited access to land means women must overcome major obstacles to meet food, fuel, and housing needs. Privatization of land often limits the access of the poorest women to adequate land to meet their families' subsistence needs; it also closes opportunities to use common land.

Limited access to land constitutes one problem for women, but the long-term degradation of soil and water and the immediate health effects of this degradation may produce more severe problems for rural people. Highly mechanized, specialized, and chemically dependent agricultural systems pose particular problems for women. Women and children, especially those of color, suffer disproportionately from nitrate- and pesticide-related illnesses. Pregnant and lactating women, and children as well, experience greater susceptibility to the health effects of nitrates and pesticides. These agricultural problems make women work harder to provide clean water and healthy food for their families. Finally, many women fight environmental problems through their efforts in the sustainable agricultural movement.

5

Women's Work with Plants

The decision to feed the world
is the real decision. No revolution
has chosen it. For that choice requires
that women shall be free.
I choke on the taste of bread in North America
but the taste of hunger in North America
is poisoning me.

—Adrienne Rich, from "Hunger," 1978

First as plant gatherers and then as the early inventors of horticulture, women have traditionally studied and cultivated plants. With the shift from hunter-gatherer and horticultural societies to agricultural societies, men began raising crops and gradually appropriated control over crop production (Stanley, 1982). Several factors characterize agricultural versus horticultural production. Agriculture is more extensive, is performed in fields rather than gardens, and often involves practices such as plow cultivation, irrigation, and fertilization. Intensive commercial agriculture tends to eliminate the use of fallow periods and reduces the diversity of crop rotations. Exactly why men gained control of crop production with the switch from horticulture to agriculture is subject to debate. Boserup's (1970) now classic argument suggests that the plow, with its heavy physical labor demands, signaled the switch from female to male farming systems. Lourdes Beneria and Gita Sen's (1981) thorough critique of Boserup's technological determinism points out that shifts in the sexual division of labor occurred not only with the introduction of the plow but also as a result of changes in the appropriation of land, capital accumulation, and women's reproductive capacity. A. Stanley (1982) asserts that Boserup fails to explain why men should plough rather than women. She attributes men's takeover as the confluence of factors including women's more frequent childbearing, exclusion from agricultural technology (the plow and large-scale irrigation), and decline of matrilineal support networks.

Theorists can point to no single factor that explains men's appropriation of crop production. In most areas of the world today, men control agricultural production, although women remain deeply involved in the daily labor. Despite, or perhaps as a consequence of, male control, women continue to provide the majority of manual labor in nonmechanized crop production. Gender divisions of labor in crop production vary by region, class, race, and the labor that individual crops require. However, certain commonalities can be noted that characterize gender relations in crop production, which include designation of specific crops by gender and division of tasks in cropping systems.

Women's and Men's Crops

In most farming systems, specific crops are designated as "women's" crops, whereas other crops are "men's." Crops are associated with the gender that controls the management and disposition of the crop rather than with those individuals who actually work on the crop. The gender assignments and designations vary from place to place, but characteristic patterns, documented in studies across the globe, tend to differentiate between men's and women's crops (Table 5:1). Men's crops are more likely to be of the following types: grain or tree; nonfood; raised for market; and raised for export. Women's crops are typically of this sort: vegetable or root; food; raised for subsistence; or raised for local consumption. There are exceptions to these patterns, and control of crops may be much more complex. For example, we find circumstances under which maize or rice are women's crops, women raise crops primarily for the market, or crops do not belong to one gender or the other.

Grain crops, such as wheat, corn, and rice, and specialty export crops often fall under men's control; by contrast, women usually assume control over vegetable crops like beans and over root crops like yams and cassava. Control over a crop by men or women does not directly coincide with a strict gender division of labor; often women provide substantial labor in men's crops, and men sometimes provide labor in women's crops. For example, in Swaziland, maize is designated as a men's crop,

TABLE 5.1   Characteristics of Men's and Women's Crops

	Men's Crops	Women's Crops
Crop type	Grain/trees	Vegetable/roots
Product	Nonfood/luxury	Food
Use	Market	Subsistence
Market location	International/national	Local

despite the fact that the women do the majority of labor. Men decide how much to plant, direct the labor of women, and control the marketing or distribution of the crop. However, the pattern of control over crops is more complicated, because some varieties of maize, especially those that are consumed fresh, belong to women, whereas other varieties, especially those that are sold, belong to men.

In many localities, men raise field crops for the market, and women raise crops that provide both food for the family and for sale. With expanding commercialization and capitalization of agriculture, use of land and labor for men's cash-crop production takes precedence over women's cropping systems. In a wide array of countries, the transition to cash-crop production has been detrimental to the poor, to women, and to the environment. Successful cash-crop production, usually controlled by men, depends on capital investment, for example, on mechanical equipment, fertilizers, pesticides, and access to the best natural resources, such as high-quality soil and adequate water. Frequently landowners devote the best land in any given region and on any particular farm to cash crops. Women seldom have access to high-quality land or to the credit and the capital necessary to adequately invest in cash-crop production. Ignoring women's responsibility in crop production, governments target information, training, and credit programs at men in rural areas. Consequently, women are both marginalized from cash-crop production and suffer a decline in their subsistence production because the land they use and their labor as well is allocated to cash crops under men's control.

Men usually control specialty, luxury, or "after-dinner crops" such as coffee, cotton, tobacco, tea, cocoa, sugar, and, more recently, flowers, all of which are produced for export markets and do not directly provide food for the producers. Writing in 1939 about cotton and tobacco production in the southern United States, Margaret Hagood touched on most of the problems that continue to plague small farmers who rely on a single cash crop: "When a farmer spends so much of his time on one of these crops that he cannot raise his food and feed, when he plants one of them consecutively without crop rotation and exhausts the soil, then he stakes his all on one crop which may in any year fail to yield a living income, the single cash crop system is at its worst" (Hagood, 1977:7).

Because these cash crops are usually sold on the global market, times of local or worldwide recession mean that farmers suffer when prices for commodities drop or fluctuate unpredictably. Declines in the prices of coffee, cacao, and cotton on the world market in the 1980s and 1990s have lowered farmers' incomes in many parts of the world.

Social relations that develop around export crops vary by agricultural and social systems in particular localities and countries. Export crops grow on large estates, plantations, farms dependent upon hired labor, and small family farms. The organization of production controls women's

Woman with child watering cabbages for market in Swaziland

involvement in agriculture. On large commercial farms, women often provide wage labor in the cultivation of labor-intensive, export crops. For example, in Sri Lanka, Tamil women harvest tea on large estates. In Swaziland, women perform field tasks on large-scale pineapple farms. On family farms, in numerous localities, women regularly provide labor for cash crop production but often lack control over the profits. For example, women in Cameroon assist their husbands in cacao production, but the crop belongs to the men. In Zimbabwe, women provide much of the labor in small-scale coffee plots, but the coffee marketing board issues checks to the family member, almost always a man, who holds a grain-marketing card.

Cash-crop production can raise producers' standards of living and is not inherently detrimental to rural women. Nevertheless, there are barriers to transforming income from cash crops into improved living standards for families. First, farmers receive minimal profits compared to their costs. Second, in societies where men are not obligated to contribute money from cash crops for their families' subsistence, women and children's standard of living often suffers with cash-crop production.

Raising crops for cash diverts women's labor from growing food for their families and performing other subsistence activities; nonetheless, in most rural areas women continue to produce subsistence crops as one

Women harvesting tomatoes on large tomato farm in Egypt

aspect of their responsibility for domestic and reproductive activities. However, in many rural households, as the need for cash pushes farmers to produce for the market, subsistence production is no longer the central activity. On U.S. farms, women persisted in producing food for their families long after men redirected their efforts toward commercial crops. Although almost all U.S. farms are geared toward market production and have sufficient incomes to purchase food, approximately 90 percent of contemporary U.S. farm women raise produce or animals for family consumption (Rosenfeld, 1985:57). There is no doubt these women's gardens are less extensive than those of their mothers or grandmothers, but women hold on to food production for the family to insure supplies of adequate and high-quality food. In Africa, Asia, and Latin America, colonial policies and more recent agricultural development projects and policies promote the transition from subsistence to commercial agriculture. By removing land and labor from the subsistence sector, the commercialization of agriculture disrupts women's subsistence production. Nevertheless, women, who lack other means of obtaining food, continue to produce their family's food supppply. Women's limited access to land on which they can raise food for their families has contributed to the food crisis in Africa. In Zimbabwe's coffee-growing regions, for example, the best land has been planted in coffee trees, so women produce vegetables and maize for family consumption on the remaining land. In Zambia, the introduction of new cash crops for men resulted in declining yields of cassava and groundnuts, women's subsistence crops (Muntemba, 1982). In Asia, Latin America, and Africa, declining possibilities for producing food means less food and higher incidence of malnutrition for rural families.

Gender Division of Tasks by Cropping Systems

In most cropping systems, tasks fall either to men or to women. Gendered division of tasks varies by class, by ethnicity, and by crop locality, but some clear general patterns emerge. Typically, women are more likely to do the work, the closer food is to the table. In almost all locations, women cook and process food. Labor-intensive activities such as transplanting, weeding, and harvesting often fall to women. Land preparation activities go to men whether performed with a tractor, chain saw, oxen, or water buffalo.

I will examine the diversity of women's activities and their knowledge of different crops by discussing their involvement with three specific crops—corn, rice, and coffee. In addition, I will discuss their work in gardens and with wild plants. Focusing on women's work, knowledge, and experiences with particular crops provides a basis for a historical and comparative understanding of women's work with plants and offers possible clues for ways to solve problems of malnutrition and develop more sustainable agricultural systems. I chose these three crops for several reasons. First, rice and corn constitute two of the three major grain crops in the world and are raised in a substantial proportion of the world's cultivated land area (Table 5.2). Second, farmers raise both crops as subsistence crops as well as cash crops, and both are grown in a variety of farming systems. Third, rice and corn are staples: rice in Asia and in particular regions of Africa; corn in southern and eastern Africa and in many areas of Latin America. I do not include wheat, despite its significance in the global food system. In her excellent work, Harriet Friedmann (1988) has thoroughly discussed the social relations that bear on global wheat production.

TABLE 5.2   Annual World Production of Major Grain Crops, 1985

Crop	Production (million tons)
Wheat	450
Corn	400
Rice	395
Barley	180
Oats	65
Sorghum	60
Millet	50
Rye	35

SOURCE: Food and Agriculture Organization.

Finally, I address coffee production, a nonfood crop raised primarily in Latin America and Africa. Although many North Americans and Europeans are convinced they could not survive without coffee, it is a luxury crop rather than a staple type of crop. I include a luxury nonfood crop to highlight the social relations involved in such production and select coffee because of its importance in the economies of many countries.

In researching and a writing about women's work in agriculture, I have learned a great deal and, simultaneously, have discovered several dangers. First, by examining a specific crop the researcher follows the reductionist tendency of Western science and development efforts of focusing narrowly on particular commodities and missing the broader context of social relations that produce these commodities. Second, women rarely organize their lives around production of one particular crop; instead they engage in multiple productive and reproductive activities. Third, this kind of research obscures women's multicropping strategies. Finally, given the diversity of cropping systems and gender relations, my approach does not cover the multitude of contexts in which women produce these crops. To address the first two difficulties, I look at women's work in particular crops as that relates to the broader social context. I also try to consider women's work in crop production in relation to the other aspects of their lives. In my discussion of women's gardens, I describe a context that is familiar to many women, one that crosses geographical and cultural boundaries. For each crop, I examine cropping systems in at least two regions.

From Three Sisters to Corn Monoculture

Corn is life. Its life is the life of men. . . . It is the eternal Mother, at once beneficent and terrible, on whose fecundity man must depend for his existence, but of which he is forever deeply afraid.

—Dorothy Giles, 1940

Corn or maize (*Zea mays*) has been the staple food crop of numerous people and cultures in the American and African continents. The search for the origins of corn long puzzled botanists because of the pervasiveness and diversity of maize varieties. Attempts to locate corn's ancestry led botanists to Mexico and the Andean highlands. Finally, in 1977, a wild perennial species genetically compatible with corn was identified in southwestern Mexico (Benz, 1990). Today, maize grows in virtually all regions of the world, with the largest areas of cultivation being in the Far East, North America, and Latin America. In 1990, corn was raised on 129 million hectares of land (Food and Agriculture Organization, *Production Yearbook*, Rome: FAO). Table 5.3 shows the distribution of maize hectares

TABLE 5.3   Regional Distribution of Maize: Hectares and Production, 1990

Region	Hectares	Percent of World Hectares	Production per 1,000 Metric Tons	Percent of World Production
North America	30,700	24.9	208,542	43.86
Europe	11,738	9.1	43,375	9.12
Oceania	73	0.0	362	0.00
USSR (former)	4,905	3.7	9,465	1.99
Other developed	3,063	2.3	16,000	3.36
Africa	12,452	9.7	19,916	4.18
Latin America	25,471	20.8	50,090	10.53
Near East	2,055	1.6	7,538	1.58
Far East	37,709	29.4	120,136	25.26
Other developing	3	0.0	5	0.00

SOURCE: Food and Agriculture Organization, Production Yearbook 44 (Rome: FAO,1991).

in different regions of the world. Corn's versatility and storage capacity has made it a favored grain in an extremely wide range of ecological regions, from the tropical lowlands to the northern plains, from 58° northern latitude in Canada and the USSR to 40° southern latitude in South America and in altitudes from below sea level to 12,000 feet in the Andes. Biologically, corn holds many advantages over other grains as a cereal crop for humans. Farmers harvest corn over an extended time period. People eat green corn as a vegetable early in the season and later as a hard grain. The husk surrounding the unusually large seeds provides protection from birds and rain and facilitates storage and transportation.

Corn in North America

> Indigenous like corn, [and also] like corn, the mestiza is a product of cross-breeding, designed for preservation under a variety of conditions. Like an ear of corn—a female seed-bearing organ—the mestiza is tenacious, tightly wrapped in the husks of her culture. Like kernels she clings to the cob; with thick stalks and strong brace roots, she holds tight to the earth—she will survive the crossroads. (Anzaldua, 1990:38)

Native American women in North, Central, and South America raised corn, beans, and squash—the three sisters. Among New England's agricultural tribes, the three-sisters agricultural production system provided the major food source. Women played the major role in planting, weeding, harvesting, and distributing corn, beans, and squash in most eastern woodland tribes in North America (Merchant, 1989). In the 1600s, Roger Williams of Rhode Island described Native American women's high yields of corn: "The woman of the family will commonly raise two or

Maize varieties in Peru

three heaps of twelve, fifteen, or twenty bushels a heap which they dry in round broad heaps; and if she have help of other children and friends, much more" (as quoted in Merchant, 1989:80). According to Merchant's estimates, corn provided about 65 percent of the calories for adult Indians (1989:80).

Women's multicropping systems for corn, beans, and squash used throughout the Americas had advantages in terms of nutrition, food availability, and increased yields. Native women planted maize and beans in hills, with the maize plants providing support for the climbing beans. They planted squash between the hills, providing a cover to keep weeds out and soil moisture in. Modern nutritional science later revealed that the combination of corn and beans in the diet results in a desirable protein balance not obtainable by consuming corn and beans separately. Corn supplies carbohydrates, small amounts of protein, and fat; beans supply proteins and contain tryptophan and lysine, in which corn is deficient, as well as riboflavin and nicotinic acid; and squash provides vitamin A and fat (Mangelsdorf, 1974). In addition to providing nutritional efficiency, this cropping system makes an efficient use of land, especially for people who do not use draft animals for tillage. Multicropping reduces pest problems, weed infestations, and assures the availability of some food if one crop fails. Long after the Native Americans developed these inter-cropping strategies, studies in agricultural science found that corn needs high levels of nitrogen to produce good yields and that beans or other legume crops fix nitrogen in the soil. Looking at these systems today from the standpoint of science, we find the complexity of the corn-beans-squash triad ecologically, nutritionally, and economically sound.

In mythology and ritual, the Corn Mother embodies the spiritual and material importance of corn production to Native American women. Eastern tribal myths of the Cherokee, Creek, Natchez, Iroquois, and Seneca Indians linked the origin of corn to a corn mother (Merchant, 1989; Jensen, 1991). The Corn Mother, a mythical woman whose body was placed in a clearing after her death, mysteriously caused corn to grow in the clearing. Different tribes produced variations on the myth, but the stories always included reference to women as the mother of corn. Indians' worship of the Earth Mother and deification of the corn plant were particularly troubling to Christians who attempted to halt Indian worship practices as early as 1560. Corn rituals still remain important ceremonies for many Native American tribes. In the American Southwest today, from Taos to Albuquerque, summer is punctuated by daylong corn dances and feasts.

European colonialists disrupted Indian agricultural systems and established their own. Prior to Columbus' journey to the Americas, Europeans knew nothing of corn. However European settlers in America, learning from the Native Americans, quickly saw the value of corn, and it is ironic that they used this knowledge against the Indians to further their colonization efforts. The ability of English settlers to survive their first years in Plymouth and Jamestown has been attributed to the presence of maize (Sargent, 1899). Europeans learned from Native Americans how to cultivate maize without extensive land clearing or plowing and learned how to prepare corn cakes and porridge; such skills enabled them to survive their first years in America. Later, corn provided the major food on ships carrying slaves from Africa to the Americas. Thus, maize seeds selected over the centuries by Native American women contributed to successful European colonization of the Americas and eventually greatly facilitated the long-distance African slave trade. The Native American women who provided Europeans with seeds and cropping systems unwittingly provided them with the ideal food for fueling European colonial efforts to subjugate both Native Americans and Africans.

Corn became the primary staple crop for the majority of Europeans in America in the eighteenth and early nineteenth centuries. In contrast to the Native American pattern of women producing corn, both men and women participated in corn production. Land preparation, no longer carried out by women with hoes, was now performed by men with oxen and plows. The three-sisters cropping systems disappeared, replaced by male-controlled European cropping systems using plow cultivation and planting single crops in rows. Women worked in the grain fields when necessary, especially during harvesting (Jensen, 1986), but field crops most definitely fell under male control. However, from the standpoint of labor, corn remained as much a women's and children's crop as it was men's. Criticizing men's reliance on women's labor in corn production in Virginia in 1728, William Byrd wrote: "Indian corn is of so great increase, that a little Pains will subsist a very large Family with Bread . . . The Men, for their Parts, just like the Indians, impose all the Work upon the poor Women. They make their Wives rise out of their Beds early in the Morning, at the same time that they Lye and Snore" (as quoted in Hardeman, 1981:37).

Corn was also a mainstay of the diet in the southern United States. We often overlook the importance of corn for southern plantation economies; it fed the slaves, animals, and fueled the cotton economy. In her travels through the southern United States, Harriet Martineau lauded the importance of corn in the South in 1837, claiming "a man who has corn may have everything. He can sow his land with it; and, for the rest, everything eats corn from slave to chick" (as quoted in Cummings, 1970:15). Plantation owners often gave slaves corn plots of their own to raise food for their families and feed for their animals..

Immigrant women on the western frontier contributed heavily to fieldwork. European disdain for white women's participation in fieldwork continually conflicted with the need for women's field labor in corn and wheat production. On the western frontier, corn also composed a major part of the diet, although it was not viewed as the preferred staple. As one Kansas frontier woman described it, "our living at first was very scanty, mostly corn coarsely ground or made into hominy. After we had raised a crop of wheat and had some ground, we would invite the neighbors, proudly telling them we would have 'flour doings.' Next it was 'chicken fixings.' And when we could have 'flour doings and chicken fixins' at the same meal we felt we were on the road to prosperity" (as quoted in Stratton, 1981:63).

As can be gleaned from this Kansas woman's story, wheat was the preferred food crop; indeed, corn was viewed as a poor food substitute. The European woman's attitude toward corn contrasts with a Native American woman's description of raising corn around the turn of the century in the Dakotas: "we cared for our corn in those days, as we would care for a child; for we Indian people loved our fields as mothers love their children. We thought that the corn plants had souls, as children have souls and that the growing corn liked to hear us sing, as children like to hear their mothers sing to them" (as quoted in Jensen, 1981:21).

Over time, wheat supplanted corn as the major grain staple for most Americans, except in the South. The persistence of corn as the primary food grain in the southern United States attests to the association of corn with poverty. The preference for wheat, served as bread, remains the symbol of elite status throughout the world. Corn, as a staple, is consumed primarily by the poor; in fact, the majority of the world's corn is fed to animals, which are then consumed by humans.

Breeding Corn—New Varieties, New Work, and Environmental Issues

Native women throughout the Americas were the first breeders of corn; over the centuries they improved and selected corn varieties. Writing in 1923, prior to the introduction of hybrid corn, Paul Weatherwax, a botanist who studied corn as his life's work, recognized Native American expertise: "All the fundamental varieties of maize in existence today, as determined by the nature of the endosperm, seem to have been known to the various Indian tribes. The choice among available varieties of the one best suited to a particular set of conditions seems to have been made about as intelligently then as now" (Weatherwax, 1923). Although Weatherwax praises indigenous use of diverse corn varieties, he goes on say that "the Indian's taste for the gaudy kept in common use a wider range of colors than is known to the average American today—white, red, yellow, purple maintained in single variety" (Weatherwax, 1923). His patronizing interpretation of the technique of breeding various colors of maize may have blinded him from understanding strategies used by Native Americans to maintain genetic diversity.

The work of Native American women in breeding corn was followed by several centuries of farmers and scientists' extensive work on improving corn varieties. Early in the twentieth century, corn production changed drastically with the introduction of hybrid varieties. Plant breeders in the land grant universities and the seed industry developed hybrid varieties with higher yields and more stable production than farmers' open-pollinated varieties. Hybrid corn, bred for increased yields, also had characteristics that fit into a management system that relied on mechanical harvesting and application of chemicals (Kloppenberg, 1988). Open-pollinated varieties proved difficult to harvest mechanically, because of irregular shape and a tendency to lodge in the machinery. Breeders shaped plants for the machine by developing varieties resistant to lodging, that is, varieties that ripened uniformly and held their ears at a specified height when mature (Kloppenburg, 1988). The use of hybrid seed in conjunction with mechanization, and fertilizer and pesticide use resulted in phenomenal increases in U.S. corn yields, which rose exponentially from 24.5 bushels per acre in 1931 to 86.8 bushels per acre in 1971 to 118.5 bushels per acre in 1990 (Table 5.4). At the same time that yield per acre increased, the labor demands of corn production decreased. Exactly what role women's labor plays in this more capital intensive corn production system in the United States remains difficult to pinpoint.

TABLE 5.4   Corn Acreage, Production, and Yield in the United States, 1931–1990

Year	Acres (000)	Bushels (000)	Yields (bu/ac in hybrids)	Percent Acres
1931	91,131	2,229,903	24.5	0.1
1941	77,404	2,414,445	31.2	15.0
1951	71,191	2,628,937	36.9	78.0
1961	57,634	3,597,803	62.4	94.0
1971	63,819	5,540,253	86.8	95+
1981	74,524	8,118,650	108.9	95+
1990	74,171	7,933,068	118.5	95+

SOURCE: R. Jugenheimer, *Corn: Improvements, Seed Production, and Uses* (New York: John Wiley and Sons, 1976), p. 14; J. Kloppenburg, *First the Seed: The Political Economy of Plant Biotechnology, 1492–2000* (New York: Cambridge University Press, 1988); U.S. Department of Agriculture, *Agricultural Statistics* (Washington, DC: USDA, 1991).

The extent of women's labor in contemporary North American corn production is difficult to estimate. Although data on women's labor specifically in U.S. corn production are not available, there are data on women's work in field crops. The most recent national study of U.S. farm women, conducted in 1980, provides detailed information on women's involvement in various farm tasks (Rosenfeld, 1985). Although it is commonly assumed that women do not work in field crops, the national farm women's study displays contradictory evidence. Thirty-seven percent of farm women regularly or occasionally did planting, disking, cultivating, or planting with machinery. In fact, 51 percent of women regularly or occasionally participated in harvesting. The study showed that of the tasks performed in farming women were least likely to apply fertilizers, herbicides, or insecticides. Although women's participation in applying fertilizers and pesticides is limited, these activities are central to these production systems and cause major environmental problems in intensive agricultural regions.

Environmental problems associated with current corn production systems include soil erosion and depletion and high levels of pesticide use. Farmers raise corn in large-scale monocultures with limited crop rotation and heavy applications of nitrogen fertilizer. Under such conditions, corn becomes susceptible to insect and disease damage, resulting in the need for dramatically increased use of pesticides. Soil erosion and soil depletion often go hand in hand with intensive corn production. In efforts to simultaneously decrease soil erosion and labor, farmers have adopted no-till cultivation that involves planting corn seed with a special seed drill directly into the untilled field, rather than plowing the ground. They spray their fields with herbicides prior to planting to kill weeds that might compete with the corn, and after the corn emerges, they spray a selective herbicide that does not damage the corn but kills major weeds. Herbicide use in corn cultivation systems has skyrocketed, with 97 percent of corn acres treated with herbicide in 1990, compared to only 11 percent in 1952 (U.S.D.A., 1990). In the United States, more than half of all herbicides used on crops are applied to corn (Pimentel et al., 1991). Two herbicides, alachlor and atrazine, often used to control weeds in corn production, appear frequently in groundwater. Groundwater contaminated by pesticides poses serious health problems. As a recent Environmental Protection Agency study reported, 10 percent of community wells and 4 percent of rural wells are contaminated with at least one pesticide above the minimum level (Holmes, Nielsen, and Lee, 1988). Thus, the new production systems that replaced the three-sisters method bring high yields, use minimal labor, but they do tremendous environmental damage.

Solving Hunger: Hopes and Frustrations of the Green Revolution

In the 1960s, plant breeders firmly believed that increasing food crop yields for small farmers would reduce poverty and eliminate hunger in the developing world. Based on early work beginning in 1941 at a research station established by the Rockefeller and Ford Foundations in Mexico, hopes were raised for increasing corn and wheat yields and thereby preventing world hunger. In 1964, the Mexican research station officially became the International Centre for the Improvement of Maize and Wheat (CIMMYT), the second international agricultural research center, after the founding of the International Rice Research Institute (IRRI) in 1961 in the Philippines (for the purpose of increasing rice yields and food production in Asia). Researchers praise both centers for their extremely successful work in increasing yields, and spreading maize and rice hybrids and new varieties of wheat, all of which effort has resulted in what has become known as the green revolution. Since 1964, the Rockefeller and Ford Foundations (in conjunction with bilateral and multilateral institutions) have set up numerous other agricultural research centers and in 1971 formed the Consultative Group in Agricultural Research (CGIAR) to coordinate an intricate network of international agricultural research centers focusing on various crops, animals, and ecosystems. These research centers focus on food crops and have the explicit goals of increasing world food production and reducing world hunger.

To their credit, these international agricultural research centers have indeed been successful in increasing grain yields in maize, rice, and wheat. However, these successes have not solved the problems of rural poverty or hunger. Limited attention to women's efforts in growing crops and feeding their families surely contributes to this failure. Soon after the spread of high-yielding varieties of maize in Africa and Latin America and rice and wheat in Asia, critics noted that the green revolution had severe consequences for the rural poor and the environment (Pearse, 1980; Dahlberg, 1979). New varieties and their input packages brought higher yields for farmers who had sufficient resources; however, increased production for wealthier farmers coincided with growing inequities among farmers, increasing landlessness, and dependency on unstable markets. The new varieties perform well for wealthier farmers who have the capital to purchase seed, fertilizer, pesticides, and machinery. In addition, new varieties perform best in irrigated or high rainfall areas and on good soil; thus, the research advances failed to benefit poorer farmers on marginal land with minimal rainfall. Furthermore, increased fertilizer and pesticide use contaminate water sources frequently used for drinking water.

Genetic diversity in corn has decreased dramatically from the time of the Native American women's corn breeding. Genetic uniformity of germ plasm poses an ominous threat for worldwide and regional crop failures, because genetically uniform plants exhibit susceptibility to diseases, insects, and climatic conditions. Despite these social, economic and environmental problems, developers and scientists continued to maintain the hope that increases in corn production could help resolve problems of hunger, malnutrition, and poverty in Africa in the 1970s and 1980s.

Transferring Maize Cropping Systems to Africa

Researchers saw improving corn production as a key to solving food problems in southern and eastern Africa in the 1970s and 1980s. Although most regions of the world have increased or maintained food production per capita, many African countries produced less food per capita in the mid 1980s than ten years earlier (McMillan and Hansen, 1986). Multilateral and bilateral agricultural development efforts in numerous countries, including Kenya, Zaire, Zimbabwe, Cameroon, and Swaziland, looked to improvements in maize production to solve local food problems. Unfortunately, agricultural planners failed to recognize women's primary responsibility for maize production.

Generally, women raise maize for their families' consumption. Maize, now the staple food crop in many rural areas in Africa, appears in written records in West Africa as early as 1502. Portuguese slave traders brought maize from the Americas and reportedly raised maize in West Africa for food on the slave ships. Over the centuries, maize has replaced indigenous grains such as sorghum and millet. In many regions of Africa, men prepare the land, and women plant, weed, harvest, and process the maize. Women typically intercropped maize in fields with cowpeas, beans, peanuts, pigeon peas, squash, yams, and cassava; however, Western agricultural scientists viewed African women's version of the three-sisters cropping system as inefficient and as a barrier to adequate agricultural development. In addition, they found women's responsibility for farming to be an impediment to increasing agricultural production. Through programs that granted legal title of land to men, that provided men with credit to purchase hybrid seeds, fertilizers, and pesticides, and that trained them in the use of these new technologies, governments hoped to increase production of maize as a cash crop. Here, a Zimbabwe woman describes men's control over land and the demise of their intercropping systems of production: "No, we don't have control over the land. The land is controlled by men. I say so because we are given two and a half acres to plough, but our husbands do not allow us to plant anything else except maize. So where shall we plant monkey nuts, beans and fruit that are good for our families" (as quoted in Batezat and Mwalo, 1989:14).

Many of these programs designed to increase maize production failed to achieve their goals and raised many questions, especially concerning the ecological and social contexts of maize production in Africa. Those designing the programs also failed to see that improvement in maize production depended on women's access to land, credit, capital, and training.

In Africa, farms produce maize under quite different circumstances than farmers encounter in the United States. In Africa, farmers work small plots; they often use marginal land, leaving the best land for various export crops. In Cameroon, families typically raise maize in plots smaller than one hectare and produce less than one ton per hectare (Ayuk-Takem and Atayi, 1991:15). Africans produce maize primarily for direct human consumption, in contrast to U.S. farmers, who produce corn primarily for animal feed or other processed products. Table 5.5 shows the distribution of corn production between developed and developing areas and the use of corn for animal feed or human food. In developed countries, farmers raise 89 percent of corn for livestock feed, compared to only 38 percent in developing countries, where farmers raise corn primarily for direct human consumption. Although farmers raise corn principally as a food crop in developing regions, agricultural scientists encourage farmers to switch to corn

TABLE 5.5   Percent of Maize Produced by Developed/Developing Regions by Use, 1984

Region	Total	Livestock Feed	Food
Developed	63%	89%	11%
	(240)[a]	(213)	(27)
Developing	37%	38%	62%
	(140)	(64)	(76)

[a] Parenthetical statistics are in million tons.
SOURCE: CIMMYT, *Research Highlights* (Mexico City: 1984).

production for animal feed in numerous regions. CIMMYT recently reported that the "decline in food use of maize and the increase in its use for feed in developing countries is a favorable consequence of economic development" (CIMMYT, 1984:111). Therefore, research on maize has focused on varieties suitable for animal feed rather than for direct human consumption. The switch from raising maize for direct consumption to raising maize for animal feed will likely have negative consequences for small women producers and the nutritional status of poorer families.

Introduction of high-yielding varieties of maize to African farmers required a major shift in African cropping systems. First, farmers had to purchase the new hybrid seeds rather than use the seeds that women had saved from the previous year's crop. The new varieties performed best with fertilizer and pesticides that the farmers had to purchase. Because the new maize varieties quickly shaded out the beans, farmers discontinued intercropping of beans and corn. Tractor plowing replaced traditional land preparation with oxen and hoes. Increased weed growth from fertilizer use required more intensive weeding, as farmers struggled to attain higher yields from the new varieties. Thus, the new varieties required more capital for farming and changed labor patterns. Women's limited access to capital and increased labor expectations brought problems for women maize farmers.

Also, few people foresaw the ecological problems associated with these new cropping systems. Drought-prone climates and poor-quality African soils proved to be unstable ecosystems for producing continuous crops of corn. Traditional African systems of shifting cultivation may have been better suited to the ecosystem. Some agronomists now recognize that indigenous methods of cultivating the fragile African soils, such as heaping, ridging, intercropping, and minimum tillage, are preferable to deep plowing, which results in leaching, erosion, and deterioration of soil structure (Lal and Greenland, 1979). Lack of attention to gendered relations in crop production led many development programs in inappropriate directions. This disregard for women's knowledge has caused problems for women farmers, and in some instances women resist involvement in development programs. Several examples illustrate problems for women farmers.

In many regions of Africa, men leave rural areas to seek employment in mines and towns and return periodically with their cash earnings. Few, however, are able to provide the entire income and subsistence needs of the family. Women farmers often find themselves delaying planting as they wait for their husbands to send money for seeds or fertilizer or possibly to return home to plow. In maize-based production systems, women and children do three-fourths of the farm work in Zimbabwe. Men plow and will often return to their rural homes from elsewhere to plow. Women maize farmers frequently delay planting dates (resulting in lower yields), until men are available to prepare the land. Zimbabwean men explain that women cannot plow with oxen, although the women say it is much easier than weeding, an arduous task done with hoes (Pankhurst, 1989). However, as elsewhere, the farming community accords significant social status to plowing, and men seek to retain control over this activity.

Although some observers see women as mere passive victims of development projects; women also resist. A maize production project in the southeastern Shaba region of Zaire failed to meet its goals, partially because project implementers neglected the roles and status of women (Schoepf, 1986). Project planners viewed men as the household heads and assumed men could direct the labor of women, but women protested that the maize project recommendations required too much of their labor and conflicted with their other activities. Women offered limited cooperation in cash-crop maize production. They preferred to work in their own cropping systems, providing their families' food through a steady supply of vegetables, buying their cooking oil, salt, and fish in small amounts.

A recent maize project in Malawi introduced hybrid varieties of dent maize for animal feed. This was of little use to the residents who allocated only 3.5 percent of their plots to dent maize. Project organizers failed to acknowledge that the remainder of family plots were planted with flint maize to provide white flour for food. Genetic research, extension programs, and farmer training are directed at men, despite the fact that women perform much of the work in maize and also are heads of 30 percent of the households. Women have adopted some hybrids but continue to focus their production on white maize for home consumption (Jiggins, 1986:45).

Complete switching from traditional varieties to hybrid maize may not be the wisest strategy for African households, especially for women. Hybrid maize, adopted fairly rapidly by African farmers in certain regions, did not totally replace local varieties. Farmers normally save seeds of local open-pollinated varieties rather than purchase them and saved seeds perform well with minimal inputs. Families find many of the dent maize hybrids suitable for sale but not desirable for home consumption. In most locations, men have control over the output and income from hybrid varieties (Lipton, 1989), whereas women maintain more control over the distribution of local maize varieties. This is even the case where traditional varieties of maize have been raised by women, for example, in eastern Africa.

Plant geneticists and seed collectors have long disregarded women's knowledge and the value of their seed stores. In fact, as Lipton (1989) points out, plant breeders emphasize qualities that bear little relation to those poor farmers need. Poor farmers, many of whom are women, select seeds based on their cross-crop effects, stability, multiple uses, and maturation dates; by contrast, plant breeders emphasize specialized market qualities and quantity of grain. The locally desirable traits have been ignored by most agricultural scientists (Jiggins, 1986). Women have selected maize seeds for their compatibility with beans, not for their individual performance in monocultural stands. Also, women often raise early maturing varieties in their gardens, because they provide food during the slack season and offer less susceptibility to insects and diseases. Plant breeders tend to neglect these early maturing and low-yielding varieties.

Scientists working with maize often focused on uniformity for easy, mechanized harvesting and increased yields. Barbara McClintock's work with maize illustrates a different approach to studying maize. McClintock spent her life working on maize genetics. Although she conducted basic research (rather than attempting to increase production), her perception of maize stands in contrast to reductionist and controlling views of nature. As Evelyn Fox Keller (1983) puts it, McClintock approached her work with "feeling for the organism." In describing her work with maize, McClintock said, "I start with the seedling, and I don't want to leave it. I don't feel I really know the story if I don't watch the plant all the way along. So I know every plant in the field. I know them intimately, and I find it a great pleasure to know them" (as quoted in Keller, 1983:198).

McClintock's intimate acquaintance with the plants, kernels, and chromosomes enabled her to understand intricacies of genetics that won her a Nobel Prize. Her feeling for the organism, the corn plant, in her approach to science, bears a resemblance to the Native American women's intimate connection to their plants: McClintock and Native American women knew and cared for corn.

Rice

As with corn, many women grow rice, know about it, feed it to others, and eat it themselves. Rice, indigenous to the valleys of Central Asia and the swampland of western Africa, provides basic nourishment for over one-half the world's population. Botanists place the origins of rice (*Oryza sativa*) in India and southern China; references to rice-growing appear in Chinese writings of 5,000 years ago (Grist, 1986). The African species of rice (*Oryza glaberrima*), indigenous to swamps in the Gambian river basin, has largely been replaced by the Asian varieties. Rice production, although concentrated in Asia, provides important, if limited, production in areas of Africa and in South and North America (Table 5.6). As with maize, farmers raise rice in a wide range of climatic conditions, from 45° North to 40° South and in altitudes ranging from below sea level to 10,000 feet in the Himalayas (Grist, 1986:12–13). Rice is typically raised in flooded

Women's Work with Plants

TABLE 5.6   Hectares of Rice Harvested by Region, 1990

Region	Hectares Harvested (per 1,000)
World	145,776
Asia	131,470
Africa	5,750
South America	5,583
North/Central America	1,778
USSR	610
Europe	456
Oceania	129

SOURCE: Food and Agriculture Organization, *Production Yearbook* 44:72–73 (Rome: FAO, 1991).

fields, known as paddies, and its cultivation by this method depends on water supplied by irrigation or rainfall. Rice cultivation is concentrated in flat lowlands, river basins, and deltas that have high temperatures and plentiful sunshine. In some upland areas, however, farmers grow rice without flooding. Irrigated rice production requires an elaborate infrastructure and cooperation among farmers to construct dams, canals, and coordinate planting times. Many of these rice-growing infrastructures have been in place for centuries, although others have been developed more recently, facilitated by elaborate irrigation schemes such as the Mahaweli Dam in Sri Lanka. Efforts to intensify rice production through the introduction of green-revolution technologies and large-scale irrigation projects have been heralded as the solutions for world food problems, especially in Asia. These efforts to intensify rice production have differential impacts on men and women, and they have mixed results for women in different classes and ethnic groups.

Because of the heavy labor demands and coordination necessary for irrigation, rice cultivation depends on efficient cooperative production or on the availability of large numbers of agricultural workers. In many areas of rural Asia, social relations are organized around the demands of rice production. Rice-growing regions in South Asia, Southeast Asia, and western Africa illustrate historically distinct patterns of labor organization. In South Asia, members of lower castes or tribes traditionally worked in rice cultivation; today, people with limited or no access to land perform much of the work in rice paddies. In contrast, in Taiwan, Vietnam, and China rice production typically occurs on cooperatively held land or on land owned by family members. In western Africa, women have controlled rice production, raising their crops on cleared swampland.

Women's labor forms a central component of rice production in all regions of the world, although the particular forms of gender division of

Man and woman preparing rice paddy in Sri Lanka

Men preparing rice paddy with water buffalo in Sri Lanka

labor vary by region. In irrigated rice, the most common pattern calls for men to prepare the paddy; thereafter, women plant and weed (Blumberg, 1981). Men and women work together harvesting and threshing, then women winnow and process the rice. Many women who work in the rice paddies do so as hired laborers and are not members of the landowner's family. Although this gender division of labor illustrates the most typical pattern, it is by no means universal; many cultures, in fact, have strict rules that preclude women from performing certain tasks in rice production. Women's contribution varies; they provide one-half of the labor in rice production in Nepal and India, approximately one-third in Southeast Asian countries, and from 30 to 40 percent in Malaysia, South Korea, and Japan (Unnevehr and Stanford, 1986). In West African countries, women contribute the vast majority of labor. Several detailed examples of gender divisions in rice production should reveal the complexities of gender and class variations.

In the Krian region of Malaysia in a village that depends largely on rice production, women put in more days than men in paddy production. However, both men and women have specific responsibilities (Ng and Mohamed, 1988). Much of men's and women's work tasks are complementary rather than independent. During land preparation, men slash weeds with scythes and women rake the weeds onto the bunds, although in richer households, landowners hire men to do this work and the women work within the household. After men prepare the land, men pull the seedlings from the nursery and women transplant the rice seedlings, usually cooperatively exchanging labor with other households. However, a shortage of male labor due to male migration has resulted in the hiring of women to pull and plant seedlings. Women typically weed. Both male family members and hired males thresh, and female family members and hired women reap. Men handle the sale of produce.

Vietnam's major crop, rice, serves as both the major food staple and export crop. Men and women cooperate in rice production; unlike in Malaysian rice-growing, Vietnamese women shoulder the heaviest workload in most phases of agricultural production (Thi, 1993). Women make a tremendous contribution in the rice paddies, where transplanting and weeding requires standing and working knee-deep in water. Concerning planting, 82.5 percent of Vietnamese farmers reported that women do much more than men. Regarding the care of plants there was less consensus: 55 percent reported that wives do more than husbands, 35.1 percent said that husbands and wives do the same amount, and 11.1 percent responded that husbands do more than wives (Tien, 1992). In addition, women retain almost exclusive responsibility for processing and drying rice.

With the opening up of the Vietnamese economy, western development efforts to improve agricultural production in Vietnam are focusing on increasing rice yields through the adoption of new seeds, fertilizer, and pesticides. For example, a recent World Bank (1990) report states that increased use of fertilizer and wider use of high-yielding rice varieties will likely prove the most important factors in increasing rice production. The World Bank has suggested improved agricultural extension services as the major initiative in the move to help farmers adopt new seed varieties and techniques of production. In an effort to modernize agricultural production, Vietnam seems to be following the green-revolution path to increasing rice production. As an alternative, Vietnamese agricultural policymakers might do better to consider the mixed results that green-revolution rice production technologies have had in other countries like India and the Philippines.

In West Africa, we can observe a set of gender relations governing rice production that do not resemble those in Malaysia, Vietnam, or other Asian countries. In eleven case studies of rice-farming systems in The Gambia, Ivory Coast, Senegal, Upper Volta, Mauritania, Zanzibar, and Madagascar, women played major roles in rice production. Consider, in contrast, the Asian family farms, where men controlled farm production, where women and men frequently worked in the same fields and pooled their resources. Household organization in many West African groups revealed separate granaries and fields for men and women. The community expected women to grow sufficient subsistence crops for their families.

Judith Carney and Michael Watts's (1991) detailed study of historical shifts in gender relations in Gambian rice production emphasizes the centrality of women's efforts. Before colonization, Mandinka women largely controlled rice production in the Gambia River Basin. In the 1850s, women cultivated the African species of rice (*Oryza glaberrima*) in swamps; men prepared the swamps for cultivation. Rice, a women's crop, was raised by the female members of the community principally for food consumption, whereas men worked primarily in groundnut production for export. The possibility for expanding rice production in The Gambia appealed to the British colonizers, who introduced improved Asian rices in the 1920s, funded mangrove clearance, and introduced new methods of seedbed preparation. They met their goals, in part, by the mid-1950s, when swamp rice cultivation expanded to 49,000 acres and rice imports were reduced by 80 percent from the 1920s. Colonial officials realized that further expansion of rice production depended on the extent to which they could persuade males to participate in rice production. However, "the mechanisms to compel men into the rice fields were singularly lacking, and men successfully resisted efforts to intensify their labor on the grounds that rice was 'a woman's crop'" (Carney and Watts, 1991:661). After World War II, the colonial and Gambian governments implemented large-scale and small-scale irrigation schemes. All of these irrigation schemes depended heavily on women's labor. The most recent effort, the Jahaly Pacharr project, consists of a large-scale irrigation scheme of 1,500 hectares with a centralized water delivery system. The original productivity goals of the project explicitly relied heavily on women's work: "Women are better than men as far as transplanting is concerned and they are also better than men as far as working in the water . . . so quite frankly we expect a lot of labour from women, more so than from men" (Jahaly Pacharr project manager, as quoted in Carney and Watts, 1991:272). However, although women's labor intensified with the irrigation scheme, their control over paddy cultivation declined because men controlled the income from rice. Gradually men entered rice growing, but women's labor and knowledge still remains central to production. In many cases, women resisted efforts to intensify their labor, and some women withdrew their labor entirely. Gender-based struggles over land, labor, and working conditions accompany rice production intensification (Carney and Watts, 1991).

After leaving paddies and swamps, women process rice. Mechanized rice processing mills largely replaced women's hand pounding of rice in many regions of Asia. Hand pounding of grain, a difficult labor-intensive task that warranted relief, afforded jobs for poor, landless women. The large-scale rice processing mills displaced 1.2 million jobs in Java and 7.7 million jobs in Indonesia (Cain, 1981:134). Ten years after the Javanese adoption of rice-processing mills, Bangladesh introduced rice-processing mills that produced a similar outcome for women as in Java. In Bangladesh, women from poor, landless households lost their rice-processing jobs, and men filled the positions in the newly created jobs (Begum, 1985). Thus, technologies that replace labor and reduce drudgery have mixed results. For poor women, technologies such as rice-processing mills have consistently undermined their limited available opportunities to earn incomes.

New Rice Varieties, Women's Knowledge, and Access to Income

Established in 1960 to improve rice varieties and increase rice production, the International Rice Research Institute (IRRI) in the Philippines quickly developed new varieties of rice with dramatically improved yields by the mid 1960s. Farmers with irrigated land adopted the new short-strawed, fertilizer-responsive varieties; the new varieties accounted for one-fourth of the increase in rice production in Asia between 1965 and 1980 (Unnevehr and Stanford, 1985). These new varieties grow in shorter seasons and enable farmers to plant two and sometimes three crops a year. More intensive cultivation of this sort brings higher yields per year but not without problems such as soil salinization, diseases, and pests that were not common with less intensive cultivation (Capistrano and Marten, 1986). Labor requirements change dramatically with double-or triple-cropping, often demanding more labor from women.

Scientists select high-yielding varieties of rice primarily for their grain yield, whereas they ignore many other qualities that vary among rice varieties, such as taste, nutrition, and biomass. For small producers, rice supplies not only grain, but straw. Women use rice straw for thatch, mats, and fodder; they use husks for fuel. Higher-yielding rice varieties, selected to reduce lodging (falling over), are shorter and provide less straw. Improved varieties have a grain-to-straw ratio of 45 to 55 as compared to 30 to 70 for traditional varieties (Khush, 1985). Although women and poorer farmers may value nongrain products such as straw and husks, they are not valued as world trade commodities and have consequently been overlooked by international researchers.

As with maize, new rice varieties are introduced to farmers as part of a package of green-revolution technologies, including seeds, fertilizer, insecticides, fungicides, and herbicides. In most regions of the world, development efforts involve the attempt to transfer these technologies to men by providing credit for them to purchase new products such as new seeds, fertilizers, and pesticides. Typically, agricultural extension services target information about new technologies and agricultural practices at male farmers.

Scientists and agriculturalists often consider women's knowledge about seeds, plants, and production techniques irrelevant and backward. They argue that "scientific knowledge" must replace women's ways of knowing. Although women have historically been the savers and storers of seeds, their knowledge and seed stores have long been disregarded by plant geneticists and seed collectors. Plant geneticists have bred rice with little consideration for women's knowledge, needs, and appreciation of diversity.

Janice Jiggins (1986) comments that it has been extremely difficult to convince scientists at the international research centers that women possess different skills, knowledge, and experience with seeds than do male community members. The IRRI funded the Women in Rice Farming Systems Program, which was focused on institutionalizing women's concerns in national agricultural research and extension systems and in agricultural universities. This research program resulted in numerous case studies being conducted on women's participation in rice-farming systems and in the publication of two collections on women's work in rice farming (IRRI, 1985; 1988). Based on observations in India, Nepal, Bangladesh, Thailand, Indonesia, and the Philippines, Gelia Castillo (1988) surmises that although the physical visibility of women's work in rice farming has increased, women's work remains conceptually and culturally invisible. Although researchers have documented women's input concerning various tasks and have conducted detailed time allocation studies, we still know little about the extent of women's knowledge regarding particular agricultural practices.

In her review of women in rice farming in The Gambia, Ivory Coast, Senegal, Upper Volta, Mauritania, Zanzibar, and Madagascar, Jennie Dey (1985) was struck by the enormous breadth of women's skill and knowledge about rice cultivation that is traditionally passed from mother to daughter. Women share detailed knowledge of soil types, soil toxicity and salinity conditions, water sources and fluctuating water levels, and different seeds and their suitability for various ecological and labor conditions. Considering that supply and control of water is the most important aspect of paddy cultivation, D. H. Grist (1986) points out that women in The Gambia impressed engineers and planners with their knowledge and awareness of technical problems relating to water. However, when engineers and water management planners built causeways, they ignored women's advice and concerns and consequently constructed causeways that were not used by the women.

Perhaps most impressive are the Kpelle women rice growers in Liberia who use and recognize 100 different varieties of rice. Jiggins found that in describing rice varieties, "Women used categories which formed a clear and systematic framework for describing rice. They mentioned such features as husk and seed colour, length of hair at the tip of the rice, size of the grain, ease with which the husk can be removed, length of time required to cook, and suitability to different types of soil and terrain. They knew their business" (as quoted in Jiggins, 1986:18). Similarly, among the Ifugao in northern Luzon in the Philippines, women have responsibility for selecting rice seed and are more knowledgeable about rice than local men.

A rice development program in Ivory Coast exemplifies the frustrating problem of managers who ignore women's knowledge and responsibilities in rice production. The project provided men with rice fertilizers, despite women's responsibility for rice production. Project personnel did not show women how to use fertilizers; men used the fertilizers on cacao or threw them away (Dey, 1985).

Although scientists and researchers regularly overlook women's detailed knowledge of rice cultivation, they have considered the impact of high-yielding varieties on women's labor and income-earning abilities. Development planners concerned with women debate whether green-revolution technologies increase or decrease the demand for women's labor and whether the new technologies raise or lower women's incomes. Clearly, the impact of the new varieties and associated technologies varies by women's class position. Women from landholding families frequently benefit because their households gain greater access to income as a result of higher yields, but women's access to this income depends on their ability to control household resources. Landless women in rural Asia earn much of their income as wage workers in transplanting, weeding, harvesting, and processing rice. For example, in the major rice-growing states of India, rice harvesting provides more than one-third of the income earned by women (Unnevehr and Stanford, 1985). Cultivation of high-yield varieties increases demands for labor in transplanting, weeding, and post-harvest activities. Hired women workers, often from landless or near-landless households, frequently perform 'this labor. In Java, Bangladesh, and India, landless women contribute approximately one-half of household cash income and work longer hours in both wage labor and household production than men (Unnevehr and Stanford, 1985). Technologies in rice production that reduce the demand for women's labor can have devastating effects on the income of landless families if there are no alternative means to earn income. Government policies in many Asian countries have cheapened capital inputs relative to labor through subsidization of inputs for farmers (Unnevehr and Stanford, 1985). Also, research on rice has focused on labor-saving rather than labor-using technologies. Development agencies and planners promote and introduce labor-saving technologies such as tractors, threshers, and herbicides that eliminate many jobs in particular areas of Asia. For example, in Taiwan, where rice production has become almost fully mechanized, new technologies have eliminated women's work in rice paddies, and men now have primary responsibility for rice cultivation: "In southern Taiwan, one seldom sees groups of women transplanting rice because of widespread use of rice transplanters" (Gleason, 1988:244). Further, herbicide use has replaced the demand for women in weeding.

Several environmental and health problems emerged the with intensification of technologically oriented rice production. Heavy applications of commercial fertilizer in rice production have proven questionable, as the technique brought quick profits in the first few years but was followed by degeneration of the soil (Grist, 1986). As a result, scientists are now promoting use of organic and green manures in rice production in addition to commercial fertilizers. Another problem with the intensive, high-yield approach to rice production has been the neglect of the importance of fish in rice paddies. Fish have typically provided a protein source in rice-producing regions, especially for poor households. Fertilizer and pesticide use in the paddies has decreased the abundant fish population and made paddy fish unsafe as food. Finally, women who spend long hours working in sprayed paddies report both acute and chronic health problems as a result of exposure to chemicals in the water.

Coffee: Men Drink the Coffee Money

Coffee is critical to the export economies of many African and Latin American countries. In many regions, women contribute much of the labor in coffee production, but they rarely have control over coffee earnings. Fluctuations in the world market prices for coffee result in vulnerable and fragile national, local, and household economies that depend on coffee production. High coffee prices do not guarantee easier lives for women, because often, as Kenyan women say, "men drink the coffee money."

Coffee is an evergreen shrub that grows at high elevations in the tropics. Growers raise coffee for its berries, and it remains second only to oil as a source of foreign exchange in world trade. Coffee is produced primarily in Latin America and Africa—largely for coffee drinkers in Europe and the United States. Europeans and North Americans accounted for 94 percent of the world's coffee consumption in 1991 (FAO, 1993:38); oil fuels the cars and coffee fuels the workers in advanced industrial economies.

Coffee is indigenous to Africa, but the bulk of the world's production comes from Latin America. In 1992, Latin America produced 65 percent of the world's coffee; Africa, 20 percent; Asia, 15 percent (see Table 5.7). Many countries in both Africa and Latin America rely heavily on coffee for foreign exchange. Brazil has historically been the world's leading producer of coffee, although its share in world production has declined, moving from 68 percent in 1948–1952 to 47 percent in 1979–1981, and decreas-

TABLE 5.7   Coffee Production, 1987–1989 and 1992

	1987–1989 Average	1992	Percent of World
	Million tons	Million tons	1992
World Total	5.90	5.69	100
Latin America	3.87	3.70	65
Brazil	1.78	1.44	25
Colombia	0.74	0.99	17
Guatemala	0.19	0.18	3
Mexico	0.31	0.25	4
Africa	1.22	1.13	20
Ivory Coast	0.24	0.22	4
Ethiopia	0.20	0.18	3
Kenya	0.12	0.10	2
Uganda	0.17	0.18	3
Asia and Oceania	0.81	0.86	15
Indonesia	0.40	0.45	8

SOURCE: Food and Agriculture Organization, *Commodity Review and Outlook* (Rome: FAO, 1993), p. 38.

ing to 25 percent in 1992. In Colombia, El Salvador, Burundi, Ethiopia, Rwanda and Uganda, coffee's share of the export market is over 50 percent (Lucier, 1988). Although many of these countries contribute only a small fraction of the world's coffee, their economies are heavily dependent on coffee. African nations that depend almost entirely on export crops for foreign exchange earnings substantially lost their share of world commodity markets (including coffee) in the 1970s. In 1970, Africa produced 34 percent of the world's coffee, only 23 percent in 1979 and 20 percent in 1992 (Timberlake, 1985:70). Prices for coffee, set on the world market and subject to low and fluctuating prices, cause severe burdens for coffee economies, both at the national level and the farm level. For example, the price for arabicas declined from 109 cents per pound in 1987–1989 to 57 cents per pound in 1992. Thus, the value of coffee exports has declined substantially in all countries in the past five years (FAO, 1993:39).

Coffee is raised under varying types of social relations. Coffee production in most countries entails a dual production structure, with both estates and smallholders producing it. In Brazil, 47 percent of production comes from farms of over 100 hectares, compared to Africa, where diversified smallholders produce most of the coffee (de Graaff, 1986:112).

Coffee in Brazil

Women's participation in coffee production varies in different regions and in different production systems. An excellent study of the changing gender relations on coffee plantations in the Sao Paulo region of Brazil by Verena Stolcke (1988) provides insight into how changing political and economic conditions have affected women. From the mid-nineteenth century until the 1960s, planters employed permanent family laborers (*colonatos*) to work on the coffee estates in the *colonato* system. The *colonatos* worked in coffee, but planters also allotted them some land to raise their food crops. Planters allowed the workers to intercrop beans and maize in new stands of coffee, and during difficult economic times they allowed intercropping of food crops in the mature stands of coffee trees. Thus, as Stolcke points out, coffee did not replace food crops under this system; instead, planters encouraged a symbiotic relationship between coffee as a cash crop and native food crops. Women, men, and children worked in coffee production and also produced their own food. Males maintained authority in the household and controlled what little family income entered the home.

During the 1960s a shift occurred that changed coffee production forever. Planters began to hire casual wage laborers instead of permanent family laborers, causing the demise of the *colonato* system. A complex web of political, economic, and technical changes brought about this change in the social relations of production on coffee plantations. In this new system, women became the preferred workers in coffee picking. As both the planters and the women explained, women work harder than men and often work for lower wages. As more men sought jobs elsewhere or became unable to earn enough to support their families, women were compelled to work for wages. Women had to perform jobs previously performed by men and often expressed their resentment toward the men. As one woman explained: "We have already dug so many ditches, there aren't any more men in the world. I think there are more women now in the world. The men [that] there are take up other jobs, they don't go after weeding any more, they seek better jobs where they earn more and don't have to make such an effort. For women, there is only the possibility to work as a maid and they earn the same as in the fields" (as quoted in Stolcke, 1988).

The transformation of women and men to casual wage laborers on coffee estates erodes the authority structure in the family but seldom enhances women's autonomy or alters gender roles in significant ways. Rather, women have to work for wages while their domestic responsibilities remain unchanged. Men maintain authority in the household but are less able to provide as much toward the family income. Stolcke found that the women were amazingly resilient emotionally as compared to the men, who became despondent due to their inability to support the family. The men's despair often led to alcoholism and in some cases to violence against women, but these women's resilience enabled them to continue to earn income and support their families under adverse circumstances.

Coffee in Africa

Coffee provided one of the cash crops that formed the backbone of colonial economies in Africa. White-owned farms or plantations produced cash crops, among them coffee, tobacco, and tea; African peasants raised other cash crops, among them peanuts, cotton, cacao, and palm products. In some countries, for example, in Kenya, whites restricted Africans' right to raise coffee for export.

In the 1990s, many African economies rely heavily on a single type of crop for the majority of their export earnings. For example, coffee provides over 50 percent of the export earnings in Burundi, Rwanda, Ethiopia, Uganda, and Kenya (Timberlake, 1985:70). Land allocation, scientific effort, and agricultural policies are geared toward production of export crops such as coffee, cacao, tea, sugar, cotton, tobacco, and oil palms. Until recently, food crops, such as maize, received limited attention from agricultural scientists or agricultural policymakers in Africa.

A typical example is a Kikuyu village in Kenya, where coffee is the major cash crop for families (Stamp, 1990). Families cultivate small plots of coffee, ranging in size from several hundred bushes to larger plots of several acres. On the remaining land, families raise maize, potatoes, and beans for home consumption and cash. Women provide much of the labor in coffee and vegetable production, and men habitually migrate from the village in search of work. Due to male landownership and policies of the Coffee Marketing Board, women do not have access to the income from coffee. Women contribute labor in coffee, but they explain that "men drink the coffee money." Therefore, women prefer to raise vegetables for sale. Working cooperatively, women in the village have also organized self-help groups, originally with the goal to save money for fertilizer. They have expanded the groups to try to raise money to establish a nursery school, to lay water pipes and facilitate other community improvements, to fund small businesses, and to create a rotating credit society. However, the women explained that "men fear women when they are in a group" and reported that some men beat their wives for participating in their self-help groups (Stamp, 1990:83).

In Zimbabwe, growers raise coffee on large estates and rely on both male and female wage labor. In the Mutare Valley, the government has encouraged small producers to plant coffee trees on land previously devoted to food crop production. Women do much of the labor in coffee harvesting but receive few of the benefits. Farmers sell coffee to the Coffee Marketing Board, but few women have been issued the official cards in their own names that would allow them to directly receive payment for their coffee. Women farmers complain that they do not receive payment when they bring their coffee to the Coffee Marketing Boards; instead, the checks come in one lump sum payable to their husbands, and they frequently never see the money.

Gardens

You cannot justify a garden to nonbelievers. You cannot explain to the unconverted the desire, the ravishing need, to get your hands into the soil again, to plant, thin, train up on stakes, trellis onto pea fence, hill up to blanch, just plain admonish to grow.

—Maxine Kumin, 1994

In most regions of the world, rural women raise a wide diversity of plant species in gardens on small plots of land near their houses. Until recently, Third World development planners overlooked women's home gardens and shifting systems of cultivation as important food sources. The patch of mixed plants abutting the house seemed insignificant in the quest to solve hunger problems with new food-producing strategies. Coinciding environmental and food crises have redirected attention to traditional mixed cropping systems, which women tend to practice in their gardens. Compared to monocropping, mixed cropping systems provide balanced diets, serve a variety of household needs, spread labor and harvest requirements, and reduce food shortages. Diverse cropping patterns also resist environmental changes, use vertical as well as horizontal space, and provide weed, disease, and insect control (Marten and Saltman, 1986).

In the tropics of Southeast Asia, women's home gardens on the average occupy 1,000 square meters and mimic the tropical forest. Women intercrop perennials and annuals, tree crops, grains, vegetable crops, herbs, spices, and root crops. These gardens provide many of the nutritional needs of families, and this produce both supplements and complements the rice in the local diet.

Farmers in Asia, Africa, and Central and South America, use the swidden plot for home gardens, a temporary plot produced by cutting back and burning off vegetative cover. Women traditionally raise diverse crops on one or two hectares. In Sri Lanka, the women's role included major responsibility for *chenna* (swidden) cultivation, whereas male farmers worked primarily in rice production. In *chennas*, women produce diverse crops, usually millet, green gram (a type of legume), maize, cassava, and vegetables for their families' food. Large-scale development projects have focused on paddy production, and in some areas *chennas* have disappeared. Without the *chenna*, women have limited access to land to raise food crops. Men, who control the income from paddy production, may or may not choose to spend this income on food for the family. The result is chronic undernutrition (Schrijvers, 1988). In Cameroon's tropical forest, women's home gardens surround their compounds and provide much of the household's food supply. Multistory intensive gardens in Cameroon include cassava, groundnuts, cocoa yam, yam, sweet potatoes, papaya, banana, plantain, and sugar cane. Scientists and development planners now interested in agroforestry, have begun to focus attention on the benefits of multiple cropping and multiple-use strategies used by women in their home gardens.

Researchers and policymakers overlook the importance of home garden crops such as cassava in meeting the food needs of rural households. Because it is associated with women, cassava has been undervalued as a food crop (Hawthorne, 1991). Flora Nwapa's poem emphasizes the importance of cassava for women farmers in Africa:

> *You, Mother Cassava*
> *You deserve recognition*

> *You are no cash crop*
> *But you deserve recognition.*
> *You don't fetch*
> *The All Mighty foreign exchange*
> *But you feed*
> *All your children.*

—Nwapa, 1986

Women's gardens often enable families to survive during difficult times, for instance, during periods of drought or in seasons when grain crops are in short supply. Foods raised by women contribute to the health of family members by supplementing and diversifying diets, and nondomesticated plants are also used to supplement the food needs of rural households.

Wild Plants

Women have always gathered wild plants and continue that tradition in modern times. Uncultivated areas provide food, medicine, building materials, tools, and utensils in subsistence economies (Cecelski, 1987). Although wild plants seldom provide the bulk of a subsistence diet in societies today, wild plants collected by women often supply important nutritional supplements and provide a fallback during droughts. Women in rice-growing regions pick greens on rice bunds and women in Africa use wild greens for their families' food. In many African and Asian regions, women and children gather fruits and nuts from common land. Also, women and children often collect fodder for animals from communal lands and forests.

In hunter-gatherer societies in Africa, wild plants constitute a major source of the required daily calories. Fruits, nuts, berries, gums, roots, and bulbs gathered by !Kung women contribute 60 percent of the daily caloric intake and many of the essential vitamins needed by these Kalahari Desert people (Lee, 1979). However, hunting and gathering societies represent less than 1 percent of Africa's population, and the importance of undomesticated plants as food for indigenous African agricultural societies has not been adequately investigated (Lee, 1979).

Numerous agricultural societies depend on wild plants as supplementary food. Collected foods include leaves from bushes, trees, and herbs; honey; fruit; and mushrooms. For example, a study in Tanzania found that wild leafy plants compose four-fifths of all leafy green vegetables eaten. Tanzanians eat such vegetables at almost half of all meals (Timberlake, 1985:104). In Zambia, wild leafy vegetables and caterpillars provide major sources of protein and mushrooms, and caterpillars supply important sources of cash income for women (Rocheleau, 1988). In Swaziland, the majority of the population consumes wild greens at least twice a week (Malaza, 1994). During periods of famine or drought or in seasons when staple crops are not available, women collect other plants for food. In Laos, much of the families' welfare depends on materials women gather in the forest, according to Carol Ireson. Women regularly gather food, medicine, and material for household items. In interviews with 120 women, Ireson found that women gathered 141 different types of forest products, including bamboo shoots, mushrooms, sarsaparilla, and rattan. Twenty-five percent of Laotian women gathered from the forest every day, and 75 percent gathered at least once a week (Freson, 1991:30).

Uncultivated plants also provide a major source of fodder for many of the world's animals; women perform much of the work in collecting such fodder. Development planners and policymakers often overlook uncultivated land as a source of fodder. Instead, they implement programs converting marginal, fodder-producing land to agriculture. Carol Carpenter (1991) conducted a fascinating study in Pakistan to investigate the complex linkages among women, livestock, fodder, agriculture, and uncultivated land. Pakistani women have primary responsibility for collecting fodder from both cultivated and uncultivated land. This is a time consuming task, and many women spend close to four hours a day collecting and processing fodder. Typically, women collect fodder in groups, and in most areas women "manage" uncultivated land for fodder production. They make daily decisions about which grasses and tree branches to cut; such skills and knowledge are taught by mothers and other women to younger women. Carpenter argues that development programs fail to recognize the value of uncultivated land for fodder production. The attempts to convert marginal land to agricultural production are likely to "increase demands on women's labor, decrease supplies of fodder and fuelwood, decrease supplies of manure, and in the long run endanger the productivity and sustainability of agricultural land and threaten the viability of rural households, especially land-poor households" (1991:76). The Pakistani study demonstrates that land privatization and the decline in common land in many regions of the world limits women's access to undomesticated sources of food.

Conclusions Concerning Women and Plants

In their relations to crops and plants, rural women vary tremendously by their class, region, ethnicity, locality, and the gendered relations that surround labor and control of particular crops. Global shifts in agriculture have more often than not disrupted women's and men's crop production systems. In the case of maize, the three-sisters method of agriculture has been and continues to be replaced by monoculture, by high-input use, and by large-scale corn production systems. Corn, once a women's crop raised in multicropping systems for family consumption, is now a global commodity raised primarily for animal feed, enabling North Americans to live on a meat-based diet. However, intensive corn production systems have severe environmental consequences such as soil erosion, pesticide runoff, nitrogen leaching, and genetic uniformity. Transfer of these intensive maize production systems to Africa has yielded mixed results, partially because of agricultural planners' ignorance about and indifference to women's extensive participation in agricultural production and because of their insistence upon directing agricultural development efforts towards men. Agricultural scientists, viewed as the experts on corn production, largely disregard women's knowledge about seeds, soil fertility, and intercropping strategies.

Intensification of rice production through the introduction of new rice varieties, production practices, and processing technologies changes gender and class relations. Uneven access to the benefits of new technologies has been particularly burdensome for women from landless and poor households. Labor-saving technologies like rice-processing mills and mechanical harvesters arrive with mixed blessings for women; new technologies that replace female labor reduce the amount of arduous physical work, but they also reduce opportunities for landless or land-poor women. Environmental and health problems emerge with the intensification of rice production. We are only now recognizing the negative implications of these western, male-centered approaches. Scientific and development failures have led planners to consider other possibilities. They should now be able to see that indigenous people, and women in particular, know their local situations and can provide insights into plans for environmentally sustainable agriculture systems. Agricultural science has ignored women's knowledge of seeds, their multiple uses of crops, and their multicropping strategies in crop improvement programs. Seldom has women's knowledge been incorporated into science or development planning; this has resulted in the loss of valuable knowledge and in wasteful, erroneously planned projects. To achieve sustainable agriculture, researchers and planners must include women's knowledge and practices. If taken seriously by Western-trained scientists and development planners, women's alternative strategies may provide key components in projects that meet food needs without destroying the natural environment.

6

Women's Work with Animals

The difference between men and women is like that between animals and plants. Men correspond to animals, while women correspond to plants because their development is more placid.

—Hegel, as quoted in Adams, 1990:37

Women's work with livestock receives less attention from development planners, social scientists, and feminist scholars than women's work with crops. Thus, the extensiveness and economic importance of women's animal-raising activities for rural households and communities remains concealed. Several factors explain the invisibility of women's work with animals: dismissal of women's small-scale livestock work as being limited to feeding a few chickens, cultural images that associate men with livestock, and general neglect of women's household and small-scale activities (Hecht, 1985). Recent feminist writers further muddy the waters as they focus on the connection between women's rights and animal rights, but they largely fail to fully understand and explore the daily experiences of rural women who work with animals.

In fact, both men and women raise animals; women in rural areas regularly raise and care for domestic animals such as chickens, pigs, cows, goats, or sheep for home consumption or for the market. As in crop production, the division of labor between women and men who work with animals has often been pronounced. Work with certain animals and specific tasks, such as milking, herding, collecting eggs, feeding, and butchering, are often gender specific. Increasing commodification and the shift from small-scale animal raising to large-scale animal production systems disrupts women's animal-raising systems, shifts gender divisions of labor in livestock raising, and alters the organization of labor. In some cases, women no longer work with animals. More commonly, women's labor remains essential, but their control over the work process and product of their labor diminishes.

Women's and Men's Livestock Systems

Women as well as men care for domestic animals, however women and men raise animals under different types of systems and circumstances. Table 6.1 displays general trends in the gendered division of animal production. Women raise poultry in many regions of the world, and in regions where cattle are raised, these are typically men's animals. Women also frequently raise goats, sheep, and pigs. However, in some regions men care for these animals. Women typically tend small-scale livestock operations, whereas men are more likely to control production of a larger number of animals. For example, as raising chickens changed from small-scale flocks on family farms to large-scale chicken confinement operations in the United States, control of production shifted from women to men. Women work with animals raised principally for products other than meat, for example, for eggs, milk, or wool, and women tend to care for newborn animals. Women's animals typically live close to the household, often subsisting on household waste products, whereas men's animals graze on pastures or rangeland. these gendered systems, though not universal, are typologies based on general trends. In fact, women's and men's work varies by locality, class, ethnicity, and race. For example, some cultures forbid women to milk animals, and in other regions some women regularly perform typically male tasks with animals.

Changes in Animal Production Systems

Industrialized animal production systems that are characterized by increasing concentration, specialization, and confinement are replacing smaller, more diverse animal production systems in many regions of the world. Harriet Friedmann and Philip McMichael (1989) identify an intensive meat production complex consisting of soybean, maize, and meat producers connected by contracts to corporate processors. Expansion of large-scale confinement operations, most notably in the United States,

TABLE 6.1   Women's and Men's Animal Production Systems

	Women	Men
Type of animal	Poultry, small ruminants, goats, sheep	Large ruminants, cattle, dairy cows
Number of animals	Small	Large
Products/uses	Non-meat, milk, eggs, wool	Meat, draft power
Value per animal	Low	High
Feed source	Scavengers, household waste	Pasture, grains
Range	Free-ranging, near household	Pastures, rangelands, distance from household
Land needs	Minimal	Extensive

replaces farms or ranches with crop, pastures, and animals. Increasingly, animal and crop production occurs on separate farms and in distinct regions. For example, cows and poultry raised in southeastern Pennsylvania consume grains raised in the midwestern United States. Promoted as being more efficient system, separation of crop and livestock production reduces labor and decreases costs for producers and consumers. Large industrial capital operating across national boundaries integrates crop and livestock production, in contrast to earlier systems that integrated crops and livestock at the farm or regional level. Lack of integrated crop and animal production at the farm level affects the environment, the animals, and the social relations of production. Livestock concentration produces more animal wastes than can easily or ecologically be spread on surrounding fields. Animal manures, valuable sources of fertilizer in mixed crop and livestock systems, create problems of waste disposal in concentrated livestock systems. In areas of the United States and Europe, cows and poultry raised on limited acreage cause nitrogen runoff into groundwater and streams, resulting in serious water pollution problems. Simultaneously, crop farms without livestock lack animal manure to improve soil fertility and must rely exclusively on chemical fertilizer.

Leading the way in large-scale confinement operations for chickens, turkeys, hogs, and cattle, the United States exhibits a long history of industrial production of meat. As early as the 1880s, meat packers such as Swift and Armour vertically integrated their operations (Kim and Curry, 1993). Since then, mass production systems, scientific innovations, and declining prices have contributed to the increase of meat consumption in the United States, particularly beef. Although dairy production still occurs predominantly on family farms, large-scale dairies are beginning to replace smaller family dairies. Animals in confined environments pose such major problems for the livestock industry as how to dispose of waste, how to maintain animal health, and how to address animal rights issues. These "factory farms" are targets of animal rights activists, including feminists, advocating the ethical treatment of animals. Large-scale animal operations are only beginning to be introduced into developing countries, where small-scale livestock production still thrives.

In Africa, Asia, and Latin America, small-scale farmers rely heavily on livestock. Susannah Hecht (1985) explains how small producers in Latin America use livestock to buffer various agricultural risks, for example, climatic difficulties, pest or disease problems, and commodity price fluctuations. During difficult times, farmers can sell animals and secondary animal products. Hecht explains that women work and manage small-scale livestock economies in Latin America. Expansion of the large-scale, capital-intensive and land-extensive livestock sector, which includes primarily cattle, is largely controlled by corporations using male wage labor and harms rural women by limiting their access to land and jobs. Unfortunately, little information and few studies exist on women's involvement in livestock production (Hecht, 1985). To begin to address the impact of changes and variations in women's involvement in animal-raising practices, I focus on changes in chicken and dairy production in different regions and briefly discuss rural women's relationship to hunting wild animals.

Which Comes First, the Chicken or the Egg?

"Why do you keep putting off writing about me?" It is the voice of a chicken that asks this. Depending on where you are, you will laugh, or not laugh. Either response is appropriate.

—Alice Walker, 1991

Women raise chickens in many areas of the world. Poultry-raising attracts women because they can easily raise a small number of chickens on minimal land, without capital investment, credit, or the assistance of men, and usually they control the income from their chicken enterprises. The United States, China, Brazil, and Europe produce the bulk of the world's poultry. Table 6.2 shows the total amount of poultry meat produced in specific countries, but care should be taken in interpreting these data—many chickens that are produced for household consumption or sold in the informal economy may not be counted in certain regions.

Chickens in the United States

Until the 1940s, U.S. farm women cared for chickens, marketed chickens and eggs, and maintained control over the income. Referred to as "pin money," farm women's earnings from poultry enterprises brought sub-

TABLE 6.2   Poultry Meat Production in Specified Countries, 1990

Country	Poultry (1,000 metric tons)
United States	18,878
China	3,229
Brazil	2,416
France	1,651
Japan	1,451
United Kingdom	1,087
Thailand	595
India	334
Egypt	235
Guatemala	94

SOURCE: U.S. Department of Agriculture, *Agricultural Statistics* (Washington, DC: USDA, 1991), p. 338.

stantial income to their farms. For example, in 1848 in Delaware County, Pennsylvania, women raised 80,000 hens, 24,000 chicks, and 6 million eggs on their family farms (Jensen, 1991). Eighty years later, farm women produced the majority of poultry in the United States. A 1929 Iowa State Extension publication described women's importance in the poultry industry: "Practically all the eggs produced in Iowa come from farm flocks. The farm flock is cared for and managed by farm women. The poultry industry of Iowa is a farm woman's enterprise" (Fink, 1986:135). Women raised flocks of chickens for both eggs and meat to sell or barter or to feed their families. Eggs, farm women's most common and reliable source of income, were traded with local grocers for food and dry goods, and were also sold for cash. As a farm woman in Iowa explained: "You'd bring the eggs to the grocery store and you'd get one cent more for them than you would get at the produce store. They did that to get the trade. . . . They knew they were going to get paid for their groceries" (as quoted in Fink, 1986:139–140). During hard economic times and especially during the depression years, women's egg money saved many farms when men's commodities provided little or no income (Fink, 1986).

In the early 1900s, poultry scientists and cooperative extension services around the country hoped to shift poultry production from women's small flock production to larger-scale male-controlled enterprises (Fink, 1986). Scientists recognized women's stake in resisting this transition: "The farm experts reckoned you could not compete with a system in which labor was free, feed was free, and the farm wife was counting on this whole thing for her spending money" (as quoted in Fink, 1986:138).

Large-scale egg and broiler production gradually pushed women out of the poultry industry. Despite women's resistance, poultry and egg production changed dramatically during and after World War II. New varieties of chickens, early sexing of poultry, and artificial hatching of eggs facilitated the separation of meat and egg production. Farm women often continued to raise chickens long after they ceased to make money, but after a time they reluctantly gave up their poultry enterprises. By 1945, women no longer traded eggs for groceries in Iowa, and shortly thereafter, they discontinued their egg enterprises. In an excellent analysis of changes in the chicken industry, Chul-Kyoo Kim and James Curry (1993) explain how restructuring of broiler production relates to changes in consumption and processing. By 1960, contracts or coordination between growers, hatcheries, feed mills, and processing plants characterized broiler enterprises. In the United States today, large-scale confinement operations contract with poultry agribusiness firms to raise chickens and eggs with feed concentrates. The twenty largest broiler companies account for 79.3 percent of broiler production and the top four broiler firms increased their share of the market from 23 percent in 1980 to 45 percent in 1990 (Kim and Curry, 1993:65).

Farmers no longer raise chickens in all regions of the country; instead, large-scale enterprises are concentrated in particular regions, especially in the southeastern states and California. In 1987, the South accounted for 76 percent of United States broiler production, with Georgia, Arkansas, and Alabama producing nearly one-half of all U.S. broilers (Table 6.3).

Regional shifts in chicken production followed poultry processing plants south. Labor-intensive plants locate in the south to minimize labor costs and avoid environmental regulations. Growers raise chickens and give sub-contracts to processing plants. Typically, processing firms will not sign contracts with growers beyond 25 to 30 miles of the plant (Heffernan, 1984:249). Thus, growers must locate their operations close to processing plants.

Kim and Curry's insightful analysis of the broiler industry fails to recognize the centrality of gender and race issues in the dynamics of this process. Women workers, especially African Americans and Latinas, perform much of the work in chicken processing plants, as will be discussed in a later chapter. Although women have lost control over poultry production and income, their labor remains essential to the success and profitability of the poultry industry.

Chickens in Africa and Asia

The extent and organization of poultry production in Africa is not well documented; however, as in earlier periods in the United States, women usually raise chickens. Rarely confined or fed, chickens largely fend for themselves consuming vegetable tops, sweet potato or yam vines, grasses, and insects. Free-ranging chickens in Africa produced an average of 2.2 kilograms of meat per bird in contrast to 19.1 kilograms in U.S. confinement operations. In response to this, scientists and development planners propose confinement of chickens and introduction of new breeds as a

TABLE 6.3   Top Ten Chicken-Producing States in the United States, 1990

State	Chickens Sold (per 1000 head)	Value of Sales (in $1,000)
North Carolina	12,000	12,439
Arkansas	18,200	11,805
Georgia	14,200	10,338
Alabama	9,800	7,977
Pennsylvania	15,600	7,391
California	20,000	4,920
Mississippi	5,200	4,259
Indiana	18,200	3,949
Oklahoma	2,800	3,246
Total U.S.	208,085	94,540

SOURCE: U.S. Department of Agriculture, *Agricultural Statistics* (Washington, DC: USDA, 1991), p. 339.

Women's poultry cooperative in Zimbabwe

strategy for increasing meat availability in Africa, especially for urban markets. In some areas of Africa, women are beginning to respond to increased urban demand for poultry by keeping their chickens in more confined areas, raising new breeds, and feeding grain products (Simpson and McDowell, 1986:213).

Women's poultry cooperatives, established by nongovernmental development agencies in several African countries, are designed to simultaneously meet increased urban demand and expand rural women's income earning potential. In Zimbabwe, women in the land resettlement areas typically raise indigenous free-ranging chickens. They have formed cooperatives to raise new varieties of chickens in more confined environments. A farmers' school in the resettlement area teaches classes introducing small-scale cooperative poultry raising to groups of women willing to initiate these new poultry enterprises because they control the earnings from their efforts. Three of these cooperatives, which I visited in 1991, organized their operations slightly differently. In each cooperative, groups of women provided cooperative labor, and using indigenous building material, constructed chicken houses and confined areas for chicks. However, access to the relatively small amounts of cash required for investment in these new enterprises posed problems for cooperative members. In one cooperative, eight women constructed their chicken house but remained unable to complete their structure until they saved enough money to purchase chicken wire. Another cooperative had completed its chicken house and was raising chickens. Some of the women also produced chickens at their own homes. Women with access to cash purchased hybrid birds, feed, and construction materials for the chicken houses, but poorer women improvised. One poorer female household head showed me how she had constructed a pen from sticks to hold chicks she had raised from her own stock. Although she lacked money to purchase hybrid chicks and grain to feed them, she had experimented and had discovered how to successfully raise her own chickens using some of the suggested methods. These newly formed chicken cooperatives were struggling, and it was not at all clear whether the women could overcome problems of transport, access to cash, and markets. Nevertheless, the women proceeded enthusiastically, explaining they controlled the income from poultry, in contrast to earnings from crop production, which were controlled by men.

In socialist China, chickens provided a source of cash for rural women. Studying women working on rural communes, Margery Wolf (1985) found that women's collective labor put them at an economic disadvantage because women were frequently assigned to work groups that received less pay than men's groups. Even in cases where both sexes performed the same tasks, women were paid less than men. Rural women clearly saw these inequities and developed strategies of sideline enterprises, such as raising chickens and selling eggs, pigs, and seedlings to earn extra income. In three out of four of Wolf's field sites, sideline products provided households with more yearly income than average male wages. Also, because much of the collective labor was paid in food allotments rather than cash, sideline activities frequently provided the major source of food as well as cash for households.

Although women raise most poultry in Asia and Africa on small-scale family enterprises, the U.S. model of factory farming of chickens is beginning to be exported to other regions of the world. In Thailand, Japanese agribusiness firms have established processing plants and subcontract with local growers to produce broilers for the Japanese market. The U.S. firm Tyson Foods and C. Itoh of Japan launched a joint venture with Mexican capital to establish new production facilities in Mexico to serve East Asian and Mexican markets (Kim and Curry, 1993). Little information is available on the composition of the labor forces in these plants, but most likely young rural women are the workers in the poultry-processing plants.

Rural women in many contexts rely on chickens as an important sideline income source. Control of poultry has shifted from female to male hands in the United States with concentrated production, but many poor rural women in other parts of the world raise poultry for both subsistence and cash income. Internationalization of the chicken industry may well begin to shift control of production from women to men in Asia and Latin America as well.

Cows

People raise cattle for meat, draft power, and milk, often under quite different production systems. Cattle production systems vary by ecological zones, social organization, and use of cattle. Pastoral systems and ranches predominate on rangelands in semi-arid or arid regions. In areas with higher rainfall, cattle act as sources of draft power, fertilizer, or converters of grain in mixed livestock and cropping systems. In the United States and Europe, dairies, cow-calf operations, and feedlots are typical enterprises.

In most of these production systems, men own and control cattle. Cattle ownership in Africa, the United States, and South America lends men status and power. For example, in southern Africa, men's cattle ownership brings status and wealth and the ability to pay bride prices. In the Americas, cowboys epitomize masculinity, as is ubiquitously portrayed by the Marlboro Man. Although women seldom own cattle, they often care for cattle, especially for calves and dairy cows. In discussing women's association with cattle, I focus specifically on dairy cows because women work most extensively with them.

In 1989, over 222 million milk cows composed 17 percent of the world's cattle stock (Ensminger, 1993:2). The largest number of cows are found in the former Soviet Union, India, Brazil, and the United States (Table 6.4). Yield varies widely, from an average of 6,642 kilograms of milk per cow annually in the United States to 890 kilograms per cow in India. Lactose intolerance in a large proportion of the population in Japan, Thailand, and the Philippines, combined with the ecological expense of raising cows

TABLE 6.4   Number of Cows and Milk Production in Selected Countries, 1990

Country	Milk Cows (per 1,000 head)	Yield per Cow (in kilograms)
Australia	2,100	3,095
Brazil	14,800	959
China	2,164	1,827
France	5,489	4,810
India	28,500	890
Mexico	6,410	1,456
Soviet Union (former)	42,000	2,605
United States	10,127	6,642
World total	158,217	

SOURCE: U.S. Department of Agriculture, *Agricultural Statistics* (Washington, DC: 1991), p. 309.

diminishes extensive reliance on dairy products for food in those countries.

Dairy animals require daily attention at regular hours year round; people milk cows at least once a day and usually twice a day. This routine contrasts with the discontinuous and seasonal work demands of raising crops or nondairy livestock. In many regions of the world, women often perform the daily tasks of milking cows, tending milk animals, and providing fodder.

Dairying in the United States

Women's work has always been crucial to dairying in the United States. Joan Jensen's (1991) excellent study of women in the butter trade in the Philadelphia hinterland documents the extensiveness of women's early work in dairying, as they developed and dominated the butter industry in the late eighteenth century. Butter was an important commodity on farms. It provided income for women, food for the family, and a cushion against hard economic times. At a time when men's grain and animal production in the East had become less profitable due to competition from western agriculture, "not only was the role of women central to agricultural development in this region, but also women's flexibility and ingenuity in producing marketable products allowed these farms successfully to survive tremendous market pressures and to reproduce the family farm as well as the farm family" (Jensen, 1991:171). By the mid-1800s women had established a steady and stable butter market. Men, with mechanized equipment, then began to establish creameries and factories on farms.

Jensen comments that "butter making was a traditional female task, having been performed by countless women over the ages, with increasingly complex skills that were passed by oral tradition from mother to daughter, mistress to servant, neighbor to neighbor. As the demand for butter increased, however, and market competition increased for livestock and grain, men began to join increasingly in dairying with women" (Jensen, 1991:181). Men gradually took over dairying and butter making in the East as the status and profitability of these enterprises increased.

Over the next one hundred years, dairies gained more cows per farm, higher milk production per cow, and new milking machines. In the 1920s and 1930s a substantial proportion of U.S. households kept 1 or 2 milk cows. During this time period, women milked cows primarily for family consumption; only 62 percent of farms with cows sold milk, cream, or butter (Manchester, 1983:22). In 1929, one-half the U.S. cow herds had only 1 or 2 cows and 78 percent of herds contained less than 10 cows. By 1936, the average farmer in the Northeast and Great Lakes states milked 17 cows, and 86 percent of farmers in the Northeast milked by hand. Herd sizes expanded as the number of dairy farms declined. From 1950 to 1989, average herd size increased 1,020 percent from 5.8 to 49 cows per farm, and the number of dairy farms declined by 90 percent from 3,648,000 to 205,000 (Ensminger, 1993:10).

Dairy farming in the United States today consists of two distinct systems: large industrial dairies, and smaller family dairies (Gilbert and Akor, 1988). One-half of all milk produced in the United States comes from five states: California, Minnesota, New York, Pennsylvania, and Wisconsin. Large-scale industrial dairies in southern California raise herds of 600 or more cows on approximately 80 acre drylots. Large industrial dairies thrive in other regions of the country, for example, in Florida and in the Southwest. These dairies purchase feed, specialize exclusively in milk production, and depend on hired workers. In comparing California industrial dairies with Wisconsin dairies, Jess Gilbert and Raymond Akor (1988) report that 343 animals compose the average herd size in California, compared to 44 per herd in Wisconsin. California dairies hired an average of 4 workers, compared to 0.8 workers on Wisconsin farms. These authors point to increasing structural divergence in United States dairy operations. Other evidence suggests that the dairy industry in all parts of the country may undergo major transformations in the near future, with large industrial dairies becoming more common in all regions. Exactly how this transformation might affect women remains unclear.

On U.S. dairy farms today, women work in but rarely control dairy enterprises. Dairy farming and other types of livestock enterprises demand constant labor and use women's labor more intensively than cash-grain farms (Rosenfeld, 1985). Schwartzweller (1991) found extensive participation of women in farm work in his study of Michigan dairy farms. During the busy season, 32 percent of women spent more than 40 hours per week in farm work and another 23 percent worked more than 20 but less than 40 hours. Tasks on dairy farms were divided by gender, with women more likely than men to clean milking parlors (62 percent), pay bills (61 percent), keep accounts (49 percent), care for calves (29 percent), and do milking (27 percent). Men were more likely than women to be involved in the following tasks on dairy farms; over 75 percent of men milked, fed cows, fixed fences, repaired equipment, monitored calving, and oversaw cow health. In general, women on dairy farms typically perform such female tasks as bookkeeping and cleaning, though many participate in all aspects of the operation. Men manage the operation, participate in a wide range of tasks, and often take sole responsibility for such typically male tasks as equipment repair.

On family dairies in Pennsylvania, women work extensively (Sachs, 1988). Despite the importance of their labor, women often minimize or downplay their contribution in describing their work in the dairy barns. A woman on a small dairy farm explained: "I don't help a lot. I care for the calves and bottle-feed them. Every day, I carry the milk out. Also, I drive the tractor when my husband needs me. I shovel corn at harvest time. During haymaking, I'm out there every day. And sometimes I work in the fields" (Sachs, 1988:128).

Why do women downplay their involvement? Their multiple responsibilities for household work, farm work, and off-farm work as well as their flexibility and willingness to "fill in" obscure the importance of their work on the farm. One woman explained to me that she decided to take a part-time job to earn extra money for the family but then quit because she realized she was needed at the farm. She described the flexibility of her schedule on the 240-acre dairy farm milking 63 cows as follows: "I milk every day except on weekends. Every now and then, I get the weekends off since the boys are home. In the summertime, I don't have to milk every night. During school, I milk every morning except weekends, and then in the evenings, if they have track meets, I fill in; or in the fall when they have field work that they're doing, I work then. It's just kind of a part-time thing in the evenings. It's not a definite [thing] that I have to be there every night" (Sachs, 1988:127). Although she is clearly a major player in her family's dairy operation, this woman viewed herself as filling in when her husband or sons were busy with other activities.

Large and technologically sophisticated family farms produce the bulk of milk in the United States as smaller and medium-sized dairies either go out of business or expand. Hired workers, usually men, milk more cows in elaborate milking parlors. Average milk production per cow has increased substantially. New technologies, such as the genetically engineered hormone, bovine somatotropin (BST), have been developed to increase milk production per cow. BST, one of the first triumphs of biotechnology in agriculture, is a growth hormone found in cows' cells that has been isolated and manufactured by the Monsanto chemical company to increase milk production. When injected regularly, the hormone boosts cows' appetites by diverting food from metabolic to milk-producing functions (Hynes, 1989). Smaller dairies are resisting the introduction of BST, realizing that this new technology will bring disproportional benefits to larger dairies. These farmers question the utility of a technology that increases milk production per cow when they receive low milk prices and are forced out of business because of an oversupply of milk. Concerns over animal health have also surfaced as research evidence suggests that BST may detrimentally affect cow health, for example, by increasing mastitis and heat sensitivity while decreasing fertility and longevity. Exactly what impact BST will have on the dairy industry and on cow health remains unclear.

Dairying in India—the White Revolution

In India, the "white revolution" has reshaped dairy production and under-mined women's centrality (Shiva, 1988). Cows, which are sacred in Indian culture, provide draft power, manure to improve soil fertility, and milk products. In addition, they are symbols of stored wealth and their dung is used for cooking fuel. Development planners introduced the white revo-lution, a western development strategy patterned after the green revolu-tion in rice and wheat production, to increase dairy production. The white revolution, called Operation Flood, is a huge dairy development effort that was introduced to India in 1970, heralded for its potential to improve dairy production, feed urban dwellers, increase the income of rural people, and build an infrastructure for the dairy industry. India's 240 million bovines comprise 18 percent of the world's cattle stock and 50 percent of the world's buffalo population. Despite large numbers of cows, low milk pro-duction per cow limits India to production of only 6 percent of the world's milk. India's dairy development strategies are based on the premises that India has too many zebu cows, whose milk production level is too low, and that a successful dairy industry would optimally result in a decline in the overall number of cattle and an increase in milk production. Operation Flood introduced new breeds of cattle and dairy processing plants to rural India, an action that often displaced rural women's traditional dairy indus-tries. The results of Operation Flood are mixed. Wealthy urban consumers buy more and higher quality milk, but the rural poor cannot afford to pay increased prices and consume less milk. Landless people either abandon milk production or purchase high-cost fodder from landed people. Also, because new breeds of dairy cows eat grain to increase milk production, less food grain is available for human consumption. R. Crotty (1980) argues that administrators of the program and European Economic Community farmers who are able to dispose of their dairy surplus in India benefit from Operation Flood.

Vandana Shiva criticizes the reductionist strategies of the white revolu-tion for introducing inappropriate breeds of cattle, undermining inte-grated agricultural systems, and depriving women of income. Cross-breeding of indigenous cattle with dairy cows such as holsteins and jer-seys often proves inappropriate for farmers with limited resources in tropical climates because the crossbreeds are sensitive to heat, are less hardy as draft animals, are vulnerable to disease, and are dependent on resource-intensive inputs like clean water and high-quality feeds. Shanti George recognizes the inappropriateness of crossbred cows in a country where the majority of milk producers cannot afford to provide adequate nutrition and health care for their children: "In many parts of India, indeed, it must be more comfortable to be a largeholder's crossbred cow than to be a small farmer's child. We are told, for example, that while most rural Indians have to drink from the pond, crossbred cows get clean water. In the Anand region that boasts the most elaborate and efficient veterinary system in India, they say it is easier to get a doctor for a sick animal than for a sick human being" (as quoted in Shiva, 1988:171–172). As George further describes the problems of a reductionist approach, "The trouble is that when dairy planners look at the cow, they see just her udder, though there is much more to her. They equate cattle only with milk, and do not consider other livestock produce—draught power, dung for fertilizer and fuel, hides, skins, horn and hooves" (as quoted in Shiva, 1988:168).

Narrow reductionist development approaches focusing on increased production of a single commodity, milk in this case, fail to consider the multiple uses of animals and therefore frequently decrease the economic well-being of rural households. Eighty million work animals meet two-thirds of India's agricultural power requirements. Cattle and buffalo produce over 700 million tons of usable manure, one-half of which is used for fuel and one half for fertilizer(Shiva, 1988:166). Farmers and rural people cannot afford to replace these energy sources with purchased oil, charcoal, or fertilizer.

Dairy processing plants replace rural women's household dairy processing operations. This means that women lose control of the income from milk products and have less access to milk products for their household consumption. The story resembles that of the displacement of women from butter-making in the United States one hundred years earlier. Rural women traditionally produced ghee, buttermilk, curds, and cottage cheese. Ghee was usually sold on the market, whereas buttermilk, its by-product, was consumed locally. Farmers now take their milk to the new dairy processing plants, where it is processed into butter, cheese, and dried skim milk—products typically consumed by the urban elites, thus diverting nutritional resources from rural areas. Rural women no longer obtain income from dairy processing, nor do they have buttermilk to feed their families.

Operation Flood claims that 8 million women have been emancipated by bringing them into the mainstream of dairy development. George questions the Food and Agriculture Organization and other advocates' enthusiasm, citing one author's assertion that Operation Flood has helped women: "Amul dairy not only organizes special picnics for women on its premises but boasts an affiliated village dairy cooperative whose membership is wholly female" (George, 1985:196). Such token efforts to include women in dairy development do not negate the shift away from women's primacy in dairying—women compose only 10 percent of members in the dairy association and although the workers in the dairy cooperative cited are all female, all staff employees are male. From George's

(1985) perspective, the industrialization of dairying has eroded women's position in dairying and also rural women's ability to feed their families.

Dairying in Zimbabwe

Attempts to improve dairy production in Zimbabwe have followed similar strategies as in India. Zimbabwean women typically milk cows for local consumption. Small dairy collection and processing plants, located in rural areas, attempt to increase milk production. Farmers bring their milk to dairy collection depots in response to incentive programs that provide some farmers with new breeds of dairy cows. One dairy distribution center that I visited had large-capacity bulk tanks for milk storage but never used the tanks because they lacked sufficient quantities of milk from local farmers to fill them. Nearby, women produced minimal amounts of milk, but they lacked the means to transport the milk to the center and of course had no refrigeration. Thus, rather than take their milk to the collection center, most of the women sold their milk on the local market or used it for their families. One woman, with a larger farm than most of the other women, hired a boy to carry milk to the distribution center on a daily basis. When I asked her if she had any problem with dairy production, she explained that she needed more cows and proudly showed me her single cow—all that she could afford. The poverty of the farmers and lack of infrastructure in rural Zimbabwe limit the success of the white revolution; consequently, women in rural areas continue to produce milk and receive income for their products.

Hunting Wild Animals

Women's and men's knowledge about, relations with, and practices that concern wild animals are different, as they are with domestic animals. Hunting wild animals is a prototypical male activity. Anthropologists and archaeologists viewed the early distinction between men as hunters and women as gatherers as the original basic division of labor between men and women. For example, Ashley Montagu explains, "Up to about nine thousand years ago all human populations lived by hunting and most of them also by fishing, supplemented by the picking of berries, fruits and nuts, and the digging of roots and tubers. Perhaps the first division of labor between the sexes was that the male became the hunter and the female the food gatherer" (1969:134).

Recent feminist scholars criticize the focus on man as hunter as the major evolutionary step for humans. For Margaret Ehrenberg (1989), the focus on man as hunter obscures the importance of women in human evolution. Human evolution has traditionally been discussed in terms of the role that "'Man the Hunter' played in devising weapons and tools for catching and slaughtering animals for food, how he needed to walk upright on two feet to see his prey above the tall savanna grass, and how he was more successful than other species in his hunting exploits because he teamed up with other men and learnt the value of cooperation. And what of 'woman', meanwhile?" (1989:41). Anthropologists cast male hunters as heroic providers while dismissing women's gathering activities as insignificant.

Collard takes another tack in her criticism of social scientists for glorifying the hunt as a major evolutionary step and decries hunting as the modus operandi of patriarchal societies. From her perspective, romanticizing and glorifying the hunt justifies a "culture of brutality toward and rape of all that is viewed as 'fair game.' Moreover, hunting as a sport serves as the paradigm activity in which the reenactment of the hunt and the kill reinforces the normalization of a violent act. By playing hunter, man ritualizes what he sees as his greatest glory: His passage from ape to human and the consequent creation of a category of domination, the politics of which have changed the face of the earth and the quality of our lives" (Collard, 1988:34).

Although Collard has no sympathy for romanticized portrayals of early hunters, she is particularly critical of contemporary rationalizations for the hunt, among them love of nature, protecting animals, food provision, and concern for people. She contends that such rationalizations conceal men's pleasure in the stalking and killing of animals, which brings status and an assurance of masculinity. In the United States, the vast majority of the 20.6 million registered hunters do not kill for survival (Collard, 1988:52). Rather, hunting more commonly encourages male comraderie and bestows status or trophies on the successful hunter—the killer of the season's largest bear, deer, fish, or turkey. Her critique of the hunt as sport that glorifies male brutality is on target, but Collard fails to consider other incentives for hunting or to detect the women's role in the hunt. For example, many rural people in the United States rely on venison, duck, turkey, and rabbit to supplement their families' meat supply. Ethical claims decrying the hunt as sport may be inappropriate for local people who live under particular circumstances in the United States, but most certainly these views must be rethought in relation to rural people in Africa.

Africans rely heavily on undomesticated animals for food. At present, people in many regions of sub-Saharan Africa consume more game meat than domestic meat. Studies in the 1960s reported that game made up 80 percent of the fresh meat consumed in Ghana and 50 percent in the Congo. In the 1970s, wild animals composed 80 percent of animal protein consumed in Botswana (McGlothlen, Goldsmith, and Fox, 1986:222). In southern Nigeria, 80 percent of the population eats game meat regularly.

Most of the meat comes from small game animals, such as springhare and grasscutter, animals that may be hunted without licenses and are not controlled by government agencies. When fish are included under the rubric of wild meat, people in Benin, Congo, Ghana, Liberia, Senegal, Sierra Leone, Togo, and Zaire receive more than 50 percent of their daily protein from wild meat (Timberlake, 1985:156). Men and boys usually hunt. Although women's role in hunting has not been well-documented, some women hunt, and women often process hunted animals.

Hunting large game is increasingly off-limits to rural Africans. Large tracts of land, set aside for game parks for use principally by wealthy foreigners, provide minimal benefit to local people (Myers, 1981). Arguments for wildlife preservation emphasize the value of such parks for tourism or species conservation. Such arguments hold little meaning for local people, as most of the profits and benefits from game parks leave Africa or go to the African elites. National parks and wildlife preserves typically displace or exclude rural people who traditionally considered the land as belonging to their communities (Kiss, 1990). Also, antipoaching laws turn subsistence hunting into a crime, and local people are prevented from killing animals that destroy their crops and livestock. Rural people bear the costs of living with wildlife but receive few of the benefits.

Zimbabwe leads the way in developing strategies for maintaining indigenous animals and simultaneously benefiting local people. Sound policies on indigenous animal populations offer the possibility of solving both ecological and food problems in some regions of Africa. The overgrazing by cattle, sheep, and goats creates major ecological problems, for example, erosion and soil degradation, in many areas of Africa. Mixed indigenous animals use more of the vegetation than do domestic animals because diverse species eat different levels of vegetation and different parts of plants (McGlothlen, Goldsmith, and Fox, 1986). Indigenous grazers eat grass more completely and are less destructive in grazing habits than cattle, in general creating a balanced, nondestructive system of animal production. The carrying capacity for unimproved, low-quality rangeland is at least three times higher for wild game than for cattle. In Zimbabwe, ranchers previously active in eliminating wildlife to make room for their livestock are now replacing cattle with kudu, impala, blesbok, bushbuck, springbok, wildebeest, zebra, francolin, guinea fowl, and ostrich. For example, in the southeast low veld, the amount of land allocated to wildlife on private ranches increased from one-fourth in 1986 to one-half by 1989. During that same time period, most cattle were removed from the Matetsi area, and in the Gwaai Valley the cattle herd has been reduced from 12,000 to less than 4,000 (Kiss, 1990:164). Initially established for safari hunting, these ranches now promote spectator tourism as well. Little data exists on women's involvement in these activities, but it is probably safe to assume that men are the principal ranch owners and hunters.

CAMPFIRE (Communal Areas Management Program for Indigenous Resources), an innovative program in Zimbabwe, simultaneously conserves wildlife resources and allows local people to use these resources on a sustainable basis (Murindagomo, 1990). Local decision-making bodies were established to mediate the conflict between agricultural production and wildlife. CAMPFIRE gives control of wildlife management to rural communities and allows profits from the wildlife enterprises to be used by the community or distributed among community residents. Little information is available on women's participation in decisionmaking in CAMPFIRE, but clearly given gender differences in control of resources and labor, women's and men's interests diverge. CAMPFIRE is considered a model for developing wildlife management programs with local community control. However, in establishing these programs in Africa and other regions of the world, consideration must be given to women's interests, and women should be involved in the decision-making groups.

Wild animals provide food and income for many rural people in the world, especially in Africa. Feminist and ecofeminist analyses of the hunt should sort out the different intentions, situations, and relations between people and wild animals. For rural people, who depend on meat in their diets, consuming wild animals may be more ecologically sound in particular circumstances than eating domestic animals. The complexities of class and economic issues must be incorporated in understandings of human relations with wild animals. Governments obtain foreign exchange from safaris, poachers gain huge profits, tourists receive animal trophies, and local people may obtain subsistence or income, or alternatively, they may be completely excluded from the benefits of wildlife.

Summary on Women and Animals

Work with animals is gendered even though both women and men raise livestock. With industrialized and concentrated livestock production, as exemplified in chicken and dairy production, women's control over the production process and access to income are minimal. Shifts in dairy and chicken production from small family enterprises in the United States to large-scale intensive dairying and poultry factories has displaced women's labor and participation in decision-making. In India, a similar shift transferred women's small-scale dairy enterprises and processing operations to men as milk collection and processing became increasingly profitable and geared to nonlocal markets. Despite similarities in the shifts, the severe consequences in India result in poor women and their families losing access to adequate nutritional resources. Women's knowledge, practices, and skills related to the multiple by-products of raising cows disappear in these transitions.

Recently, feminist theorists have pointed to the connection between violence against women and violence against animals, suggesting that a feminist agenda must include attention to animal rights. The call for vegetarianism as necessary for the feminist agenda may be appropriate for upper- and middle-class Western women, but for many women in the world, animal-raising activities, especially for poor women, contribute substantially to their income, and access to animal products improves their families' nutritional status. In particular regions, raising animals may be the most ecologically sound way for humans to live on resources. Thus, the call for vegetarianism as an essential component of the feminist agenda fails to adequately consider the context of women's involvement in animal production and consumption.

7

Women on Family Farms: A Reappraisal

In many rural areas of the world, life revolves around the family farm. Patriarchal relations on family farms set the context for gender relations in rural areas, but with changes in family farms, patriarchal authority is shifting and loosening. The extensive literature on the demise of the family farm, on its persistence or on changes within it rarely acknowledges the centrality of gender relations in maintaining and changing these systems, with the exception of work by women scholars and women farm activists. Failure to explicitly discuss patriarchal authority and the importance of women's work for the survival of family farms limits theoretical understandings of family and peasant farms. Studies by feminist scholars on women in agriculture focus on documenting women's work on family farms with the intent to make women's work visible, to redirect policy, and to improve farm women's lives. A decade of scholarship devoted to measuring women's work in agriculture has resulted in serious attempts to reconceptualize and understand women's work on farms and has led to the realization that merely documenting the extent of women's work fails to destabilize patriarchal authority. Agrarian ideologies continue to bolster patriarchal authority and privileges in rural areas through idealized portrayals of agrarian and rural life that conceal the oppressive living conditions of women. I discuss here how the centrality of gender relations can be incorporated into theoretical understandings of family farms, and review methodological and strategic lessons learned in conceptualizing gender divisions of labor on farms. I also suggest that agrarian and domestic discourses have romanticized, subordinated, and misinterpreted women's lives on family farms.

Theorizing About Rural Production Systems

Agriculture stands at the heart of rural production systems; rural life has been organized around agriculture for centuries. The social relations that pertain to producing agricultural goods vary over time and space; they include peasant, feudal, slave, family, collective, and capitalist modes of production. Two types of production systems in agriculture have gained predominance worldwide: the peasant or family farm, and capitalist enterprises. Vestiges of other agricultural systems remain, but they usually survive in combination with one of these two predominant systems. With the demise of socialist economies in Europe and Asia, collective and state-operated farms are breaking up and agriculture is restructured according to family or capitalist-based systems.

Attempts to explain the transformation of agrarian populations tend toward two divergent interpretations within the Marxist tradition; one focusing on proletarianization and the other on the persistence of family farms (Long, 1984). On the one hand, theorists see the penetration of capitalism as displacing rural people from the land and forcing them to seek their livelihoods outside of agriculture. Mechanization of agriculture and concentration of landownership result in the emergence of a small landowning class, more and more agricultural wage laborers, and a massive migration of people from rural areas. These processes of urbanization and proletarianization can occur in advanced economies as well as Third World nations.

On the other hand, some scholars focus on what is perhaps most striking about family farms—their ability to survive in capitalist economies. Sociological and economic theories in both the Marxist and modernization schools clearly expected household production to disappear in modern or capitalist societies. Thus, recent studies of social relations in agriculture in advanced capitalist societies devote considerable attention to the viability of family farms. The inability of capitalism to completely penetrate agricultural social relations elicits a theoretical as well as a practical concern in developing countries in what has become known as the mode of production debate. Despite, and also because of, early colonial and later development efforts to capitalize agriculture in Africa, Asia, and Latin America, peasant production systems survive. Here, I discuss arguments describing the resiliency of family farms in advanced capitalist societies and peasant production in developing countries with consideration of the importance of gender relations in these production systems.

The Family Farm in Advanced Capitalism

Why has the family farm survived? Scholars employ two major lines of argument to explain the tenacity of the family farm in advanced capitalist economies. The first line of reasoning emphasizes that the uniqueness of agriculture prevents capitalist organization of production on the farm. Unsuited to industrial organization, the biological nature of agricultural production must be sequential, and time must pass for biological processes, such as plant and animal growth, to occur. S. A. Mann and J. M. Dickinson (1978), major proponents of this view, argue that there is such a disjuncture between labor time and production time that labor must be mobilized at certain times and dispersed at others, thus inhibiting the capitalist organization of production.

The sequential and seasonal nature of agricultural production influence the gender division of labor and the use of land and capital (Flora, 1988). Discontinuous labor requirements depend in some cases on women acting as a critical reserve labor force on family farms and in other instances, on men migrating to perform seasonal labor on corporate farms. Also, women's small multiple-cropping systems and income-generating activities often subsidize land-extensive cropping systems during periods of inadequate income and contribute to capital needs in the lag between planting, harvesting, and marketing.

The second line of reasoning, referred to by Sarah Whatmore (1991) as the resiliency thesis, derives from Karl Kautsky's analysis suggesting that the family farm survives because the interplay between household and enterprise allows the "exploitation" of family labor. In an insightful theoretical and empirical analysis, Harriet Friedmann (1988) argues that the uniqueness of family farms derives not from biological processes, but from (1) the organization of labor by kinship, and (2) the combination of labor and property. Agriculture's connection to nature is not unique; rather, all production processes can ultimately be traced back to biological processes. Friedmann criticizes theoretical arguments equating capitalism with industrialization for improperly defining agriculture as non-capitalist. As she explains, agricultural production need not be organized in the same fashion as industrial production to be capitalist. Gender is not at the center of Friedmann's analysis, but she discusses how unique features of family farms effect gender relations. In discussing women's role on Canadian farms, she states that women have an equal, if not more important, role than men in maintaining family enterprises; in addition to farm work they also manage the household, mediate conflict, and maintain political and community liaisons. Property relations based on kinship often legally deny women equal rights to the farm enterprise. The confluence of labor and property in the family farm holds different meanings and opportunities for men and women.

Whatmore's (1991) analysis of theoretical approaches to the family farm goes beyond these two arguments; she suggests that the family farm can best be understood through a combination of a poststructural approach and feminist theory. From her perspective, both the biological and resiliency arguments fail to adequately conceptualize (1) empirical diversity; (2) human agency, ideology, and lived experience; and (3) family and gender relations. To address these issues, she proposes a theoretical framework for analyzing a "poststructuralist agrarian political economy." Elements addressed within this framework include the biological nature of the production process, the level of commodity orientation in farming, the agro-industrial complex as well as the farm, and how commodity orientation and the social relations on farms are produced through the daily life activities of farm family members. After presenting this poststructural model, Whatmore finds that the model cannot adequately account for social relations on the family farm. She then turns to feminist theory and theories of gender relations to construct a theory that incorporates family relations. The three major points in this framework are that (1) patriarchal gender relations are socially constructed through an active process that subordinates women to men, (2) reproduction is intimately connected to production and varies by historical and class conditions, and (3) the family is an "ideologically-loaded composite of kinship and household relations which is historically and culturally varied in form and the conjugal household, centered on a monogamous heterosexual couple, defines the intersection of kinship and household on family farms" (Whatmore, 1991:43). Whatmore's fresh approach in understanding rural production systems transcends biological-resiliency approaches and captures the centrality of gender as a factor in explaining the persistence of family farms.

Family or Peasant Farming in Developing Regions

The mode of production debate in developing regions takes on a similar, though slightly different, cast as compared to the debate over the place of family farms in capitalist economies. Different, less orthodox approaches have recently appeared. Typically, scholars view family-centered production in developing regions as either resistant to the penetration of capitalism or as serving the interests of capital through exploitation of family labor.

The crisis in African agriculture concerns family-centered agriculture. In the 1970s, African agriculture production declined, and since then it has stagnated. Rural farmers, national and local food supply, and governments' ability to earn foreign currency have suffered from this stagnation. Debates concerning causes and solutions to the crisis revolve around three key issues: the mode of production, dependency, and the role of the state (Barker, 1984). The mode of production debates and further debates that concentrated on the concept of the articulation of the modes of production were initiated to explore the complexities of agrarian transition in Africa, but such discussions increasingly lack political relevance and occur in ever-more obscure and inaccessible language (Booth, 1985). Rather than becoming bogged down in the theoretical semantics that others engage in, I undertake a more straightforward, though perhaps less theoretically sophisticated, discussion of rural production systems.

Currently two types of agricultural production systems prevail in Africa: the agroindustrial system and the family-local system (Barker, 1984). The agro-industrial system, an outgrowth of earlier colonial models, consists of a network of government agencies, transnational firms, and international development agencies involved in supplying or monitoring the inputs, producing, processing, marketing, and transporting of agricultural goods for the international market. By contrast, the family-local system consists of kinship groups, women producers, and local small-scale traders providing food for local markets and family subsistence needs. Jonathon Barker notes that erroneous interpretations of the independence of these two systems present peasants as resistant to capitalist values (Hyden, 1980), as fully integrated into market production, or as totally subordinated to capital. Barker suggests an alternative, building on the articulation of modes of production analysis, and he elaborates on the many interactions that occur between the agro-industrial and family-local systems of production, with many households participating in both systems. There is growing tension between production for the agro-industrial system and the family-local system, which is played out on a number of levels that range from international and national policy debates to negotiations for land and labor within households.

Policy discussions rarely note the centrality of gender in this tension, despite feminist scholars' emphasis on the importance of gender relations in shaping rural production. The different positions of men and women make it possible for households to be simultaneously involved in production for the agro-industrial system and for the family-local system. For example, men may engage in export-oriented agriculture either as wage workers or farmers, and women may produce food for family and local consumption. In Cameroon, for example, men produce cacao for the export market and women grow maize, beans, cassava, and vegetables for local markets. Men, relying heavily on women's labor, usually control household production of goods for the agro-industrial system. Women maintain more autonomy in their efforts to produce for local markets and for subsistence. In most regions of Africa, patriarchal systems of land allocation prevail in the face of capitalist development. For example, men in Zambia and Nigeria used precapitalist systems of control to gain access to the land, the capital, and the women's labor required for successful export commodity production (Afonja, 1990). Governments or local chiefs allocate land to individual male household heads who usually make decisions about use of land for specific crops and also reallocate their land to their wives and sons. Thus, men control export-oriented production, and women produce food for local consumption and their families.

Peasant households in Latin America clearly differ from those of Africa because of the greater diversity of Latin American cultural systems and the highly uneven land distribution (Deere and Leon de Leal, 1981). Gender relations in peasant households help maintain the survival of family farms and simultaneously bolster the capitalist system. Women, especially those from the poorest households, remain on minifundias, or small family farms, to raise food for the family, and they provide uncompensated reproductive labor while their husbands earn incomes below family subsistence wages on latifundias or in towns. Thus, peasant production, particularly women's labor, furthers the development of the capitalist agricultural sector while contributing to the continued viability of family farms.

Women's Work on Family Farms

Don't ask me what I has done, but what I ain't.

—Lettice Boyer, as quoted in Jones, 1988

Ester Boserup's book *Women's Role in Economic Development* (1970) was the groundbreaking work on women's involvement in productive activities in developing countries. Boserup highlighted the significance of women's work in agricultural systems, especially in Africa, and warned of the detrimental impacts of capitalist development on women's status and on their ability to feed their families. The significance of her work extends beyond her actual conclusions, which have been contested. Her work opened the door to research on women and inspired two decades of research on women's work and on development policies.

The serious undercounting of women's labor identified by Boserup put in motion a nearly worldwide effort to document women's labor contribution in agriculture. Researchers' extensive attempts to make the work of rural women visible by quantitatively documenting their work in North America, Europe, Africa, Asia, and Latin America prompted Carmen Deere and Magdalena Leon to suggest that the U.N. Decade for Women in Latin America might more aptly be called the "decade on measurement" (1987:3).

Reviews of national-level census data in almost every country investigated found extreme undercounting of women's labor. Ruth Dixon (1982) and Lourdes Beneria (1982), among others, sought to redress problems with national-level census data to more accurately account for women's labor. National-level surveys, such as the national farm women's study funded by the United States Department of Agriculture (USDA), documented the extensive participation of women on farms (Rosenfeld, 1985). In contrast to data from the U.S. agricultural census in which only 8 percent of farmers were reported as women in 1980, the national survey found that 54 percent of farm women considered themselves major operators of their farms (Sachs, 1983:75). A multitude of local studies in various regions of the world showed in more detail the deep level of involvement of women in agricultural systems.

Scholars hoped that making women's work visible would reorient agriculture development policies and programs to improve women's status and lives. This early optimism, and in some senses, liberal naïveté (with the implicit assumption that hard work should be rewarded), soon met with the realization that documentation of women's important labor contribution in agriculture was not enough to change national policies or to improve the lives of rural women. Researchers then reshaped research questions in their attempt to more fully understand women's participation in agriculture and to develop strategies appropriate to improving women's lives.

The first new research tenet was that extensive labor on the part of women failed to translate into control over income, equal participation in decisionmaking, or improvements in women's status. In fact, women frequently perform agricultural labor either under men's direction or to increase male income. Thus, women's heavy work often reinforces or reflects their subordination to men rather than improving their social position.

Despite the plethora of empirical studies after the publication of Boserup's study, government agricultural policies in Africa continue to direct agriculture development efforts toward men. African policymakers are by no means ignorant of women's labor contribution. On the contrary, they recognize women's critical labor contribution to African families and economies, but they expect women to perform this work for the benefit of men and the wider community: "Politicians in public speeches and writers in poems and novels pay homage to their mothers, without whose hard work, determination, dedication, and courage they would not have achieved prestige, status, or power. It is public knowledge that the poorest man is one without a wife to work for him, since women's work is indispensable for producing both subsistence and wealth" (Obbo, 1990:222).

Although government officials may acknowledge the importance of women's labor contributions, they only rarely seek to redress policies and practices that reinforce men's control of land, women's labor, and income from agricultural products. A story told to me by a male agricultural scientist while I was visiting farmers in Cameroon reveals the recognition but low level of respect accorded to women's work. He jokingly said that a male farmer had told him he was thinking of marrying a third wife, to which he replied that two wives were enough for a man. The farmer responded that he figured three wives were about the same as a tractor—and the scientist then saw the logic in the farmer's strategy.

A second major research shift on farm women's labor occurred when scholars realized that emphasis on women's contribution to production neglected women's reproductive work. The first research on women's productive contribution on farms, overcompensating for earlier research traditions that viewed farm women exclusively as domestic workers, placed minimal emphasis on women's domestic contributions to the farm household. Studies showed that regardless of their level of responsibility for agricultural work, rural women almost everywhere spent many hours in domestic work. Efforts to categorize farm women's work as either production or reproduction were frustrating: First, the two types of work are intricately interrelated, especially for rural women, who often work outside the formal wage economy; and second, such distinctions were not helpful in understanding how rural women interpreted the daily activities in their lives.

Researchers initiated various approaches to more accurately assess and understand gender divisions of labor in agricultural households. Surveys estimated women's and men's participation in specific tasks, seasons, crops, fields, and household chores. Also, scholars looked at work in the broader agricultural system, such as processing, food preparation, and marketing, rather than merely focusing on production. Renewed emphasis on women's reproductive work required methodological strategies to evaluate these activities.

Evaluation of labor usually measures wage labor by using time or money as standards. However, standard methods of evaluating work that rely on these measures have little relevance for measuring work on farms that is not based on wages (Whatmore, 1991). The attempt to separate the categories of farm and farm household, the site of both production and reproduction, to measure women's work is artificial. Women perform productive and reproductive tasks simultaneously or a single task might include elements of production and reproduction. For example, on Pennsylvania farms many women take their infants and young children to the barn with them when they milk cows (Sachs, 1988). How should such work be counted—as farm work for the family's dairy business, as child care, or as both? An English farm woman clearly described this dilemma: "You see, you develop the knack of being able to do two or three things at once. I mean most people don't realise that . . . that's why when you sit down and talk about it it's very hard to separate " (as quoted in Whatmore, 1991:90). During many of the interviews I conducted with farm women, women engaged in various activities while we talked: folding clothes, cooking lunch, changing diapers, washing dishes, watching children, weeding, or sorting vegetables for farmers' markets. All of these activities, including their generosity in talking with me, are unpaid for, but they clearly support the farm household. Women's multiple responsibilities often result in the necessity of doing at least two things at a time. Attempts to categorize this work as either productive or reproductive labor or to measure time allocated to a particular task are inherently problematic.

Describing African women's perception of their work, Christine Obbo explains: "Women work all the time, juggling several tasks. Gardening is constantly interrupted by guests or children needing attention. Nursing a baby is usually welcomed by women who need a break, but it can also be resented because the constant interruptions prolong the workday. . . . A mother has to carry (her baby) on her back, which slows her down" (1990: 213).

Distinguishing between productive and reproductive activities is also difficult because a single task may serve both purposes. A Pennsylvania woman who raises livestock for sale and for the family explains, "I market pigs that we raise. I do the marketing, make sure they get butchered and distributed. It's not a big thing; it really pays for what we raise, and I get it for nothing really. We usually buy extra steers or whatever and raise them and sell them. We don't make extra, but it pays for what we got. It pays for our steer, or it pays for our pork" (as quoted in Sachs, 1988:131). From her perspective, she raises and markets livestock to pay for the family's meat. Does her work in raising and marketing livestock count as market or subsistence production? In Swaziland, women typically attempt to raise enough maize for their families; if they have surplus maize, they sell it locally. They work in planting, weeding, harvesting, and storage simultaneously for both market and subsistence.

Thus, it has become important to many researchers who are attempting to understand women's work to transcend both quantitative estimates of women's contribution to agricultural work and efforts to categorize work in dualistic categories. Instead, researchers ask what work means to the women themselves. Scholars now emphasize how these activities affect women's consciousness: How do they view their work? Confronted with English farm women's accounts of their activities, Whatmore noted the tricky problem of interpreting accounts of research subjects "whose everyday activities and ways of making sense of the world are structured within and reproduce the ideological apparatus of a patriarchal sex-gender order" (1991:47). In my earlier research on farm women, I listened in amazement to farm woman describe the array and extent of their work, which they then defined or minimized as "helping." For example, the Pennsylvania woman quoted above who raised pigs and steers downplayed the significance of her contribution. Similarly, Obbo argues that African women's interpretation of their work is an articulation of their subordinate position. Women internalize and reiterate the pervasive ideologies that control their labor and sexuality. These examples illustrate the way women's activities shape their own perspectives and also shape men's consciousness. As Dorothy Smith (1987) argues, the more successfully women perform their work, the more invisible it becomes to men. Their ability to juggle tasks and simultaneously perform productive, reproductive, and emotional labor provides them with different angles of vision than men. Also, as a result of women's work, men are free to attend to other issues and activities and need not consider feeding or clothing themselves or attending to the immediate needs of other household members. As Haraway (1991) suggests, the problem for women is how to see from below. The perspective of a person in such a position is often distorted and clouded by various modes of denial like forgetting, repression, depression, and other disappearing acts. Agrarian and domestic ideologies contributed to the distortion of women's interpretation of their lives and denial of their interests.

Agrarian Ideology

Deborah Fink's (1992) recent book on Nebraska farm women traces the impact of agrarian thinking on women's lives. Agrarian ideology in the United States, often traced to Thomas Jefferson, promotes an agrarian democracy based on family farms. The superiority of farm life over urban life, long a theme in Europe, influenced Jefferson. He saw even greater possibilities for agrarianism in the United States, a country without feudal traditions. From Jefferson's standpoint, the prosperity and moral character of family farms formed the backbone for a democratic society. Rural people seemed healthier, happier, and more moral than urban dwellers. Variants of this agrarian theme appear in other historical periods, as well as in different national contexts (Fink, 1992).

As Fink clearly explains, agrarianism, embedded in a political and economic context purported to benefit family farmers, disproportionately benefited political and economic elites. Settling North America with family farms enabled the expansion of U.S. territory and economic interests. Focus on the supposed moral attributes of family farming distracted attention from the fact that the U.S. government drove Native Americans off their land. Destruction of Native American cultures as well as ecological systems was recast as a moral endeavor to establish family farming. Agrarian ideology often promotes the interests of privileged classes and racial groups, but rather than being explicit, these interests are often veiled by extolling the moral superiority of family farms.

Farm women, supposedly in a special position in this agrarian ideology, lived hard lives offset by the benefits of country life, including closeness to nature, relief from the pressures of city life, and love of their families. Deborah Fink criticizes the view that rural life is unique and that rural women are privileged in contrast to urban women. "Whereas agrarian ideology has proclaimed that women were liberated rather than limited by their service within the family farm, my analysis indicates that rural women lived the same basic contradictions as nonrural women, although the circumstances of rural life put a unique stamp on the form of these contradictions" (1992:2). Fink goes on to explain that agrarianism, as a gendered ideology, projects different ideals for men and women. Agrarianism views farming as a superior way of life and defines the appropriate moral position for farm women as wives and mothers who support their husbands and raise their children to continue the farm tradition. The subordination of farm women was expected and "no one publicly questioned the assumption that farm women would interpret their lives in terms of their duties as wives and mothers in service to the overarching good of the farm" (Fink, 1992:29).

At the same time that the agrarian ideology exemplified farm people as the moral backbone of society, proponents of the domestic ideology singled out urban and middle-class women as the defenders of morality. Proponents of agrarianism and domesticity viewed capitalism, industrialism, and urbanism as morally suspect in contrast to the values of rural people and women in the home. The domestic ideology, which prevailed during the late nineteenth and early twentieth centuries, emphasized the importance of women's role in the home. As capitalist social relations increasingly separated the workplace and the home, proponents of the domestic ideology called upon women to remain in the home to provide labor and emotional support for their families. The proper role for a woman in urban areas was as a housewife and in rural areas as a farmwife.

However, only upper- and middle-class women successfully adhered to the domestic ideology. Confined to the household sphere, women of the privileged classes were guaranteed certain protections and options that women in other classes could not command (Mullings, 1986). Black and working-class women left their homes and worked for wages in factories, in service establishments, or in other people's homes. African-American women were denied the refuge of their families and households but experienced greater independence than other women and possessed the greatest degree of equality with their own men. These historical racial and class differences in women's experiences set the stage for quite different perspectives for white women and women of color in their perceptions of work and their organizing strategies around issues of work.

In an earlier work (Sachs, 1983), I argued that farm households adopted the domestic ideology, keeping women in their homes and away from outdoor farm work. Wealthy rural women attempted to mimic the model of domesticity adopted by privileged urban women, but for the most part, rural women failed to become housewives. The domestic ideology for rural women took a different twist: Rather than being housewives, they were farmwives.

Farmwives, Housewives, Farm Women, or Women Farmers

Farmwife is a term used to designate women who live on farms in many regions of the world, but the term is worth questioning. Who are farmwives, and what do they do? How do they perceive of themselves? In larger context, what changes are occurring in women's definition of themselves? What is the relation between the state and farm women?

In many parts of the world, women gain access to farming and farms through marriage. In the United States, farmwife designates women on farms; women marry farmers and become farmwives (Fink, 1992). Society-wide gender ideologies that define marriage and motherhood as the primary roles for women are imbedded in the concept of the farmwife. For farm women in England, the "role of 'wife' builds upon, and reinforces, more widely constructed subordinate gender identities of femininity and womanhood" (Whatmore, 1991:142).

To understand the emphasis on women's role as wife, it is important to look more closely at the form of the family on farms, recognizing that family types are historically and culturally variable (Whatmore, 1991). In the Western world, the concept of the family farm includes the nuclear family, especially the conjugal unit, as the strongest feature. Designation of women as farmwives defines them primarily in relation to their husbands rather than emphasizing their relation to their children, as in "farm mothers," or stressing their relation to the farm, as "farm women" or "farmers."

Farmwives, similar to housewives, perform reproductive activities that include childbearing, childrearing, cooking, cleaning, and washing. Like housewives, they are expected to express their sexuality in monogamous, heterosexual relation to their husbands. Thus, farmwives share many of the duties of housewives, but in addition, they perform various activities related to the farm enterprise, such as bookkeeping, milking cows, running errands, supervising farm labor, growing and preserving food, various farm chores, and "filling-in" or doing what "needs to be done."

Popular culture and farm communities often romanticize and idealize farm women's lives. On the one hand, these idealizations overlook the way men control women's labor, fertility, and sexuality. Both Fink (1992) and Whatmore (1991) note the paucity of research on the sexuality of women on farms or on the violence against them. In rural Nebraska, historical information and writings on women's sexuality or childbirth is rare and in rural England, there is little information on women's sexuality. For rural women, sexual independence was the least desirable characteristic for a wife or potential farmwife; respectable farm women limited their sexual activities to their husbands and did not discuss it. Discussions of unwanted pregnancies, heterosexual liaisons outside of marriage, or lesbian relationships rarely appear in the literature on rural women. People from farm households or rural communities or research findings on farm women rarely mention violence against women in farm households. Confronting spouse abuse and rape remains difficult even in urban areas and is even more difficult on farms and in rural communities. Glorification, isolation, and interdependence of farm families further mitigate against recognition and resolution of these problems for farm women. Fiction writing offers one of the few avenues for rural women in the United States to express concern about domestic violence on farms (Smiley, 1991).

On the other hand, farmwives are not merely subordinate to men; they gain economic security, respectability, and prestige from their positions (Fink, 1992). In her study of English farming women, Whatmore found women as well as men were responsible for legitimizing patriarchal production regimes and defending traditional practices on the farm. It should be remembered that farmwives, generally members of the propertied classes, hold privileges not enjoyed by members of other classes in rural areas. Although ownership of family farms typically rests in male hands with women's access to farming or land coming primarily through marriage, women do not usually perceive their husband's ownership of the farm as oppressive or problematic. In fact, many farm women fight long and hard to preserve the family farm. Interests opposed to feminist political agendas in the United States recognize farm women's stake in their families. In the mid-1980s, I attended a farm women's conference sponsored by the USDA that coincided with congressional voting on the Equal Rights Amendment (ERA). One speaker urged the farm women attending the conference to lobby their congressional representatives to vote against the ERA; she explained that the Equal Rights Amendment was supported by radical lesbians who rejected all relations with men and that this certainly was an affront to farm women who deeply valued their farm families. Through appeals to the virtues and values of the family, she attempted to mobilize farm women's particular interests against the interests of other women.

Another important role for a farm woman involves providing support for the transfer of the farm from her husband to her son(s). Since World War II, the U.S. cooperative extension service and farm journalists encouraged families to consider their farms as multigenerational enterprises (Jensen, 1991). Government and media have joined in the effort, emphasizing the importance of continuation of the farm business by passing the farm to the son rather than considering only the economic interests of the immediate farm family. Multigenerational farms seldom improve farm women's place in the farm enterprise. Jensen (1991) points out that wives and daughters on farms question the fairness of inheritance of the farm by males rather than consideration of how the farm benefits the entire family. For example, a woman who marries a man who farms with his father and several brothers often feels relegated to the sidelines in decisionmaking even if she participates in farm work. Keith Moore (1989) found that both farm women and men are recognizing new identities and values as traditional family farming declines. Several other studies in Europe, the United States (Pfeffer, 1989), and Japan (Matsuda, 1992) suggest that women resist becoming farmwives by refusing to marry farmers. In some areas, male farmers have difficulty finding women willing to assume the position of farmwife. On farms, wives and daughters are beginning to question their place in the family farm and actively participate in farm women's organizations, as can be seen by tracing changes in farm women's political activities.

Farm Women's Organizations—Raise Less Corn and More Hell

Farm women's involvement in agricultural politics often occurs in local settings at the grass-roots level, remains unrecognized, and involves maintaining conditions for the existence of family farms. In their study of women's participation in U.S. farm politics, Lorna Miller and Mary Neth (1988) find that men hold formal positions, whereas women lead in creating understanding, providing social cohesion, and building group loyalty: "Men dominated the public and political arenas, but the institutions they led were built on the structures that women created" (Miller and Neth, 1988:360). Farm women participate in the political arena in both gender-integrated groups or in women's auxiliaries. Progressive farm organizations, such as the Farmers' Alliance, the Grange, and the National Farmers' Union, all of which arose during times of agricultural unrest, integrated women into their organizations. Although women participated in these organizations, they were seldom in leadership roles.

By contrast, other types of farm political organizations, such as the Farm Bureau and commodity associations, typically had auxiliaries for women. The Farm Bureau, connected to the Federal Cooperative Extension Service, offered women's auxiliaries with agendas focusing on the home rather than on broader political issues. However, times have changed. In the 1990s, commodity groups now wield more power in Washington because traditional farm political groups have lost power. Commodity associations typically incorporate women into these organizations in auxiliaries. The mere names of these organizations reveal a lack of respect for women, not to mention minimal concern with feminist issues. For example, women associated with the National Pork Producers' Association are in the Porkettes; in the National Cattlemen's Association, women are the Cowbelles; in the Wheat Producers' Association, they are the Wheathearts. Recently some of these women's auxiliaries have merged with the men's groups, an action that may suggest that women on farms and in these organizations demand more respect for their participation in farm businesses and consider themselves partners rather than merely the wives of farmers. During the 1970s and the farm crisis of the 1980s, farm women started new organizations that were not auxiliaries or social bases for male farm organizations. American Agriwomen and Women Involved in Farm Economics (WIFE) were formed in the 1970s to bring the voices of women into agricultural politics. American Agriwomen, a coalition of farm women's organizations concerned with the well-being of family farms, primarily educates and creates networks. WIFE, a women's farm organization involved primarily in lobbying for farm policies and programs, takes positions on a variety of issues, among them major farm policies, combating the farm crisis, disposing of hazardous waste, and improving housing for seasonal agricultural laborers. WIFE sees farm women as effective lobbyists for farm bills; they place agricultural economic issues in a community and family context. One president of WIFE noted: "I have seen the power of women lobbyists. Maybe it's a surprise attack that congressmen think this sweet little farm lady is coming in and what can she know? And suddenly they find out that as they sit and listen that she indeed knows the facts and figures and knows what's going on. Farm and ranch women are living the difficulties today, so who better to talk to them? And to speak about what's happening in agriculture? National WIFE meets in Washington, D.C., every June" (as quoted in Miller and Neth, 1988:370). These women rarely take on feminist issues, but they work hard to save the family farm and support commercial agriculture. Miller and Neth applaud these new women's organizations for moving beyond merely supportive roles for farm organizations and developing voices of their own. However, Fink remains skeptical of farm women's efforts to support the family farm, believing farm women's efforts to preserve the family farm have not been progressive from women's standpoint. Farm women's promotion of agrarianism involves a degree of deference to the family and to men not in their own interest: "Agrarianism has been limited by its being a white male vision that has failed to consider the full human integrity of other persons. It has led rural people down a blind alley" (Fink, 1992:196). The blind alley, however, leads men and women in different directions.

In their study of Ohio farm women's political involvement during the farm crisis, Linda Lobao and Katherine Meyer (1992) found that women's political concerns and political involvement differed from men's. Although the majority of farm women and men were alienated from conventional politics, farm women were more so than men. Farm women maintained slightly more skepticism about an individual's ability to effect change through local electoral politics; these women more willingly supported unconventional political activities like protests. Also, farm women exhibited more concern than farm men over the declining ability of their families to purchase goods and services such as health care and clothing. With these concerns in mind, farm women favored state intervention in farm and nonfarm sectors and supported more equitable distribution of services than farm men. Farm women, more than men, thought corporate farms should pay higher taxes than family farms, taxes should fall more heavily on large corporations and the rich, the government should spend more money to create jobs, and federal health insurance programs should be available to all people. Farm women's perspective therefore differs slightly from farm men's. As Lobao and Meyer suggest, women are likely to be involved in future political struggles at local and community levels because they are situated at critical junctures where conflict and change occur.

Some feminist agrarians discard the traditional view of women as wives and propose a model of farm women as equal partners in labor, ownership, and decisionmaking on farms. What would social relations on these new farms look like? Fink perceptively realizes that once gender differences are dissolved, the farm no longer needs to be a "family farm" but could just as well consist of a group of women, a group of men, or a mixed-gender collective operating the farm. Clearly, defining women solely by their relations in the home has presented problems in the West, but application of the domestic ideology to Third World women has brought disastrous consequences.

Domestication and Housewives in the Third World

Barbara Rogers (1980) elaborates numerous problems resulting from the application of a Western concept of domesticity to Third World women. Development agencies advanced the perspective that the ideal place for women was in the home, with their work confined to domestic and child care. Underlying this approach was the moral imperative that women should be in the home to care for their children and families. Few development planners comprehended that this model of the family and women's place in it provided possibilities only for wealthy and secure households.

Various studies of women in rural Asia note a process referred to by Maria Mies (1986) as "housewifization." State policies and development programs in India, Sri Lanka, and Malaysia emphasize women's domestic role and encourage emulation of the Western nuclear family. Joke Schrijvers' (1988) analysis of malnutrition associated with the Mahaweli River Development Scheme, a large scale resettlement and irrigation project in Sri Lanka, reveals the way this focus on women as housewives can cause severe consequences. In 1981, the Mahaweli Authority established the Home Development Center with the goal of teaching rural women to become better farm housewives. Governmental and nongovernmental organizations encouraged women to take short courses on health, nutrition, sanitation, needlework, poultry, and home gardening. Such programs reached only the higher-income women, the only women who were, in fact, housewives, and consequently these programs rarely moved toward alleviating poverty or undernutrition in the area. Most of the women were farming, and the failure to focus on women producers brought devastating effects for local people.

In their study of rural women in Malaysia, Cecilia Ng and Maznag Mohammed (1988) also found that state-supported 'housewifization' programs for rural women emphasize women's place in the home. Ng and Mohammed feel the emphasis on rural women is misdirected and "instead of being dealt with as farmers, they are dealt with as farmers' wives" (1988:77).

The domestication of rural women in many areas of Asia is frequently linked with attempts to control their sexuality. For example, in Bangladesh there are increased reports of violence against women in the household. As Roushan Jahan explains, "As the bearer of the heir and the carrier of the line, women are held to be vulnerable, needing to be jealously guarded from the lust of strangers. Chastity and modesty in women are placed at a premium and early marriage is still perceived to be the best strategy to provide 'symbolic shelter' to young girls especially in rural areas" (1988: 214). In rural Bangladeshi households, husbands' violence against their wives is considered socially acceptable. Extended patrilineal households do not necessarily protect women from violence by their husbands, but rather mother-in-laws and others frequently actively aid in the husband's violence toward his wife. Thus, perhaps the bitterest task for feminists involves acknowledging adult women's complicity in socializing women to inequality and participating in violence against younger women (Papenek, 1990).

A quite different situation emerges for rural women in many areas of Africa and Latin America. Out-migration of rural men to seek work in urban areas leaves many rural women as de facto household heads. Most of these female heads of household are legally married, but their husbands remain absent for either short or long periods of time. Although these women may appear free of everyday male authority in their households, their economic situations often necessitate dependence on their absent husband's willingness and ability to contribute to the household. Studies of women household heads in Botswana, Swaziland, and Zimbabwe demonstrate that these women are the poorest of the poor and have the least access to land, animals, and cash (Fortmann, 1984).

Summary on Gender and Farm Households

Theoretical discussions surrounding family farms do not normally incorporate the centrality of gender issues in maintaining and changing family farms. Women's work and flexibility associated with gender divisions of labor in farm households contribute to and often enable the survival of farm households. Recognition and documentation of the extensive participation of farm women in agriculture in most regions of the world rarely translates into agricultural or farm policies that improve women's access to resources, thus methodological attempts to understand the multiple contexts of the productive and reproductive aspects of farm women's work should focus on the meanings of work for farm women. Although the role of family farms in producing food is declining in both advanced capitalist societies and in developing regions, gender relations in rural areas continue to be steeped in vestiges of patriarchal relations in farm households. In any given rural area, women on family farms are privileged in contrast to women from nonlandowning families, especially as agriculture becomes increasingly capitalized and tied to the global agrofood system. As these shifts occur, the basis of patriarchal authority in rural areas begins to unravel. However, patriarchal ideology continues to pervade rural areas, often under the guise of agrarian or traditional values.

8

Global Restructuring, Local Outcomes, and the Reshaping of Rural Women's Work

Restructuring of the global economy brings changes to rural women's lives in most regions of the world. Increased reliance on women workers in the formal and informal economy provides the backbone of global restructuring in both rural and urban areas (Ward, 1990). Market women in Cameroon, poultry processing workers in Georgia, strawberry packers in Zamora, Mexico, and telemarketers in Nebraska live entirely different lives already tied together through global economies; they will likely become more interconnected through the processes of global restructuring. These connections do not imply that women in Zamora will know, form alliances, or organize with women in Georgia, or that their situations will become more similar; rather, the impact of the global economy on their lives will be strengthened as corporations increasingly consider and compare the advantages and possibilities of using women's labor.

In most areas of the world, the global economy incorporates rural places and people on unfavorable terms compared to their urban counterparts. Global and national restructuring processes unfold unevenly across space and time with different local outcomes that are mediated by social, economic, and ideological forces in local environments. People in rural areas have fewer and less remunerative income-earning opportunities and experience greater poverty than people living in urban areas. Relations with the global economy differ by gender, with rural women incorporated into the global economy on the least favorable terms and with the highest likelihood of experiencing poverty.

Global economic restructuring involves trends toward transnationalization of capital, ascendence of finance capital, decentralization of industry, and reorganization of labor. Fairly rapid and dramatic shifts in global and national economies defy scholarly interpretation and outstrip the capacity of corporate or state interests to respond.

Global Restructuring

In order to examine the shifts in rural women's work, I briefly discuss three major aspects of global restructuring: ascendance of finance capital, industrial reorganization, and changes in labor market structure. Then, I focus on five causes of shifts in the global economy that have particular importance for rural dwellers' lives in different localities: restructuring of agriculture; agro-industrial development; reorganization of employment in mining and logging; movement of manufacturing away from urban centers in the West; and growth of the service economy. I discuss the impact of these shifts on rural women's lives by using examples from particular regions.

Ascendance of Finance Capital

After the 1970s, the global financial system underwent substantial reorganization and emerged as increasingly powerful and influential. For the first time in history, a single world market for money and credit now operates through a global stock market with global commodity futures markets and accelerated geographical mobility of funds. The complexity of this reorganized system perplexes many people. As David Harvey observes, "the structure of this global financial system is now so complicated that it surpasses most people's understanding" (1989:161). I confess to being one of these people and must refrain from an attempt to unravel the complex workings of this system. Rather, I briefly point to some aspects of the ways in which this system affects rural people's lives.

New financial systems give more power and autonomy to the banking and financial system relative to states and corporations. Brought about partially by the decline of U.S. control of world monetary and fiscal policy as signaled by the breakdown of the Bretton Woods agreement in 1971, the new world financial system operates beyond the control of even the most advanced nation states. States are often subject to the power of international capital and encounter tremendous difficulty in their attempts to control the flow of capital and fiscal and monetary policies. Not all nation-states are equally powerless within the global financial system, however. The United States, Japan, and Germany clearly hold sway, although diminishing U.S. hegemony clears the way for the emergence Japan and Germany as centers of financial power. Many Third World countries faced with severe debt crisis are highly vulnerable to global financial capital.

Financial capital has become less connected to industrial capital, as is evidenced by the preponderance of "paper entrepreneurialism." Profits are not necessarily linked to production of goods and services, but rather to creative financial wheeling and dealing that result in profits without production (Harvey, 1989). Corporate takeovers and mergers often occur as strategies for financial gain rather than for production or market advantages.

Cornelia Flora (1990) argues that global monetary and fiscal policies now assume more importance than trade and migration in rural-urban relations. She points to the debt crisis in Latin America as well as to the U.S. farm crisis as exemplars of the power of financial capital to shape the destinies of rural people. The current indebtedness of Third World governments can be traced to development strategies after World War II that pushed Third World nations to pursue import substitution as a way to build industrial infrastructures and decrease their dependence on foreign goods. Building infrastructures required heavy borrowing of foreign capital, resulting in huge debt loads for many nations. Repayment of debts could only be accomplished by generating foreign exchange, which depended on increasing exports. Thus, Third World countries increased their exports of traditional raw materials such as coffee, timber, cacao, sugar, cotton, and minerals to earn foreign exchange, while pursuing a long- term strategy of limiting imports and developing domestic industry. These strategies seemed promising from 1973 to 1979, when there were high commodity prices and cheap credit. However, high prices and cheap credit were short-lived, and by 1981, indebtedness brought financial disaster to Latin American and African nations and U.S. farmers. Nations scrambled to repay debts by instituting policies that encouraged export production, but the tactic resulted in overproduction of agricultural goods worldwide; consequently, world prices of most agricultural commodities fell and still remain low.

The indebtedness of Third World governments to Western financial institutions makes these nations particularly susceptible to control by such institutions. The World Bank and the International Monetary Fund, for example, require African and Asian debtor countries to pursue policies known as "structural adjustment." In Africa and Latin America this frequently involves currency devaluation and declining government investment in social services such as food programs and education. In many regions of the world, these policies have particularly devastating consequences for women and children. Further, governments no longer rely solely on traditional exports such as coffee, cacao, and sugar as sources of foreign exchange because of global overproduction and low prices. As a result, international banks and developers pressure Third World governments to implement policies of "comparative advantage" and the production of nontraditional exports like flowers and processed or frozen fruits and vegetables in the agroindustrial sector. Multilateral and bilateral institutions push indebted Third World governments to establish export-free trade zones for nonagricultural products as well.

Women work in fields and processing plants that produce these nontraditional crops and in factories that produce comparatively advantageous goods, such as textiles, electronics, and toys.

Global financial shifts brought economic recession to many regions of the world in the 1980s and 1990s and placed severe strains on rural people's lives, especially those of women and minorities. Structural adjustment programs forced governments to provide fewer services, such as health care and welfare, and without these safety nets, households and individuals developed a multitude of strategies for survival. Some of these strategies are wage work, participation in the informal economy, and subsistence production. Because rural men's earnings prove less and less adequate to financially support their families, women frequently overwork as they extend themselves to earn income and care for their families.

Industrial Reorganization

Various analysts of the global economy point to a change from the Fordist model of industrial organization to a period of flexible accumulation (Harvey, 1989) under which industries have been reorganized in a number of ways. Transnational restructuring of capital involves shifts in the importance of industrial sectors, integration between sectors, and changes in the spatial location of industries.

Geographical dispersal, decentralization, and flexibility emerge as key strategies of industrial restructuring. Industrialization in Third World countries offsets declines in the manufacturing and extractive industries in advanced industrial countries; these countries now specialize in organizational and service industries. Decentralization of industries brings about the decline of industrial cities and deconcentration of production from cities to peripheral or semirural areas (Lash and Urry, 1987).

Under the Fordist system of mass production, uniform and standardized goods are produced in large plants. This has given way to small-batch production of a variety of flexible products in smaller factories. Corporate strategies focus less on achieving advantages through economies of scale and more on economies of scope (Harvey, 1989). To achieve flexibility, large corporations often subcontract to smaller businesses, resulting in a proliferation of small businesses that are tied to larger corporate networks. Harvey emphasizes that these flexible organizational forms do not totally replace Fordist production systems; instead, we now have a mix of organizational forms. Dispersal and decentralization cannot be equated with any decline of corporate power. Rather, mergers and corporate diversifications increase the power of larger, multinational corporations. Thus, as Harvey (1989) explains, the most fascinating aspect of these changes is the way capitalism becomes ever more tightly organized through strategies of decentralization and dispersal.

Decentralization and dispersal alter the traditional relations between rural and urban areas and transform rural people's means of livelihood. Relocation of industries to rural areas in advanced countries provides new types of work for rural people, but it also generates environmental and fiscal problems in rural places (Summers, 1977). Sites of industrial development in many Third World countries are often located near urban areas and depend heavily on the migration of rural people in search of work. Concentration of expanded service industries in urban areas once again leaves rural areas with the peripheral low-wage services. Rural people have longstanding ties to the global economy due to the demand for rural resources. Extraction of natural resources—oil, coal, timber, water, and agricultural products—historically benefited urban centers disproportionately while drawing resources from the rural periphery. However, these industries also provided the cornerstone of employment in rural areas. Traditional rural reliance on employment in resource-extractive industries has declined as capital has replaced labor in agriculture, mining, and logging. For women in rural areas, shifts in industrial organization often mean they are less able to depend on men's incomes to support their families and must seek wage employment.

Shifts in Labor Markets

The restructuring of global and local economies alters the daily work activities of many women and men throughout the world. The first contribution of feminist scholars was to recognize the importance of multiple types of work and redefine what counted as work. These scholars, initially enthusiastic about documenting the extent of women's work in the formal economy, soon realized that such a focus neglected much of women's work. Traditional economic categories that define work as wage labor and employment in the formal economy inadequately capture much of women's work. Feminist scholars working in both developed and Third World nations noted that "work" is not the equivalent of paid work, employment, and wage labor. In fact, much of the women's work occurs outside of capitalist relations. Scholars working in Latin America and Africa, where women's subsistence production and participation in the informal economy provides both family survival and the expansion of capitalist production, led these scholars to rethink definitions of work. In Europe and the United States, socialist feminists recognized the value of women's housework in reproducing capitalism. Initial efforts to tackle this problem of reconceptualizing work focused on theoretical discussions sorting out how women's unpaid domestic and subsistence activities or reproductive labor contributed to capitalism. However, the domestic labor debate went the way of other mode of production debates, continuing to move toward more abstract and theoretical discussion, eventually proving less relevant to women's lives. Beneria and Sen (1981), moving beyond the domestic labor debate, recognized the complex array of work activities engaged in by rural women and noted the importance of the relation between women's productive and reproductive labor. Aptheker's (1989) work, among others, led the way in rejecting the need to fit women's work into theoretical categories developed by either liberal or Marxist economists. Aptheker criticizes these theoretical discussions as inaccessible to most women; the categories of work hold little relation to women's own life experiences. Although Aptheker admits to spending years steeped in and frustrated by these theoretical discussions, she concludes that "a preoccupation with fitting women into theories that subordinated them at their core was crippling" (1989:11). Dualistic categories, which include paid/unpaid, employed/unemployed, wage/nonwage, production/reproduction, subsistence/market rarely help interpret the real conditions of women's daily lives. Redefining what counts as work represents a major contribution of feminist scholarship.

Nanette Redclift and Enzo Mingione (1985) attribute the scholarly discovery of work outside of capitalist relations as a response to the changes produced by economic restructuring as well as a paradigmatic shift in redefining what counts as work. Both empirical changes in the organization of work and paradigmatic shifts have resulted in new theoretical approaches to work. Scholars should therefore reconceptualize work, and women's work in particular, because the nature of work has changed. Restructured economies' reliance on decentralized labor, on fewer permanent full-time workers, on expansion of the informal economy, and on women's continued responsibility for household work expands women's labor in all of these arenas.

Employers increasingly rely on flexible work regimes rather than on full-time permanent, unionized workers. Corporations that seek to maintain a flexible workforce increase their use of part-time employees and their reliance on temporary workers, and engage in subcontracting and outsourcing. These changes entail increased dependence on women's labor; women work in part-time jobs and as temporary workers. Revitalization of older systems of labor control emerges as corporations rely on subcontracting and outsourcing of jobs. Domestic, artisanal, patriarchal, and paternalistic systems of organizing labor flourish with organized subcontracting, as is evidenced by the revival of sweatshops in New York, Los Angeles, Paris, and London (Harvey, 1989). Also, informal market growth in both core and Third World countries often relies on these older systems of labor control.

Changes in types of work available to women relate to a major point of debate among feminist scholars that concerns the relation between women's incorporation into the workforce and their empowerment. Liberal neoclassical thinkers argue that employment in the formal sector improves women's lives by providing them with access to income and status. Through employment, women escape the traditional male authority of their fathers and husbands and can possibly shape more choices in their lives. However, others take issue with this argument. Studies on women's employment in wage labor in numerous locations consistently show that women's incorporation into the workforce is on unequal terms with men's (Nash, 1988). Concentrated in jobs with low pay, limited benefits, and little mobility, employed women's primary responsibility for child care and household work rarely diminishes. With the exception of elite women who can afford to hire domestic workers, employed women often work extraordinarily long days and juggle a number of activities. Cross-cultural studies of time use consistently find that women, compared to men, have shorter resting hours, greater intensity and fragmentation of work, and more frequent recourse to multiple simultaneous occupations (Redclift and Mingione, 1985). Most scholars and observers would probably agree that employment has contradictory effects on the empowerment of women.

Women's incorporation into the global economy takes different forms in various localities and among different classes and races of women in the same locality. In many parts of the world, women from minority ethnic and racial groups face completely different employment prospects and situations than do women from privileged ethnic and racial groups. Global restructuring by no means uniformly effects rural women's lives. However, key features of rural economies consistently disfavor women during the process of capitalist development. I show how global economic shifts alter the daily work lives of rural women in various economic contexts in particular localities. In the following sections, I compare rural women in the United States and Europe with rural women in the Third World to illustrate the different outcomes of global restructuring on rural women's lives as concerns off-farm employment, agro-industrial development, mining-and timber-based economies, and decentralization of manufacturing and service economies.

Off-Farm Employment

Global restructuring decreases rural people's ability to support themselves through either subsistence or market-oriented agriculture. Consequently, many rural people move to urban areas in search of income-earning opportunities. Those who remain in rural areas increasingly earn their living through nonagricultural activities; only a small proportion of them depend totally on agriculture for their livelihoods. Throughout the world, the work patterns of many people involve moving back and forth between smallholdings in agriculture and nearby capitalist enterprises (Wenger and Buck, 1988). Farm households rely on temporary or permanent migration of some family members for longer distances as a key strategy for enhancing their incomes. However, peasants and farmers have largely failed to complete the predicted transition to becoming proletarian. Analysts in Africa and Latin America describe this process as semiproletarianization. Latin Americanists who subscribe to the dependency school tradition view peasants as totally subordinated and exploited by the interests of capital. By contrast, some African scholars see this process of semiproletarianization as peasant resistance to capitalism. Strategies of agricultural households to remain on the land vary by region, locality, and class. As discussed in Chapter 7, these analysts frequently overlook the centrality of gender relations and divisions of labor in maintaining agricultural households (Staudt, 1987). In this process, gender divisions of labor are not static. The movement of people between small farms and capitalist enterprises disrupts traditional patriarchal forms; ideological forms of patriarchy become difficult to maintain under such conditions (Wenger and Buck, 1988).

Strategies of earning off-farm income take different forms in different regions of the world and vary by gender. In some regions, men migrate to urban areas, leaving women in the countryside. In other regions, young women migrate from rural areas to earn income, and in still other regions, entire households are displaced and migrate to cities. Migration patterns vary by class and ethnicity as well as by gender. In advanced industrial economies, off-farm employment of farm men and women has become widespread. Typically, both men and women remain in residence on their farms, while working at off-farm jobs. In Latin America and Africa, family members temporarily migrate to urban areas to save the rural household. In many Asian countries, peasants permanently move to urban areas, but their remittances to their families in rural areas enables the survival of rural households.

Off-Farm Employment in Advanced Industrial Economies

Off-farm employment of family members, once viewed as a transitory phenomenon, has now become persistent in Germany, Norway, England, Italy, and the United States (Pfeffer, 1989). Escalating financial stress on farms in most European countries and in the United States has increased the rate of both men's and women's off-farm employment. Farmers' dependence on fluctuating prices historically necessitated reliance on diverse income-earning and survival strategies. Whereas previously farm households often turned to alternative agricultural enterprises, such as women's chicken or egg production, to provide additional or stable incomes and to meet subsistence needs, off-farm employment now offers the most common diversification strategy for specialized U.S. farmers (Rosenfeld, 1985). Government commodity programs, vertical contracts with processors, highly specialized capital investments, and loan agreements with banks mitigate against on-farm diversification in the United States. Some European governments institute policies to encourage on-farm diversification, promoting value-added or other types of on-farm enterprises such as farm tourism, but nevertheless off-farm employment continues to expand. In only a small proportion of farm households in the United States and Europe do both husband and wife work only on the farm or in the farm household. As more farm people engage in off-farm employment, traditional gender relations on the farm and in the farm household change, but this may not necessarily improve women's status.

Prior to the 1970s, researchers and policymakers viewed men's off-farm employment as problematic and threatening to the viability of farms. However, since then some researchers have shifted their attention to gender divisions of labor on farms; they acknowledge both the increase in women's employment and the importance of their contribution to the viability of family farms. In the United States, over 50 percent of farm women had off-farm employment in 1985. Farm women, similarly to other women, have entered the labor force in increasing numbers, and farm women's income serves as an economic cushion that permits many farms to continue operating. In fact, U.S. farmwives who are employed on average contributed a higher proportion of family income than nonfarm wives (Godwin and Marlowe, 1990:26).

Researchers use the results of survey and census data to study patterns of husbands and wives' on-farm, off-farm, and household work and to identify factors that explain both genders' off-farm work. They focus attention on farm characteristics, for example, farm size, type of farm enterprise, and number of hired workers; on demographic characteristics such as education, family cycle, number of children, and age; and on labor market demand factors such as types of local industries and proximity to metropolitan areas. Findings from a number of studies suggest that farm characteristics are more likely to explain men's off-farm employment than women's (Simpson, Wilson, and Young, 1988; Buttel and Gillespie, 1984; Barlett, 1986). Men are more likely to work away from the farm on smaller farms with lower sales, whereas women's off-farm employment does not vary systematically according to farm size or sales. The most consistent factor that explains women's off-farm employment is their level of education. Women with higher education are more likely to engage in off-farm work than less-educated women. Contrary to expectations, women's off-farm employment is not related to how many children they have, although women with young children, on average, work fewer hours off the farm. Thus, studies of off-farm employment in the United States more successfully predict men's than women's off-farm employment. These studies implicitly or explicitly conclude that men's off-farm employment threatens farm success and can only be risked on certain types of farms, whereas women's contributions to the farm enterprise are expendable.

Bill Reimer (1986) criticizes radical theorists who focus only on farm work and paid labor for neglecting women's domestic contribution on farms. Regardless of the extent of their farm and off-farm work, farm women perform the bulk of domestic activities. In the United States, these domestic activities far outweigh the domestic workload of nonfarm women. Laundry, cooking, and cleaning in farm households requires more labor than in typical urban households due to the ever-present dirt and larger food preparation tasks.. Farm women are much more likely to bake goods, can vegetables and fruit, make household goods such as draperies, and sew clothing than are nonfarm women. In addition, women on farms care for family members and negotiate in conflicts between the interests of farm and family. Overlooking women's enormous contribution in these activities results in the failure to adequately explain when and under what circumstances farm women do or do not work off the farm.

A number of questions arise about changes in farm life: What happens to the traditional family farm when women or men work off the farm? How do gender relations change when work is no longer organized primarily by kinship? Do women attain more independence and power when they work off the farm? When men work off the farm, do women "take over" the farm? At least one scholar asks whether the declining economic importance of farming in the countryside results in the feminization of agriculture (Cernea, 1978). In some regions of the world, men migrate from rural areas, leaving women on farms. In studying German farms, Max Pfeffer (1989) found that when men were employed off the farm, women's work on the farm increased. However, he argues that feminization of farming has not occurred. Rather than replacing men in driv-ing tractors and doing field work, women intensify the amount of labor expended in tasks they previously performed, for example, doing both their own and their husbands' chores in milking. The persistence of the sexual division of labor in defining women's and men's work keeps women off the tractors but not out of the barns. However, Pfeffer discovered that German women's will-ingness to do farm chores was eroding, as most of them found the increased workload undesirable and young women even object to the idea of marrying a farmer. Peggy Barlett (1986) reported that women resented their husbands' working off the farm while remaining in farming in her study of Georgia part-time farms. She suggests that part-time farmers do not work to save the farm, but add farming to their full-time job as an income-earning strategy and because of their preference for farming as a lifestyle. Wives of Georgia part-time farmers express none of the strong positive sentiments about farming that women on full-time farms do. Women's objections to farming may well emerge because women acquire fewer lifestyle benefits from being their own boss or from off-farm employment than men; in fact, the overall lifestyle costs may be higher for women.

Members of landholding families in rural areas often have better off-farm employment opportunities and can earn higher incomes than their neighbors because they are likely to be more highly educated than other rural residents, Thus, farm owners sometimes take off-farm jobs and hire less-educated agricultural laborers to work on their farms. The low wages paid to farm workers often provide inadequate income, so farm workers as well as farm family members increasingly turn to nonagricultural employment to support themselves. Nonagricultural, low-skill jobs also provide inadequate incomes but are more reliable sources of income than farm work.

Off-Farm Strategies in Latin America and Africa

Declines in crop prices and increasing need for cash push many members of farm families in developing countries into adopting nonagricultural strategies for earning incomes. The search for off-farm employment in many Third World regions entails the emigration of family members from rural areas.

In Latin America, young rural women led the migration stream to urban areas beginning in the 1940s. Poor and landless young women left rural areas as their ability to contribute to their families' survival diminished. Poor peasant families frequently prefer migration of daughters over migration of sons. Families encourage men to stay because of their major responsibility for agriculture, and encourage young women to migrate because of the declining importance of their work in production of food and clothing for local markets. As previously discussed, Deere and Leon de Leal (1981) recognize the multiple off-farm employment strategies of peasant households in the Andean highlands. There were different opportunities for men's and women's employment in various regions depending on the extent of capitalist development.

In contrast to the Latin American pattern, men in southern and eastern Africa are the principal migrants to urban areas. In rural areas of Lesotho, Botswana, Swaziland, and Kenya, large numbers of males commonly migrate from rural areas; male emigration is now becoming a pattern in

West Africa as well (Staudt, 1987). On the demand side, many of the employment opportunities were in mining in South Africa; mines relied almost exclusively on a male workforce. Moreover, apartheid laws kept rural black women out of South African cities. In addition, communal land tenure systems and women's traditional responsibility for agriculture favored women remaining in rural areas to hold the land and farm until their husbands retired from wage labor. Men's work in agriculture, largely limited to land preparation, requires heavy physical labor for a relatively short length of time. Thus, men are able to return home to plow or send money to hire others to plow without seriously disrupting the agricultural system. Women and men in African households have separate sources of income, and although women expect remittances from their husbands, these are not guaranteed. Thus, men's migration often adds to the heavy burden of women's work as well as complicating their obligation to provide for their families. Married women remaining in rural areas who engage in agricultural production sometimes receive remittances from their husbands, but they frequently seek to expand their income by adopting multiple strategies that often involve activity outside the formal economy. Women in rural areas brew beer, process food, make handicrafts, and sew school uniforms to augment their income from agriculture. African women have long been engaged in these types of activities, but as the formal sector contracts during periods of economic crisis, informal activities become more widespread and critical for family survival (Newbury and Schoepf, 1989). This decline in the number of households supported solely through agriculture occurs simultaneously with the rise of agro-industrial development.

Agroindustrial Development

> let me tell you, in one end they pour
> the lives of women, of children,
> of men poor enough or brown enough
> not to count, in one end, in the hopper,
> in measured quantities,
> and some of us they pay to push the buttons
> some to read the dials, and some to sweep the floor;
> at the other end they pay us to rubber band
> the bills, by denomination and neatly
>
> and in between there is a mile of whirring blades
> bubbling vats, teeth that mesh endlessly
> a strong smell of disinfectant—whitewash—and blood
> in between there are milled surfaces meeting
> to close tolerances, hammers falling, diesels beating

the clash of rough-cut gears, the growl, the whine
this is no swiss watch I tell you
this is a combine
this is the machine

and where it passes there is damn little to glean
—**D. A. Clarke, "Farm Equipment," 1985**

Economists typically view agriculture as a distinct economic sector that stands in contrast to industry. This no longer proves helpful or valid for interpreting reality because the formation of an agrofood sector blurs the distinction between agriculture and industry (Friedmann, 1991). Transnational restructuring of the agricultural sector blurs national and sectoral boundaries, intensifies agricultural specialization for both enterprises and regions, and creates large agro-industrial complexes (Friedmann and McMichael, 1989). Harriet Friedmann describes the agrofood sector of the world economy as a series of commodity chains woven together into food complexes that link producers to processors and distributors of final goods. She delineates three such complexes: wheat, livestock and feed, and durable food. In each of these, industry subordinates agriculture in both the input and output sides of the commodity chain. On the input side, farmers must rely on feeds, pesticides, fertilizers, and equipment; they also depend on financial credit to purchase these inputs. On the output side, farmers rarely supply consumers directly with fresh produce; they sell their produce directly to food-manufacturing industries. Few studies discuss how these agrofood systems incorporate women. An exception is Irene Padavic's (1993) insightful study of U.S. women agricultural workers, which elaborates on the variation of women's incorporation into agriculture by region, commodity, and locality.

To understand the changes in women's work in agriculture, we must look beyond farms to women's work in other aspects of the agrofood systems. Expansion of food-manufacturing industries in rural areas and the heavy reliance on rural women to fill the jobs these industries have created proves particularly important. I discuss two examples of women's work in food-manufacturing industries: U.S. women's work in meat processing, and Latin American women's work in the fruit and vegetable industries. Both examples are useful in understanding how women's work is connected to the restructuring of agrofood industries.

Meat Processing

Women workers in poultry-processing plants in the United States received media attention as a result of a fire that killed 25 workers—18 women and 7 men—in a North Carolina plant in 1991. The unsafe and poorly remunerated working conditions of these workers came to light when these workers were killed. Their escape from the plant was blocked by doors locked from the outside by company owners to prevent workers from stealing chicken parts. Poultry workers at this particular plant earned an average hourly wage of $5.30. As a woman worker at the plant explained: "They treated us like dogs. The owner's son didn't care about human life, he cared about people not stealing his chicken parts" (Anthan, 1991). Conditions at this plant, especially the locked doors, may have been extreme, but other working conditions typify conditions at poultry plants.

These women work for the intensive meat complex described by Friedmann and McMichael (1989). Grain companies are at the helm of this meat complex; they expand vertically into meat production and processing by means of contracts that tie soy, maize, and meat producers closely to corporate processors. As discussed earlier, women's small-scale poultry enterprises no longer exist. Large enterprises with contracts to the large-scale poultry processors such as Perdue, Tyson Foods, ConAgra and Cargill produce approximately 99 percent of U.S. poultry. These poultry growers and poultry-processing plants, concentrated in the south, mid-South, and in the Delaware-Maryland-Virginia peninsula, rely heavily on the labor of women and people of color. Significantly, the largest increase in women's employment in the food-manufacturing industries between 1950 and 1980 in the United States was in the meat products sector, specifically in poultry processing (U.S. Bureau of the Census, 1950, 1980). In 1980, women comprised 52 percent of the employees in poultry processing in the United States (U.S. Bureau of Labor Statistics, 1982). Predominantly black and Hispanic women work in these plants, with black women often performing the least desirable tasks and receiving the lowest pay in poultry processing. A study of two poultry-processing plants in rural Virginia found that women comprised 75 percent of the labor force; work was highly gender segregated (Bryant and Perkins, 1982:204). Women worked primarily on the processing line at eviscerating, cutting, trimming, boxing, and packaging, whereas men hung, killed, shipped, stored, and supervised. In their interviews with workers, researchers found that workers justified the differences between men's and women's jobs in terms of traditional gender divisions of labor. Workers explained that men performed certain jobs because of their physical strength or because the jobs were simply "men's jobs" and not women's place. Women did certain jobs in the plants because they involved something women normally knew about and would ordinarily do as housekeepers, such as preparation of meat for cooking and consumption. Men were said to be capable of doing women's jobs, but did not do them because they were needed to do the "men's jobs."

Hog production firms hope to follow the path of the chicken broiler production industry—with increases in contracts between growers and processors. In the rural Midwest, large-scale meatpacking plants push small meatpackers out of business. In their search for cheap labor, these meatpacking plants recruit Hispanic, Asian, and black workers, primarily women, from urban areas in the Midwest and West. Few minorities have previously settled in these rural areas of Iowa, Nebraska, and Missouri, and in some areas where companies have recruited minorities as workers, racial tensions abound.

Although most large-scale meatpacking and processing occurs in the United States, some evidence points to the movement of meat-processing plants to the Third World (Kim and Curry, 1993). By contrast, vegetable- and fruit-processing plants already operate extensively in the Third World.

Vegetable and Fruit Processing

In response to severe debt loads, international financial institutions pressure many developing countries to step up production of agricultural goods for export and pursue agro-industrial development as a strategy for earning foreign exchange. Multilateral and bilateral institutions encourage increased production of such traditional export crops as coffee, cacao, and sugar as well as continued production of tropical fruits such as bananas and pineapples. In addition, these institutions push many countries to move their agro-industrial development in the direction of "nontraditional crops." Increased demand for such nontraditional crops as strawberries, vegetables, and flowers occurred in the 1980s as fresh fruit and vegetable consumption moved from their luxury market niche to a broader consumer base. These crops, increasingly raised in Latin America and Africa for European and U.S. markets, require intensive labor in production and processing. Agrofood firms in fruit and vegetable production require more labor than other segments of agriculture. They restructure their labor forces as nonagricultural industries do—through employment practices that include labor casualization and increased hiring of women (Collins, 1993). For example, in Central America, agricultural diversification strategies in the 1980s promoted such nontraditional exports as snow peas, melons, broccoli, flowers, and shrimp. These nontraditional export industries prefer women workers because they will work for lower pay than other employees. Industries use the usual arguments about women's manual dexterity to justify hiring women for labor-intensive work (Crummet, 1987). In Brazil's Sao Francisco Valley, the technical advisers at large firms use women workers in grape, tomato, and melon production. Reasons given for the preference for women workers "range from, 'they are more obedient and follow orders,' 'they are gentler and work more patiently,' to 'they are smaller and fit under the grape arbors'" (Collins, 1993:69). In Colombia, women constitute the majority of workers in the cultivation of flowers for export (Leon, 1987); in Mexico, migrant peasant women travel to Zamora to make up the majority of the workforce in strawberry production for export to the United States.

Lourdes Arizpe and Josefina Aranda's (1981) fine study of women employees in six strawberry firms offers a thorough analysis of how and why the strawberry agro-industries rely on women's labor and the consequences of this employment on rural women's lives. U.S. companies began to expand strawberry packing and freezing plants to Zamora in Mexico in the mid-1960s. The plants hire predominantly young, unmarried women from peasant households to destem, select, and pack strawberries. Women work for low wage rates, approximately 66 cents U.S. per hour, in seasonal and temporary jobs with no benefits. Almost all of the women workers live at home with their parents and one-half of them turn most of their wages over to their families. The majority of women disliked working conditions in these plants, but they preferred that work to the alternatives of performing domestic service, staying at home, or working in the fields. Younger women see the work as a stage in their life that enables them to escape the daily routines of village life prior to marriage. But high turnover and lack of avenues for promotion do little to alter the long-term opportunities for these women. Rather, the strawberry companies take advantage of the traditional values and conditions that subordinate young women both within their parental families and in their view of marriage. As Arizpe and Aranda cleverly state, "the 'comparative advantages' of this industry in the international market are closely associated with the 'comparative disadvantages' of young inexperienced, rural women who face social, legal, and economic discrimination" (1981:471). The authors note two dilemmas for a feminist analysis and program of action in this situation. Women report they prefer this work to other opportunities, but at the same time feminists recognize industry's exploitation of women. Attempts to organize the workers to achieve better working conditions will likely result in the loss of 'comparative advantage' for agribusiness, which often threatens to move elsewhere taking the women's jobs with them. Thus, the authors suggest that efforts to organize locally or nationally must also recognize the ties between women workers throughout the world.

In a study of labor arrangements in fruit and vegetable production in Brazil, Jane Collins (1993) finds that firms use a variety of labor arrangements, including contract farming, migrant labor, sharecropping, and local labor, to meet various labor needs. Agricultural firms experiment with different labor arrangements, preying on the most vulnerable segments of the global workforce. They strategically use appeals to women's

Woman sorting onions in central California packing shed. Photograph by Lyn Garling. Used by permission.

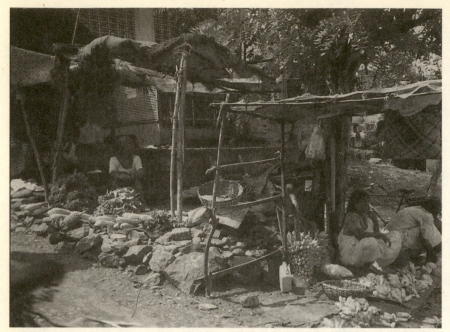

Women selling fruit and vegetables in rural Sri Lanka. Photograph by Padma Karunaratne. Used by permission.

place in the family as the justification for offering unequal pay and work opportunities to women.

In vegetable production in California, an increase in the proportion of women hired as agricultural workers has resulted from increasing harvest mechanization and tightening of vertical integration between growers, processors, and wholesalers. Women traditionally worked in fruit and vegetable canneries. With the introduction of mechanized harvesting equipment, activities such as sorting tomatoes and monitoring lettuce-wrapping machinery moved to the fields. Women, predominantly Chicanas, followed their processing jobs from the canneries to the fields. William Friedland (1991) argues that the rise of industrialized agriculture follows the model of the industrial sector and increasingly hires women as cheap labor.

Restructured agrofood industries, characterized by concentration in the food processing sector and vertical integration, rely increasingly on rural women's labor. Examples of poultry, hog, and fruit and vegetable production and processing reveal how women of different nationalities and races participate in these agro-industries in different cultural contexts. As a result of women's employment, family relations shift, but labor arrangements, predicated on inequitable rewards and labor opportunities for women based on their work in the home, often reinforce women's subordination both in the workplace and the home.

Women in Mining- and Timber-Based Economies

> *The miner is no metaphor. She goes*
> *into the cage like the rest, is flung*
> *downward by gravity like them, must change*
> *her body like the rest to fit a crevice*
> *to work a lode*
> *on her the pick hangs heavy, the bad air*
> *lies thick, the mountain presses in on her*
> *with boulder, timber, fog*
> *slowly the mountain's dust descends*
> *into the fibers of her lungs.*
>
> **—from Adrienne Rich, "Natural Resources," 1978**

Rural communities that depend primarily on extractive industries such as mining and timber pose particular sets of problems and opportunities for rural women. Regions dependent on mining and logging experience boom and bust cycles, high levels of poverty, and extreme sex segregation of jobs. Ownership of land and resources by outside corporate interests minimizes local control and local benefits. During the boom periods, men work in high-wage unionized jobs, but always with the specter of interspersed periods of unemployment as well as high injury rates. Both the mining and timber industries increasingly substitute capital for labor, often with severe environmental consequences. These industries, attempting to increase profits, implement practices such as strip-mining and clear-cutting that result in extreme damage to the environment, rely on large-scale machinery, and use less labor than other types of mining and logging operations. Because jobs are closely tied to the exploitation of natural resources, environmental issues may be hotly contested in such communities. In mining and logging areas, women lack opportunities for economic independence and often depend on male wages for income. These women, who often actively defend men's rights to jobs, remain particularly vulnerable to slipping in and out of poverty (Maggard, 1990).

Women in the Appalachian Mining Region

In the extremely sex segregated local labor markets in Central Appalachia, men work primarily in mining and women work in personal service jobs, health services, retail sales, tourism, and light manufacturing. In a study of women's work in two Appalachian coal-mining counties in Kentucky,

Sally Maggard (1990) found that employment, income-generating activities, and household work were all at high levels among rural women. However, although these women had high levels of employment, they experienced a narrow range of opportunities. For the most part, high-paying coal mining jobs excluded women.

Some women in mining regions struggle to enter the mines. In the late 1970s, over 99 percent of miners were men; women began to organize to pressure coal companies to hire women (Tallichet, 1991:38). The Coal Employment Project, a Tennessee-based women's advocacy group, provided the greatest impetus for gaining women's entry into the mines during the late 1970s. The group successfully pushed for federal legislation to force coal companies to accept women in the mines. Women entered the coal mines slowly, largely as a result of federal pressure, and often faced severe resistance. For example, in Kentucky, the number of women coal miners increased from five in 1974 to 200 in 1977 (Tallichet, 1991:34). A 1985 Bureau of Mines national sample of bituminous underground mines with twenty or more employees found that women composed approximately 2 percent of the labor force (Tallichet, 1991:126). Despite federal legislation and women's efforts, coal mining remains male terrain.

Women who overcame barriers to enter the mines face difficulties in their jobs, families, and local communities. In West Virginia, women coal miners experience difficulty entering mining and advancing on the job (Tallichet, 1991). Upon breaking the barrier, these women, who were attempting to earn higher incomes by entering the male-dominated world of mining, met the direct criticism that they were taking jobs away from men. There was extreme hostility directed at the first women who entered the mines, and it came from many directions—from community members, employers, male miners, and miners' wives. Mine owners often justify women's exclusion from mining on the grounds that mining requires heavy physical labor and is extremely dangerous. Many of the women interviewed by Suzanne Tallichet (1991) described physically difficult working conditions but reported more difficulty in establishing working relations with men. One woman miner recalled her initial entrance into mining: "I can't tell ya how scared I was. I wasn't scared of the mine, I was scared of the men. See, I don't work with women, I work basically with all men. I'm not scared of 'em now, but back in them days I was scared to death of 'em. When they gotcha down there they can do anything they want to" (as quoted in Tallichet, 1991:205).

Sexual issues play a major role in attempts to keep women out of the mines. Sexual harassment and accusations of sexual promiscuity met women who entered the mines. Co-workers and bosses sexually harassed them; bosses, miners, miner's wives and other women in their communities accused women miners of sexually promiscuous behavior. As a woman miner described the community members' view of women miners, "When we enter the coal mines, we're whores" (as quoted in Tallichet, 1991:207).

Women miners might turn to the union, the United Mine Workers, to resolve their problems. Women support the United Mine Workers, although the union harbors a mixed record on its support of women. Women miners often find union leaders and members hostile to their entry into mining and reluctant to support their efforts to end sex discrimination and harassment in the mines (Tallichet, 1991). For example, one woman miner described how the union failed to back her when the company discriminated against women in job assignments: "Well, I just think that some of the union officials that's in office doesn't approve of us women being in there. An' they won't help us, they won't stand up for us like they would a man. It's just obvious" (as quoted in Tallichet, 1991:257).

Thus, in the 1990s women coal miners' political involvement includes union activities, but they continue to turn to organizations for women miners, such as the Coal Employment Project, in their efforts to gain further entry and advancement in the mines.

Not all women in mining regions fought to enter the mines; some led struggles to keep mining jobs for their husbands. Women in mining communities, although typically excluded from jobs in the mines, often form the backbone of strike support for the United Mine Workers, one of the more militant unions in the United States. Women in these communities depend on their husbands' earnings from mining and struggle to keep this income by supporting unions and strikes. Maggard's study of women's support of the Brookside strike in eastern Kentucky illustrates the persistence of rural women. Women participated in this thirteen-month-long strike in 1973 by planning strategies, picketing, testifying in court, confronting union officials, talking with the press, devising behind-the-scenes tactics, and going to jail (Maggard, 1990). Maggard interviewed twenty women who were involved in this particular coal strike. Before the strike began, all of the twenty female respondents from Harlan County lived in traditional nuclear households that depended on a male wage earner. According to Maggard, "The ideology of the male breadwinner (i.e., coal miner) is very strong in eastern Kentucky" (1990:6), and all of the women viewed themselves as housewives before working on the strike. Their involvement with the strike brought dramatic changes into their lives, the most obvious being their entrance into the labor force. During the strike many of these women took jobs to provide the economic support for their families that their husbands' coal-mining jobs no longer provided. Husbands often contested their wives' employment, as one women describes: "He always was the breadwinner until the strike. I went to work then. But as soon as he got back to work he made me quit.

I liked working. He just always said, 'It's a man's place,' the support" (as quoted in Maggard, 1990:12).

Thus, in coal-mining communities, women's entrance into the labor force and especially into the mines clearly disrupts traditional gender relations. Involvement in strike activities in households instigated a renegotiation of gender relations that continued long after the strike ended. Men and women in the local communities view economic independence of women as threatening to family stability and as tied to women's sexual independence. In a different fashion than in Appalachia, women in mining regions in southern Africa and South America have also acted to secure men's employment in the mines.

Women in Mining Regions in Southern Africa and South America

For many years, the mines in South Africa provided the major employment opportunity for black southern African men. In southern Africa, men's employment in the mines severely affects rural women's lives. Men migrate from rural areas in South Africa, Swaziland, Lesotho, and Botswana to work in the South African mines, while their wives and families remain in the rural areas. Typically, men stay away for months at a time, returning home only periodically. Thus, females are de facto household heads. These women raise crops, brew beer, and market their produce or handicrafts on a small scale; they also depend on remittances from their husbands or other family members to support their rural households. Remittances, not always forthcoming, often prove insufficient to support the family; men receive fairly low pay and may not necessarily feel obligated to send large proportions of their income to their families. Men's absence from their homes places heavy workloads and responsibilities on women, who sometimes benefit from their husbands remittances, but at other times receive very little support.

By contrast, miners' wives counted heavily on their husbands jobs in the mines, as shown in June Nash's (1988) study of women in Bolivian mining communities. These women played crucial roles in resisting government efforts to close the mines. In the state of Oruro, tin mines formed the backbone of the economy through the 1970s. However, with the decline in the price of tin and the increase in costs of production, the mining economy fell into serious trouble in the 1980s. Nationalized mines lost thousands of dollars each month and the state lacked the resources to improve production and threatened to close the mines. Wives of union members had formed housewives' associations during the 1960s when their husbands were imprisoned. These associations gained political strength over the years, and in the 1980s, their members led protests in La Paz demanding food for the poverty-stricken people living in mining communities. However, these protests failed to influence government policy on the mining communities. As one of the presidents of a housewives' association told Nash, "It's clear that we didn't gain anything. The government only promised to help, but has not fulfilled their obligation. We still don't have any meat, we don't have bread, we don't have sugar, and we don't have rice. There are homes that have ten children and these homes suffer more than most" (as quoted in Nash, 1988:72).

After the lack of adequate government response, the women began pooling money to buy food items in bulk. Conditions in the mines deteriorated further; many men were laid off and migrated in hopes of attaining land or jobs. Despite increasing desertions of women by men, Nash found that these women continued to define themselves as housewives and to couch their appeals to the government as such: "The awareness that women without men must live on very meager resources makes them fearful of striking out on their own, and their demands continue to be phrased in terms of homemakers" (Nash, 1988:73).

Women in mining regions in the United States, Africa, and Latin America live in quite different circumstances, but several common issues emerge. Women, largely excluded from employment in mines, often rely on men's earnings to support their families. Seasonal and declining employment in mining as well as labor struggles push many women to find alternative sources of income to support their families. Also, as evidenced in Appalachia and Bolivia, women support the labor struggles of their husbands in the mines, and in some instances, their protest activities empower women in mining communities.

Women in Timber-Dependent Regions

Women in timber-dependent communities in the northwestern United States live with similar economic uncertainty as the women in Appalachia. Loggers and sawmill workers, predominantly men, work in an industry with market fluctuations, seasonality, and high accident and death rates. In-depth interviews were conducted with twenty women married to loggers in a timber-dependent community in Oregon to determine their level of stress and subsequent changes in roles as they faced the possibility of a decline in timber-related jobs due to environmental pressures to limit logging (Warren, Lee, and Carroll, 1992).

The United States: The Northern Spotted Owl and Beyond

The northern spotted owl symbolizes the ecological damage caused by cutting old-growth forests. The timber industry, loggers, and environmentalists heatedly debate protection of the northern spotted owl. When

Women and men protesting timber harvesting in northern California. Photograph by Sheila Seshan. Used by permission.

Women, men, and children supporting timber harvesting in same northern California community. Photograph by Sheila Seshan. Used by permission.

interviewed, loggers' wives expressed anger, resentment, and uncertainty about attempts of environmentalists and the state to limit the timber industry; many actively engaged in efforts to preserve their husbands' jobs. These women exhibited hostility toward environmentalists and were skeptical of their claims. From their perspective, people in logging communities, who live and work in the forest unlike urban environmental advocates, are the real environmentalists. As one women lamented, "They (the media) portray us as a bunch of rowdy drinkers . . . illiterate drunks who don't care anything for the environment, and it's so ridiculous—my husband works hard . . . and he just loves the woods—it's his life. Even when he isn't working he is out there with me and the kids, camping and fishing" (as quoted in Warren, Lee, and Carroll, 1992:13).

Women who depend on their husbands' employment in logging for their families' support have organized local and state timber advocacy groups. One woman, in describing her political involvement in supporting the timber industry, explained: "I got involved because I felt threatened . . . in some ways it's like glorified PTA only it's so much more important—and it's threatening the home front and that's the woman's area" (as quoted in Warren, Lee, and Carroll, 1992:23–24). The reactions of these women against environmentalists reveal the need to revise the ecofeminist position that women, either by nature or through their daily lives, nurture the environment. When their economic support depends on their husbands' logging jobs, they tend to support timber harvest rather than environmental protection. In this study, women married to loggers supported their husbands' right to earn income even if it meant destruction of the forest. These women defined their interests in terms of their husbands' and many of them resented resistance efforts organized by nonlocal people to protect their local forests.

Women resented that their husbands spent weeks away at a time and traveled further from home to work as loggers. They focused their resentment on environmentalists rather than on the industry, despite the fact that the timber industry was downsizing for reasons other than environmental regulations on timber harvesting. In this community, women formed a support group to help each other when their husbands were away, but the support group broke up when husbands pressured their wives to drop out. As one woman explained, "The group was really just to help with self-esteem and coping, but it was a real cop-out on the men's part—women were doing everything and getting no credit from their husbands. I mean, some men were surprised by the strength and intelligence of their wives and were really supportive, but others couldn't deal with their wives' success in running the household without them. They felt as if their wives didn't need them and it changed the power dy-namic—they decided that the support group undermined their power so they pressured their wives to drop out" (Warren, Lee, and Carroll, 1992:16).

In addition to performing the majority of housework and child care, many women worked outside the home but complained about the limited job opportunities in this logging community. As one woman commented: "Its pretty limited up here for work for women. I'm not educated enough to make it worth while to commute to a nearby city for work—between child care, gas and wear and tear on the car, what would be left?" (as quoted in Warren, Lee, and Carroll, 1992:22). Geographic isolation, responsibility for child care, limited employment opportunities, and low wages all limit women's income-earning opportunities and life options in this timber community.

I interviewed several women married to loggers in a community in rural Pennsylvania where the main industry was a paper and pulp mill. These women worried about the instability of their husbands' jobs in logging, which depended on the fluctuating timber market in the area. In response to the unpredictable employment and income situations of their husbands, these women worked as secretaries, retail clerks, and also initiated sideline activities to earn income. One woman, married to a self-employed logger, worked as a secretary in a local school and also rented out rooms in her home during hunting seasons. The boom and bust cycles in the timber industry, environmental conflicts over use of forest resources, and limited employment opportunities in forested regions are factors that place women and men in unstable economic circumstances. Conflicts over timbering affect women and men quite differently, not only in the Pacific Northwest, but in India as well.

Women and Tropical Forests

> What do the forests bear?
> Soil, water and pure air.
> Soil, water and pure air.
> Sustain the earth and all she bears.
> —traditional Chipko song

Indian women in the Chipko movement sang these words to save the forests in India. The Chipko movement gained notoriety for its demonstration of the power of women's grass-roots organizations to preserve the forests.

Worldwide attention focuses on problems associated with the destruction of the world's forests, especially the tropical rain forests, in the 1990s. Exploitation of tropical forests by northern people has a long history beginning during the era of colonialism. At present, multinational corporations and national governments continue to destroy the remaining world's forest to obtain timber and expand agriculture. Advocates of saving the forests point to the vast biological diversity in rain forests and appeal to biodiversity as a major reason for preserving forests. The environmental movement also brings to light the extent of human dependence on forests for survival at both global and local levels. Organizing strategies focus on convincing northern people that their well-being depends on the existence of tropical forests and stressing as well the importance of preserving tribal cultures. This level of interdependence comes as no surprise to rural people, who have long recognized the connection between their lives and the forest; they rely on forest plants and animals for food, housing, clothing, and fuel. In many areas of Africa and Asia, rural women collect firewood and other plant materials from the forest. These rural women and other indigenous people, often blamed for the destruction of forests, in fact often act as forest conservationists.

The Chipko movement in India achieved worldwide notoriety for its grass-roots women's efforts to protect the forest from commercial foresters. Vandana Shiva (1988) tells the story of the Chipko movement—Chipko literally means "hugging"—and emphasizes the extent of women's leadership and grass-roots participation. A poem written by the male activist Ghansyam Raturi in the 1970s represents the movement's philosophy:

> *Embrace our trees*
> *Save them from being felled*
> *The property of our hills*
> *Save it from being looted* (as printed in Shiva, 1988).

During the 1960s, women resisted commercial logging in the forests in India, and by the 1970s, were protesting widely concerning local people's right to use forest products. Deforestation increases women's workloads, as Hima Devi explained at protests against forest auctions: My sisters are busy in harvesting the kharif crop. They are busy in winnowing. I have come to you with their message. Stop cutting trees. There are no trees even for birds to perch on. Birds flock to our crops and eat them. What will we eat? The firewood is disappearing: How will we cook?" (as quoted in Shiva, 1988:75).

In 1977, Chipko activists successfully protected the forests from commercial loggers by physically embracing trees in Garhwal, Adwani, Amersar, Chanchnidhar, Dungari, Paintoi and Badiyaharh. This movement spread through various regions of India largely through the decentered leadership of local women. Shiva points out that observers overlook the centrality of women in this movement, largely because several men act as spokesmen for Chipko. From Shiva's perspective, Chipko politics shifted in 1977, becoming both an ecological and feminist movement. Up until then, women had directed their resistance efforts at outside forest contractors, but when local men began obtaining contracts for logging, local women protested. Shiva notes that "it did not matter to them whether the forest was destroyed by outsiders or their own men" (1988:76) and comments further on the way community interests are fragmented by gender. Local men were hired by companies to fell trees; however, for women, the felling of trees meant they had to walk farther to obtain water and firewood. Women therefore clearly viewed forest conservation as in their interest.

Irene Dankelman and Joan Davidson (1988) describe many other organized efforts by rural women to protect forests or to plant trees In Asia, protests against forestry programs are most pronounced in India. Tribal members, women, and hill people in India contest the social forestry programs of the Indian government and the World Bank. These groups realize that such programs promote monoculture—stands of fast-growing trees such as eucalyptus and teak—to meet the demands of a market economy rather than to provide local people with biomass, fodder, oil, medicine, and housing, needs previously supplied by their forests. As a result, grass-roots movements in Karnataka pulled out eucalyptus saplings and replaced them with tamarind and mango trees in 1983; tribal members in Jharkhand pulled out teak saplings and replaced them with saal trees in 1980. The Green Belt Movement in Kenya was begun in 1977 to raise awareness and prevent deforestation by the planting of trees; Wangari Maathai led local Kenyan women in organizing the movement. By 1982, 50 nurseries produced 2,000 to 10,000 seedlings per year, 239 green belts existed, and there were hundreds of groups with active women members. In addition, women organized reforestation efforts in Bolivia, Lesotho, Nepal, and Korea. Although women's efforts are unlikely to reverse the trend toward deforestation, groups have begun to address issues of injustice and inequality in resource use (Dankelman and Davidson, 1988).

Decentralization of Manufacturing and the Rise of Services

The instability and declining employment possibilities in the traditional rural industries of agriculture, mining, and logging undermine women's dependence on men's incomes and spur rural women in many regions to seek alternative income sources. In addition, decentralization of manufacturing industries and growth of the service sector provide employment opportunities for some women. The search by industries for cheap labor, few environmental regulations, and tax breaks in developing countries and in rural areas in developed countries has led to the decentralization of manufacturing. In the 1970s, labor-intensive industries that relied heavily on women workers moved out of cities in northern advanced industrial countries. For example, the electronics, garments, and pharmaceutical industries moved plants from the United States, Europe, and Japan to developing countries. During the same time period, labor-intensive industries, such as textiles, garments, and food products, moved from the northern cities of the United States to the South and to other rural areas in search of cheap, predominantly female labor. Nations, states, and localities competed for these transient industries by offering bargain prices for infrastructures, breaks on taxes, exemption from environmental regulations, and cheap, nonunionized labor.

As these industries left the northern nations, their economies shifted from goods-producing to service-producing economies that rely heavily on women workers. Contraction of manufacturing employment in advanced capitalist countries has been accompanied by rapid growth in the service sector. In 1981, the proportion of employment in the service economy was 66 percent in Canada, 50 percent in West Germany, 54 percent in Japan, 61 percent in the United Kingdom, and 66 percent in the United States (Harvey, 1989:157). Expansion of the service sector contributes to the large-scale movement of women into the labor force in Western countries. Although rates of pay for service jobs span the wage scale and job types range from financial adviser to data processor to hotel maid, the vast majority of jobs in the service sector pay less and are occupied more often by women than in manufacturing.

Much of the service sector activity remains concentrated in urban areas with their dense populations and large numbers of businesses. Rural areas are typically the location of lower-order services that more often rely on unskilled labor and pay low wages; service employment in large cities frequently requires higher skills and pays higher wages (Flora, 1990; Tigges and O'Toole, 1990). Cornelia Flora cautions that rural areas may become service employment ghettos for such undesirable jobs as in telemarketing. Some service industries, for instance, data processing, are already moving to Latin America and Asia. In addition, many women in the Third World work in the tourist industry as maids, waitresses, and prostitutes. They may also work in the rapidly expanding informal service economy, in activities such as food preparation and processing that are not protected or licensed by governments. The expansion of sex tourism, especially in Thailand and other Asian countries, poses particular problems for young rural women who are recruited as prostitutes. In the next section, I provide some examples of the way decentralized industries and the expanded service sector affect rural women in the United States and in the Third World.

Industrialization and Services in the Rural United States

Rural areas of the United States attracted companies with labor-intensive production needs as they sought ways to regain a comparative advantage in the face of global competition. In response to the demise of agriculture and extractive industries, rural communities often welcomed industrial expansion as the key to their economic survival. However, some observers warned at the time against the industrial invasion of the non-metropolitan United States, pointing out the minimal benefits for local residents and the high costs for local governments (Summers, 1977). Unfortunately, these warnings proved on target. Some rural areas did successfully attract industry, but the results were not impressive—primarily low-wage jobs and higher tax burdens for rural residents. One-half of the industrial and manufacturing jobs established in U.S. rural communities from 1980 to 1990 paid below poverty wages and failed to provide medical benefits (Naples, 1991–1992:8). In the United States, low-wage, less stable, labor-intensive, and routine manufacturing jobs are disproportionately concentrated in rural areas (Tigges and O'Toole, 1990). Similarly, in Italy, industries sought out areas with small farms to decentralize industrial development in order to escape well-organized urban workers (Bonnano, 1990).

Rural blacks, Hispanics, and Native Americans are highly vulnerable to the restructuring of manufacturing within the United States. These minorities gained in economic status from 1959 to 1979, but from 1979 to 1986, their economic status declined and poverty increased (Jensen and Tienda, 1989:528). The concentration of black women, black men, and white women in a narrow range of occupations characterized by low wages, high job turnover, and limited mobility is highest in rural areas (Bloomquist, 1990; Tickamyer and Bokemeier, 1988). Economic downturns and decline in government support further disadvantage rural minorities.

For example, Native American women on reservations face limited employment opportunities and precarious economic circumstances. Approximately 48 percent of Native American women, both rural and urban, were employed in 1980, but only one-third held full-time jobs (Amott and Matthaei, 1990:58). Unemployment is widespread on reservations. Native Americans are self-employed in farming, herding, or crafts; they may take jobs in clerical or social service work for the Bureau of Indian Affairs or work for corporations located near the reservations.

Mobile industries are attracted to rural areas, though they regularly move on to other locations. Janet Fitchen (1991) contends that the loss of factories in rural New York has affected the state economy more pervasively and deeply than the loss of farms. Fitchen examines several cases of industries' downsizing or moving out-of-state, as with a health care and hospital products factory employing almost 500 workers, mostly women, that moved its operations to Mexico in 1989. The New York workers earned an average of $8.00 per hour, but in Mexico, the company paid only $1.25 per hour. Workers in the New York plant wielded virtually no bargaining power with the company. When the plant closed, displaced workers had difficulty finding jobs; those who found jobs earned considerably lower wages than previously. For example, one women who liked her job at the medical products plant expressed dissatisfaction with her job at a new household appliance assembly plant. Her new job paid $2.50 per hour less than her previous job, and in addition, she is now required to work at night under dangerous work conditions.

People who work in rural areas are by and large working for less. The new jobs that are created as older industries move out of rural areas provide low wages, no health benefits, and part-time employment. This forces many women to enter the workforce to support their families. Many workers, both men and women, take two jobs. In about 10 percent of nonmetropolitan married couples, at least one spouse moonlights (has more than one job) (Whitener and Bokemeier, 1992:28). Not all couples moonlight for solely economic reasons. Less-educated couples report that underemployment and low income contribute to one or both spouses taking a second job. Despite their efforts, many rural families fail to attain the job stability, level of income, and health benefits provided by their previous jobs.

In addition to locating factories in rural areas and employing wageworkers, many corporations reach rural workers through subcontracting industrial work to informal factories or home-based workers. For example, in the midwestern United States, corporations targeted women on farms during the farm crisis for subcontracted industrial work (Gringeri, 1993). Christine Gringeri (1993) documents how home-based piecework in midwestern farm communities provided some income for farm women and their families but also placed severe burdens on women and seriously exploited their labor. Yet another consequence of global restructuring has been the growth of the informal sector, which includes economic activities that take place outside the private and public sector. Many of these informal sector workers are women. With these trends in manufacturing, rural women's involvement in wagework and the informal economy has increased in the past several decades.

Although the enormous expansion of the service sector in advanced industrial countries is much discussed, less attention is paid to exactly which aspects of the service sector expanded. In the 1980s, employment in producer services, finance, insurance, real estate, health, and education expanded, but employment in retailing, distribution, transport, and personal services remained relatively stable (Harvey, 1989). Some economic planners suggest that nonmetropolitan areas may eventually benefit from rapid advances in information technology, for example, in such telecommunications equipment as fax machines, satellites, personal computers and computer networks. Nevertheless, the majority of business services locate in urban areas. Management jobs and the large proportion of jobs in consumer and business services seem likely to remain in metropolitan centers. Other types of services, for instance, data processing for large businesses, especially insurance and banking, can be conducted in rural areas because technological advances in data processing allow the employment of low-skilled clerical workers. Services typically located in rural areas include food stores, auto dealerships, gas stations, electric and gas services, combined real estate and insurance offices, state and local governments, building materials supply companies, agricultural services, rail transportation services, private household services, and pipeline companies (Miller and Bluestone, 1988). Thus, growth in the service economy tends to bring lower-wage jobs to rural areas, whereas growth in high-paying service employment tends to bypass rural areas.

In studying rural areas in New York state, Fitchen found that over 60 percent of jobs were in the service sector. In one New York county, local people viewed prisons, nursing homes, and facilities for the mentally disabled as among the most stable employers (Fitchen, 1991:60). In tourist regions, women find jobs in hotel and restaurant work; however, as Michal Smith (1989) observes, jobs in rural resorts tend to offer low wages, minimal benefits, part-time hours, and seasonal employment. Low population density will likely limit further growth of the service sector in areas such as rural New York, consequently offering few new opportunities for women.

Retail trade offers another source of service employment for women. In rural areas, Wal-Mart symbolizes the restructuring of retail trade and the promise of new jobs, as well as low prices, for local people. Near large towns, regional and national chain stores in shopping malls replace local businesses and offer greater variety and cheaper goods. Fitchen (1991) found that in the Midwest these stores use their size and labor practices to push local stores out of business. In small towns and villages, retail businesses now consist of convenience stores, laundromats, and video stores, each providing a few local jobs. Rural women go to malls and stores primarily as shoppers, but they are also employed there. Many of these chains advertise employment policies that emphasize flexibility for employees, meaning they offer part-time jobs without or with only limited benefits for workers. Fitchen notes that malls employ entry-level, low-paid, and part-time workers, often teens, senior citizens, and mothers of young children. One respondent in a study on women workers in a small community in Pennsylvania reported that as an employee at a chain department store she received low pay and no benefits, but she appreciated the opportunity to work part-time in the evening and on weekends so that she could mind her children when her husband was at work. Women's employment in the service industry in rural areas will likely expand, but these jobs will probably offer low pay, and part-time hours and be temporary.

Women Wageworkers in Developing Countries

The massive relocation of textile, garment, electronic, and toy manufacturers to Singapore, the Philippines, Taiwan, and Korea, and more recently to Sri Lanka, Mexico, Haiti, and African nations, has relied heavily on women workers. Many multinational companies locate in urban areas or export-processing zones, hiring rural migrant women to fill jobs. Numerous excellent studies document women's entry into factory employment, particularly in Asia (Lim, 1983; Ong, 1987). Major debates on the topic among feminist scholars concern whether these jobs absolutely exploit rural women or in fact provide them with economic opportunities and employment that loosens their bonds to their patriarchal families (Lim, 19835). Early studies frequently viewed women as complete victims of international capital, but more recent studies note women's complicated strategies of resistance.

Aihwa Ong's (1987) superb study of rural women's entry into factory employment in Malaysia documents the ways in which transnational corporations manipulated the traditional patriarchal rural culture to encourage rural families to send their daughters to the factories. Electronics factories hire young women from peasant families. Factory employment releases young rural women from subordination in their families but at the same time intensifies their dependence on men in the industrial workplace. Media, politicians, and local people often accuse young rural women workers in multinational corporations of sexual immorality and conspicuous consumption, for example, Malay women factory workers are labeled as prostitutes and pleasure seekers. Ong suggests that linking working women's economic independence with their sexuality results in increasing public control over their leisure activities, while diverting attention away from the harsh reality of their working conditions. According to Ong, the factory women do not question male-dominated systems in the household or factory, in religion or society. Although they hope for improved economic positions, they do not envision sharing power with men. As one factory woman explained, "In Malay society, men ought to be at the top. Father has more authority than mother because he is male. This is as it should be. It is not surprising that at the workplace/factory all the persons in authority are men. If women get promoted along with men in the factory, then it is fine. In the house, it is not possible that women have authority because really men are the ones with power" (as quoted in Ong, 1987:192).

Still, resistance comes in many forms, as shown in the strategies of these rural women factory workers in Malaysia. Newspapers reported mass hysteria in free trade zones in the 1970s and 1980s. Ong investigates how rural Malay women indirectly resisted factory discipline and the dehumanizing aspects of capitalism, using possession as their tactic. In 1978, at an American-owned microelectronics factory, fifteen women possessed by spirits disrupted production for three days. As one factory official remembered, "Some girls started sobbing and screaming hysterically and when it seemed like it was spreading, the other workers in the production line were immediately ushered out . . . It is a common belief among workers that the factory is 'dirty' and supposed to be haunted by a datuk" (as quoted in Ong, 1987:204).

A factory worker described one of the incidents: "It was the afternoon shift, at about nine o'clock. All was quiet. Suddenly, [the victim] started sobbing, laughed and then shrieked. She flailed at the machine . . . she was violent, she fought the foreman and [the] technician pulled her away. Altogether, three operators were afflicted. . . . The supervisor and foremen took them to the clinic and told the driver to send them home". The same worker continued: "She did not know what happened. . . . she saw a hantu, a weretiger. Only she saw it, and she started screaming. . . . The foremen would not let us talk with her for fear of recurrence. . . . People say that the workplace is haunted by the hantu who dwells below . . . well, this used to be all jungle, it was a burial ground before the factory was built." In response to such incidents, management personnel often brought in spirit healers to cleanse the premises.

Ong discovered in her interviews with women workers that "spirit images reveal not only a mode of unconscious retaliation against male authority but fundamentally a sense of dislocation in human relations and a need for greater spiritual vigilance in domains reconstituted by capitalist relations of production" (Ong, 1987:207). These rural women entered a capitalist world that contradicted their values. Their wages gave them some semblance of economic independence; however, their wages were too low to give them economic independence from their families. They gained more individual freedom to move in a wider social world outside the village and family, but at the same time villagers, parents, and the media questioned their sexual morality. Ong interprets incidents of spirit possession in transnational factories as evidence of the "anguish, resistance, and cultural struggle" of factory women and suggests that their actions exemplify how Third World women's struggles can take on different forms to combat new forms of domination. All the same, many women lack effective resistance strategies.

In the short run, global restructuring makes work opportunities available to some women, but in the long run, women workers face job turnover, limited mobility, unsafe working conditions, and low wages (Ward, 1990). Kathryn Ward notes that the emphasis on women's employment by multinational corporations, although important, may distort our perception of the way multinationals affect the majority of women in developing countries. In fact, only a small proportion of women in these countries work directly for multinational corporations. Rather, many transnationals and smaller companies subcontract industrial production to informal factories or home-based workers. Women work in these informal factories or in their homes for scandalously low piece-rate pay without benefits.

In the Third World, the expansion of services occurs primarily in the informal sector. Women often compose the core of the service economy in both the formal and informal sectors. Domestic workers, primarily women, constitute the bulk of service workers in developing countries. Generally, as the formal economy falters and government programs deteriorate, the informal sector in the Third World expands. Women workers in this sector sell handicrafts, work at home-based production, and enter small-scale retail trade, food production, and other services catering to urban workers (Sen and Grown, 1987). Rural women bring their wares and those of other women to sell on the street in urban or town markets. In tourist areas, young rural women work as prostitutes, especially in Southeast Asia.

In Latin America, both the changes in agriculture and the growth of the service sector have caused women from rural areas to leave the countryside in search of work. Beginning in 1940, women began migrating to urban areas in greater numbers than men, largely to work in unskilled service occupations, principally domestic service and street vending (Crummet, 1987). Studies in Buenos Aires, Mexico City, and Santiago found rural women more likely to be in the labor market than native urban women; rural women were concentrated in domestic service occupations.

Summary

Global restructuring relies heavily on rural women's labor and transforms gender relations in the countryside. Declining employment in traditional extractive industries such as agriculture, mining, and logging decreases men's income-earning opportunities and pushes many women into the workforce. Because rural people suffer income loss in the general decline of agriculture, corporations perceive rural areas as prime locales for introducing particular industries and finding workers, particularly rural women who are willing to work for low wages under dangerous working conditions. For many rural women, employment away from their families offers one avenue of escape from the patriarchal authority of their fathers and husbands; this opens possibilities for changing power relations in households. However, employers of women frequently view women as mothers and domestics, which serves to perpetuate inequitable gender relations. In many rural areas, women employed outside the home are openly criticized for undermining male authority, appearing sexually promiscuous, and disrupting the social order based on the rural family. Control of women's morality and sexuality clearly determines the particular types of work opportunities and strategies for resistance available to rural women.

9

Conclusion

Rural women's experiences, largely overlooked by feminist and rural scholars alike, provide fresh insights for understanding gender relations and rural places. Rural women's lives have changed in many ways in response to shifts in gender divisions of labor and environmental degradation. Understanding the strategies rural women use to negotiate these difficulties furthers feminist approaches that derive predominantly from urban contexts.

Recent developments in feminist epistemology, especially the move from feminist standpoint theory to a more complicated understanding of women's situated perspectives, create new avenues for understanding rural women's lives and perspectives. For example, tracing rural women's practices and knowledge about land, crops, and animals conveys the ways in which the partial, situated perspectives of women shape their approaches to agriculture and the environment. Women's knowledge and practices, which have been marginalized by scientists and development planners, may well generate solutions to environmental and health problems. However, Haraway (1991) observes that all knowledge is partial, situated, and subject to distortions, and she wisely cautions against the simple claim that women hold the key to solving global problems. Women's knowledge might certainly inform scientists and policymakers, but it remains selective; it need not embody "truth."

Feminist recognition of multicultural differences among women suggests new strategies for analyzing complex social relations in rural places. Use of ethnic, racial, and socioeconomic variables insufficiently captures the complicated positions of rural women of different classes, races, ethnicities, and sexualities. For example, in any particular rural area, women married to men who own land, women landowners, and landless women stand in complicated relations with each other and with men. Often, feminists study women in privileged positions, for example, farm women, and neglect or marginalize other women's experiences, such as landless women in many regions and lesbians and women of color in the rural United States. Feminist scholars need to hear the multiple voices of rural women in order to shape a body of work that provides room for these women to express their pleasures, frustrations, successes, and differences with other women.

Urban-centered feminist scholarship and activism generates particular problems for feminist rural scholars. Although feminist rural scholars may convey and celebrate the multiple perspectives of rural women, the views of rural women seldom directly influence government assemblies, corporate policies, or international politics. Their strategies of resisting domination (in local places) may be indirect and difficult to see, causing problems for scholars attempting to diagnose and explain their problems. Rural women often handle their problems using less obviously confrontational strategies than urban feminist activists. Nevertheless, feminist scholars should recognize the power and political nature of these activities.

Global restructuring and changes in patriarchal forms in rural areas continually reshape rural women's lives. Few rural people can escape the demands of the market economy; many people from agricultural families take off-farm jobs. Declining employment in the traditionally male occupations of mining, logging, and farming forces rural residents to seek alternative sources of income or entirely different livelihoods. Rural women in most regions of the world can no longer rely completely on subsistence activities and male wages to support their families. In fact, changes in the global and local economies push rural women into wage-work, informal market activities, and other income-generating activities to provide for their families' welfare. Faced with patriarchal authority, increased workloads, confined sexuality, heightened poverty, and a subordinate position in the countryside, many women resist by leaving rural areas. Rural studies and feminist studies therefore should rethink simple dualistic categories such as rural/urban and farm/nonfarm and recognize that many women and men hold multiple identities in relation to place.

Women's intensive knowledge of their local environments, especially their strategies for coping with marginal land and limited resources, informs sustainable development strategies. Global shifts in agriculture alter women's and men's cropping and animal production systems and tend to favor men's control of production. Men gain control of cash-crop production, as illustrated in the discussions of corn, rice, coffee, and gardens. As livestock production becomes more concentrated, especially in chicken and dairy production, women producers lose control over income and management in many regions. Male control of new agricultural systems marginalizes women but also results in malnutrition and damage to the environment. Unfortunately, the reluctance of scientists and development planners to incorporate women's knowledge into their conception of problems and subsequent policymaking has slowed progress in solving problems of world hunger and environmental degradation.

Rural women's situated knowledge and daily work with crops, animals, land, and forests provide them with particular angles of vision concerning the natural world that clearly differ from urban women's or men's perspectives. Despite the symbolic associations between women and nature, women's access to natural resources such as land and trees is often limited by patriarchal ownership patterns and government policies. Nevertheless, women in these positions have specific knowledge that they use to survive. For example, women are knowledgeable about seeds, multiple uses of plants, and multicropping strategies. Further in-depth studies of women's knowledge of land, plants, animals, and social relations in various local contexts would enhance feminist scholars' understandings of food and environmental situations.

Environmental degradation might affect women and men in different ways at different times. For instance, rural women are often the first to experience increased workloads and health problems associated with the deterioration of local environments. In many diverse places, for example, in the United States, India, and Kenya, women, among others, have organized efforts to maintain their local environments and have led local actions to sustain forests and agriculture. It would advance scholarship to conduct more studies on the differential effects of environmental degradation on men and women and on the successes and problems encountered in efforts to confront environmental problems.

Scholars studying rural women's lives would do well to keep abreast of new developments in feminist theory and to promote scholarship that incorporates rural women's actions and knowledge into feminist theory.

References

Ackelsburg, Martha. 1988. "Communities, Resistance, and Women's Activism: Some Implications for a Democratic Polity." Pp. 297–313 in *The Politics of Empowerment*, edited by Ann Bookman and Sandra Morgen. Philadelphia: Temple University Press.

Acosta-Belen, Edna, and Christine E. Bose. 1990. "From Structural Subordination to Empowerment: Women and Development in Third World Contexts." *Gender and Society* 4(3):299–320.

Adams, Carol J. 1990. *The Sexual Politics of Meat: A Feminist-Vegetarian Critical Theory.* New York: Continuum.

Afonja, Simi. 1990. "Changing Patterns of Gender Stratification in West Africa." Pp. 198–209 in *Persistent Inequalities: Women and World Development*, edited by Irene Tinker. New York: Oxford University Press.

Agarwal, Bina. 1992. "The Gender and Environment Debate: Lessons from India." *Feminist Studies* 18(1):119–157.

Allen, Jeffner. 1990. *Lesbian Philosophies and Cultures.* Albany, NY: State University of New York Press.

Allen, Patricia. 1993. *Food for the Future: Conditions and Contradictions of Sustainability.* New York: John Wiley and Sons.

Allen, Patricia, and Carolyn Sachs. 1992. "The Poverty of Sustainability: An Analysis of Current Discourse." *Agriculture and Human Values* 9(4):30–37.

Amott, Teresa, and Julie Matthaei. 1990. *Race, Gender, and Work.* Boston: South End Press.

Anthan, George. 1991. "'Cheap' Poultry Carries Shamefully High Price Tag." Shreveport, *Louisiana Times*, September 8.

Anzaldúa, Gloria. 1990. *Making Face, Making Soul: Creative and Critical Perspectives by Women of Color.* San Francisco: Aunt Lute.

Aptheker, Bettina. 1989. *Tapestries of Life: Women's Consciousness and the Meaning of Daily Experience.* Amherst: University of Massachusetts Press.

Arizpe, Lourdes, and Josefina Aranda. 1981. "The 'Comparative Advantages' of Women's Disadvantages: Women Workers in the Strawberry Export Agribusiness in Mexico." *Signs* 7:453–473.

Ayuk-Takem, Jacob A., and Emmanuel A. Atayi. 1991. *The Cereals of Cameroon.* Yaounde, Cameroon: Institute of Agricultural Research.

Barker, Jonathon. 1984. *The Politics of Agriculture in Tropical Africa.* Beverly Hills, CA: Sage Publications.

Barlett, Peggy F. 1986. "Part-Time Farming: Saving the Farm or Saving the Lifestyle." *Rural Sociology* 51(3):289–313.

Batezat, Elinor, and Margaret Mwalo. 1989. *Women in Zimbabwe*. Harare, Zimbabwe: South African Political Economy Series.

Begum, S. 1985. "Women and Technology: Rice Processing in Bangla-desh." In *Women in Rice Farming*. Los Banos, Philippines: Interna-tional Rice Research Institute.

Beneria, Lourdes. 1982. "Accounting for Women's Work." Pp. 119–148 in *Women and Development*, edited by Lourdes Beneria. New York: Praeger.

Beneria, Lourdes, and Gita Sen. 1981. "Accumulation, Reproduction, and Women's Role in Economic Development: Boserup Revisited." *Signs* 7(2):279–298.

Benz, B. F. 1990. "Hugh H. Iltis: An Appreciation." *Maydica* 35(2):81–84.

Biehl, Janet. 1991. *Rethinking Ecofeminist Politics*. Boston: South End Press.

Blaikie, Piers. 1985. *The Political Economy of Soil Erosion in Developing Countries*. London: Longman.

Bloomquist, Leonard E. 1990. "Local Labor Market Characteristics and the Occupational Concentration of Different Sociodemographic Groups." *Rural Sociology* 55(2):199–213.

Blumberg, Rae Lesser. 1981. "Females, Farming, and Food: Rural Devel-opment and Women's Participation in Agricultural Production Systems." Pp. 24–102 in *Invisible Farmers: Women and the Crisis in Agriculture*, edited by B. Lewis. Washington, DC: Office of Women in Development, U.S. Agency for International Development.

_____. 1992. African Women in Agriculture: Farmers, Students, Extension Agents, Chiefs. Morrilton, AR: Winrock International Institute for Agricultural Development.

Bonanno, Alessandro. 1990. *Agrarian Policies and Agricultural Systems*. Boulder: Westview Press.

Booth, D. 1985. "Marxism and Development Sociology: Interpreting the Impasse." *World Development* 13(7):761–787.

Boserup, Ester. 1970. *Women's Role in Economic Development*. New York: St. Martin's Press.

Bryant, C. D. and K. B. Perkins. 1982. "Containing Work Disaffection: The Poultry Processing Worker." In *Varieties of Work*, edited by P. L. Stewart and M. G. Carter. Beverly Hills, CA: Sage Publications.

Bull, David. 1982. *A Growing Problem: Pesticides and the Third World Poor*. Oxford: Oxfam.

Butler, Judith. 1990. *Gender Trouble: Feminism and the Subversion of Identity*. New York: Routledge.

Buttel, Frederick, and Gilbert Gillespie. 1984. "The Sexual Division of Farm Household Labor: An Exploratory Study of the Structure of On-Farm and Off-Farm Labor Allocation Among Farm Men and Women." *Rural Sociology* 49:183–209.

Cain, Melinda. 1981. "Women in Technology—Resources for the Future." Pp. 3–8 in *Women and Technological Change in Developing Countries*, edited by Rosyln Dauber and Melinda Cain. Boulder: Westview Press.

Capistrano, Ana Doris, and Gerald Marten. 1986. "Agriculture in Southeast Asia." Pp. 6–19 in *Traditional Agriculture in Southeast Asia*, edited by Gerald Marten. Boulder: Westview Press.

Carney, Judith, and Michael Watts. 1991. "Disciplining Women? Rice, Mechanization, and the Evolution of Mandinka Gender Relations in Senegambia." *Signs* 16(4):651–681.

Carpenter, Carol. 1991. "Women and Livestock, Fodder, and Uncultivated Land in Pakistan: A Summary of Role Responsibilities." *Society and Natural Resources* 4(1):65–79.

Castillo, Gelia T. 1988. "Some General Impressions and Observations from Trips to India, Nepal, Bangladesh, Thailand, Indonesia, and the Philippines." Pp. 31–37 in *Filipino Women in Rice Farming Systems*. Los Banos, Philippines: University of the Philippines and International Rice Research Institute.

Cecelski, E. 1987. "Energy and Rural Women's Work: Crisis, Response, and Policy Alternatives." *International Labour Review* 126(1):41–64.

Cernea, Michael. 1978. "Macrosocial Change, Feminization of Agricul-ture, and Peasant Women's Threefold Economic Role." *Sociologia Ruralis* 18(2/3):107–124.

Chazan, Naomia. 1990. "Gender Perspectives on African States." Pp. 185–201 in *Women and the State in Africa*, edited by Jane L. Parpart and Kathleen A. Staudt. Boulder: Lynne Rienner.

CIMMYT. 1984. *Research Highlights.* Mexico City: CIMMYT.

Clarke, D. A. 1985. *To Live with the Weeds.* Santa Cruz, CA: Herbooks.

Collard, Andrée. 1988. *Rape of the Wild: Man's Violence Against Animals and the Earth.* London: The Women's Press.

Collard, Andrée, with Joyce Contrucci. 1989. *Rape of the Wild*: Man's Violence Against Animals and the Earth. Bloomington: Indiana Uni-versity Press.

Collins, Jane L. 1993. "Gender, Contracts and Wage Work: Agricultural Restructuring in Brazil's Sao Francisco Valley." *Development and Change* 24(1):53–82.

Collins, Patricia Hill. 1990. *Black Feminist Thought: Knowledge, Con-sciousness, and the Politics of Empowerment.* Boston: Unwin Hyman.

Crotty, R. 1980. *Cattle, Economics and Development.* London: Commonwealth Agricultural Bureaux.

Crummet, Maria de los Angeles. 1987. "Rural Women and Migration in Latin America." Pp. 239–260 in *Rural Women and State Policy: Feminist Perspectives on Latin American Agricultural Development*, edited by Carmen Diana Deere and Magdalena Leon. Boulder: Westview Press.

Cummings, Richard Osborn. 1970. *The American and His Food.* New York: Arno Press.

Dahlberg, Kenneth. 1979. Beyond the Green Revolution: The Ecology and Politics of Global Agricultural Development. New York. Plenum Press.

Dangarembga, Tsitsi. 1988. *Nervous Conditions.* Seattle: Seal Press.

Dankelman, Irene, and Joan Davidson. 1988. *Women and Environment in the Third World: Alliance for the Future.* London: Earthscan.

de Graaff, J. 1986. *The Economics of Coffee.* Wageningen, Netherlands: Pudoc.

Deere, Carmen Diana and Magdalena Leon de Leal. 1981. "Peasant Production, Proletarization, and the Sexual Division of Labor." *Signs* 7(2):338–360.

_____. 1987. *Rural Women and State Policy: Feminist Perspectives on Latin American Agricultural Development*. Boulder, CO: Westview Press.

de Janvry, Alain, and E. Phillip LeVeen. 1986. "Historical Forces That Have Shaped World Agriculture: A Structural Perspective." Pp. 83–104 in *New Directions for Agriculture and Agricultural Research*, edited by Kenneth Dahlberg. Totowa, NJ: Rowman and Allanheld.

Demissie, E. 1992. "A History of Black Farm Operators in Maryland." *Agriculture and Human Values* 9(1):22–30.

Dey, Jennie. 1985. "Women in African Rice Farming Systems." Pp. 417–444 in *Women in Rice Farming*. Los Banos, Philippines: International Rice Research Institute.

Diamond, Irene, and Gloria Orenstein. 1990. *Reweaving the World: The Emergence of Ecofeminism*. San Francisco: Sierra Club Books.

Dixon, Ruth B. 1982. "Women in Agriculture: Counting the Labor Force in Developing Countries." *Population and Development Review* 8(3): 539–566.

Donovan, Josephine. 1990. "Animal Rights and Feminist Theory." *Signs* 15(2): 350–375.

Edwards, Clive. 1993. "The Impact of Pesticides on the Environment." Pp. 13–46 in *The Pesticide Question*, edited by David Pimentel and Hugh Lehman. New York: Chapman and Hall.

Ehrenberg, Margaret. 1989. *Women in Prehistory*. Norman: University of Oklahoma Press.

Ensminger, M. E. 1993. *Dairy Cattle Science*. Danville, IL: Interstate Publishers.

Felski, Rita. 1989. "Feminist Theory and Social Change." *Theory, Culture and Society* 6:219–240.

Ferguson, Ann. 1990. "Is There a Lesbian Culture?" Pp. 89–108 in *Lesbian Philosophies and Cultures*, edited by Jeffner Allen. Albany, NY: State University of New York Press.

Fink, Deborah. 1986. *Open Country, Iowa: Rural Women, Tradition and Change*. Buffalo, NY: State University of New York Press.

_____. 1992. *Agrarian Women: Wives and Mothers in Rural Nebraska, 1880–1940*. Chapel Hill: University of North Carolina Press.

Fitchen, Janet M. 1991. *Enduring Spaces, Enduring Places: Change, Identity, and Survival in Rural America*. Boulder: Westview Press.

Fitzgerald, Deborah. 1990. *The Business of Breeding: Hybrid Corn in Illinois, 1890–1940*. Ithaca: Cornell University Press.

Fitzsimmons, Margaret. 1989. "The Matter of Nature." *Antipode* 21(2): 106–120.

Flax, Jane. 1990. *Thinking Fragments: Psychoanalysis, Feminism, and Postmodernism in the Contemporary West*. Berkeley: University of California Press.

Flora, Cornelia Butler. 1985. "Women and Agriculture." *Agriculture and Human Values* 2:5–12.

_____. 1988. "Public Policy and Women in Agricultural Production: A Comparative Analysis." Pp. 265–280 in *Women and Farming: Changing Roles, Changing Structures*, edited by Wava G. Haney and Jane B. Knowles. Boulder: Westview Press.

_____. 1990. "Rural Peoples in a Global Economy." *Rural Sociology* 55(2): 157–177.

Food and Agriculture Organization. 1991. *Production Yearbook 1990*. Volume 44. Rome: Food and Agriculture Organization.

Food and Agriculture Organization. 1993. *Commodity Review and Outlook.* Rome: Food and Agriculture Organization.

Fortmann, Louise. 1984. "Economic Status and Women's Participation in Agriculture: A Botswana Case Study." *Rural Sociology* 49(3):452–464.

Fraser, Nancy. 1989. *Unruly Practices: Power, Discourse, and Gender in Contemporary Social Theory.* Minneapolis: University of Minnesota Press.

Friedland, William. 1982. "The End of Rural Society and the Future of Rural Sociology." *Rural Sociology* 47(4):589–608.

_____. 1991. "Women and Agriculture in the United States: A State of the Art Assessment." Pp. 315–338 in *Towards a New Political Economy of Agriculture,* edited by W. Friedland, L Busch, F. Buttel, and A. Rudy. Boulder: Westview Press.

Friedmann, Harriet. 1986. "Property and Patriarchy: A Reply to Goodman and Redclift." *Sociologia Ruralis* 26:186–193.

_____. 1988. "World Market, State, and Family Farm: Social Bases of Household Production in the Era of Wage Labor." *American Journal of Sociology* 88:248–286.

_____. 1991. "Changes in the International Division of Labor: Agrifood Complexes and Export Agriculture. Pp. 65–93 in *Towards a New Political Economy of Agriculture,* Friedland et al., Boulder: Westview Press.

Friedmann, Harriet, and Philip McMichael. 1989. "Agriculture and the State System: The Rise and Decline of National Agricultures, 1870 to present." *Sociologia Ruralis* 29(2):93–117.

Frye, Marilyn. 1983. *The Politics of Reality: Essays in Feminist Theory.* Trumansburg, NY: Crossing Press.

Fuss, Diana. 1991. *Inside/Out: Lesbian Theories, Gay Theories.* New York: Routledge.

Gearhart, Sally. 1978. *The Wanderground.* Watertown, MA: Persephone Press.

Geisler, Charles C., William F. Waters, and Katrina L. Eadie. 1985. "The Changing Structure of Female Agricultural Land Ownership, 1946– 1978." *Rural Sociology* 50(1):74–87.

George, Shanti. 1985. *Operation Flood: An Appraisal of Current India Dairy Policy.* Delhi: Oxford University Press.

Gershuny, Grace. 1991. "Women in Alternative Agriculture." *Organic Farmer* 2(3):5–21.

Gilbert, Jess, and Raymond Akor. 1988. "Increasing Structural Divergence in U.S. Dairying: California and Wisconsin Since 1950." *Rural Sociology* 53(1):56–72.

Gilbert, Reg. 1992. "Pesticide Use: The Most Preventable Pollution." *Bulletin of Pollution Prevention* 5:1–6.

Gilman, Charlotte Perkins. 1979. *Herland.* New York: Pantheon Books.

Giles, Dorothy. 1940. *Singing Valleys: The Story of Corn.* New York: Random House.

Gleason, Jane E. 1988. "The Contribution of Women to Agriculture in Taiwan." Pp. 237–251 in *Gender Issues in Farming Systems Research and Extension,* edited by Susan V. Poats, Marianne Schmink, and Anita Spring. Boulder: Westview Press.

Godwin, Deborah D., and Julia Marlowe. 1990. "Farm Wives' Labor Force Participation and Earnings." *Rural Sociology* 55(1):25–43.

Griffin, Susan. 1978. *Women and Nature: The Roaring Inside Her.* New York: Harper and Row.

Gringeri, Christine. 1993. "Inscribing Gender in Rural Development: Industrial Homework in Two Midwestern Communities." *Rural Sociology* 58(1):30–52.

Grist, D. H. 1986. *Rice.* London: Longman.

Hagood, Margaret. 1977. *Mothers of the South.* New York: W. W. Norton.

Haney, Wava G., and Jane B. Knowles. 1988. "Making 'The Invisible Farmer' Visible." Pp. 1–14 in *Women and Farming: Changing Roles, Changing Structures,* edited by Wava G. Haney and Jane B. Knowles. Boulder: Westview Press.

Haraway, Donna J. 1991. *Simians, Cyborgs, and Women: The Reinvention of Nature.* New York: Routledge.

Hardeman, Nicholas. 1981. *Shucks, Shocks, and Hominy Blocks: Corn as a Way of Life in Pioneer America.* Baton Rouge: Louisiana State University Press.

Hardin, G. 1968. "The Tragedy of the Commons." *Science* 162:1243–1248.

Harding, Sandra. 1986. *The Science Question in Feminism.* Ithaca: Cornell University Press.

_____. 1991. *Whose Science? Whose Knowledge? Thinking from Women's Lives.* Ithaca: Cornell University Press.

Hartsock, Nancy. 1983a. "The Feminist Standpoint: Developing the Ground for a Specifically Feminist Historical Materialism." Pp. 283–310 in *Discovering Reality: Feminist Perspectives on Epistemology, Metaphysics, Methodology, and Philosophy of Science,* edited by Sandra Harding and Merill Hintikka. Dordrecht, Netherlands: Reidel.

_____. 1983b. *Money, Sex, and Power: Toward a Feminist Historical Ma-terialism.* New York: Longman.

Harvey, David. 1989. *The Condition of Postmodernity.* Oxford: Basil Blackwell.

Hawthorne, Susan. 1991. "Gold into Straw: Feminist Fiction and Cultural Transformation." *Women's Studies International Forum* 14(3):153–162.

Hecht, Susanna B. 1985. "Women and the Latin American Livestock Sector." Pp. 51–69 in *Women as Food Producers in Developing Countries,* edited by Jamie Monson and Marion Kalb. Los Angeles: University of California.

Hectlinger, Adelaide. 1977. *The Seasonal Hearth: The Woman at Home in Early America.* Woodstock, NY: Overlook Press.

Heffernan, William. 1984. "Constraints in the U.S. Poultry Industry." Pp. 237–260 in *Research in Rural Sociology and Development,* edited by Harry Schwarzweller. New York: JAI Press.

Holmes, T., E. Nielsen, and L. Lee. 1988. "Managing Groundwater Contamination in Rural Areas." *Rural Development Perspectives* 5(1): 35–39. Washington, DC: U.S. Department of Agriculture.

Hubbell, Sue. 1983. *A Country Year: Living the Questions.* New York: Harper and Row.

Huerta, Dolores. 1992. Keynote address, presented at Harvesting Our Potential conference, Des Moines, Iowa, January 31–February 2.

Hyden, Goran. 1980. *Beyond Ujamaa in Tanzania: Underdevelopment and an Uncaptured Peasantry.* London: Heinemann.

Hynes, Patricia H. 1989. *The Recurring Silent Spring.* New York: Pergamon Press.

International Rice Research Institute. 1985. *Women in Rice Farming.* Los Banos, Philippines: International Rice Research Institute.

International Rice Research Institute. 1988. *Filipino Women in Rice Farming Systems.* Los Banos, Philippines: University of the Philippines and International Rice Research Institute.

Ireson, Carol. 1991. "Women's Forest Work in Laos." *Society and Natural Resources* 4(1):23–36.

Jackson, Wes, and Marty Bender. 1984. "Investigations into Perennial Polyculture." Pp. 183–194 in *Meeting the Expectations of the Land,* edited by Wes Jackson, Wendell Berry, and Bruce Colman. San Francisco: North Point Press.

Jacobs, Susan. 1990. "Zimbabwe: State, Class, and Gendered Models of Land Resettlement." Pp. 161–184 in *Women and the State in Africa,* edited by Jane L. Parpart and Kathleen A. Staudt. Boulder: Lynne Rienner.

Jaggar, Alison M. 1983. *Feminist Politics and Human Nature.* Totowa, NJ: Rowman and Allenheld.

Jahan, Roushan. 1988. "Hidden Wounds, Visible Scars: Violence Against Women in Bangladesh." Pp. 199–227 in *Structures of Patriarchy: State, Community, and Household in Modernizing Asia,* edited by Bina Agarwal. London: Zed Books.

Janiewski, Dolores. 1988. "Making Women into Farmers' Wives: The Native American Experience in the Inland Northwest." Pp. 35–54 in *Women and Farming: Changing Roles, Changing Structures,* edited by Wava G. Haney and Jane B. Knowles. Boulder: Westview Press.

Jellison, Katherine. 1993. *Entitled to Power: Farm Women and Technology, 1913–1963.* Chapel Hill: University of North Carolina Press.

Jensen, Joan. 1981. *With These Hands: Women Working on the Land.* Old Westbury, NY: Feminist Press.

_____. 1986. *Loosening the Bonds: Mid-Atlantic Farm Women, 1750–1850.* New Haven: Yale University Press.

_____. 1991. *Promise to the Land: Essays on Rural Women.* Albuquerque: University of New Mexico Press.

Jensen, Leif, and Marta Tienda. 1989. "Nonmetropolitan Minority Families in the U.S.: Trends in Racial and Ethnic Economic Stratification." *Rural Sociology* 54(4):509–532.

Jiggins, Janice. 1986. *Gender-Related Impacts and the Work of the International Agricultural Research Centers.* Washington, DC: World Bank.

Jodha, N. S. 1992. *Common Property Resources.* World Bank Discussion Paper 169. Washington, DC: World Bank.

Jones, Jacqueline. 1985. *Labor of Love, Labor of Sorrow: Black Women, Work and the Family from Slavery to the Present.* New York: Basic Books.

_____. 1988. "'Tore Up and A-Movin': Perspectives on the Work of Black and Poor White Women in the Rural South, 1865–1940." Pp. 15–34 in *Women and Farming: Changing Roles, Changing Structures,* edited by Wava G. Haney and Jane B. Knowles. Boulder: Westview Press.

Jones, D. W. and R. V. O'Neill. 1993. "Human-Environmental Influences and Interactions in Shifting Agriculture When Farmers Form Expectations Rationally." *Environment and Planning* 25(1):121–136.

Jugenheimer, Robert. 1976. *Corn: Improvements, Seed Production, and Uses.* New York: John Wiley and Sons.

Keller, Evelyn Fox. 1983. *A Feeling for the Organism: The Life and World of Barbara McClintock.* San Francisco: W. H. Freeman.

_____. 1985. *Reflections on Gender and Science.* New Haven: Yale University Press.

Khush, Gurdev S. 1985. "Improved Rice Varieties in Retrospect and in Prospect." Pp. 455–460 in *Women in Rice Farming*. Los Banos, The Philippines: International Rice Institute.

Kim, Chul-Kyoo, and James Curry. 1993. "Fordism, Flexible Specialization and Agri-industrial Restructuring." *Sociologia Ruralis* 33(1):61–80.

King, Ynestra. 1989. "The Ecology of Feminism and the Feminism of Ecology." Pp. 18–28 in *Healing the Wounds: The Promise of Ecofeminism*, edited by Judith Plant. Philadelphia: New Society Publishers.

———. 1990. "Healing the Wounds: Feminism, Ecology, and the Nature/Culture Dualism. Pp. 106–121 in *Reweaving the World: The Emergence of Ecofeminism*, edited by Irene Diamond and Gloria Orenstein. San Francisco: Sierra Club Books.

Kiss, Agnes. 1990. *Living with Wildlife: Wildlife Resource Management with Local Participation in Africa*. Washington, DC: World Bank.

Klein, Renate D. 1991. "Passion and Politics in Women's Studies in the Nineties." *Women's Studies International Forum* 14(3):125–134.

Kloppenburg, Jack. 1988. *First the Seed: The Political Economy of Plant Biotechnology, 1492–2000*. New York: Cambridge University Press.

———. 1991. "Social Theory and the De/Reconstruction of Agricultural Science: Local Knowledge for an Alternative Agriculture." *Rural Sociology* 56(4):519–548.

Kumin, Maxine. 1994. *Women, Animals, and Vegetables*. New York: W. W. Norton.

Lal, Rattan, and D. Greenland. 1979. *Soil Physical Properties and Crop Production in the Tropics*. Chichester, England: John Wiley and Sons.

Lash, S., and Urry, J. 1987. *The End of Organized Capitalism*. Oxford: Oxford University Press.

Lee, Richard B. 1979. *The !Kung San: Men, Women, and Work in a Foraging Society*. Cambridge: Cambridge University Press.

Leon, Magdalena. 1987. "Colombian Agricultural Policies and the Debate on Policies Toward Rural Women." Pp. 84–104 in *Rural Women and State Policy: Feminist Perspectives on Latin American Agricultural Development*, edited by Carmen Diana Deere and Madalena Leon. Boulder: Westview Press.

Lim, Linda. 1983. "Capitalism, Imperialism and Patriarchy: The Dilemma of Third-World Women Workers in Multinational Factories." Pp. 70–92 in *Women, Men, and the International Division of Labor*, edited by June Nash and Maria Fernandez Kelly. Albany: State University of New York Press.

Lipman-Blumen, Jean. 1986. "Exquisite Decisions in a Global Village." Pp. 42–65 in *New Directions for Agriculture and Agricultural Research*, edited by Kenneth Dahlberg. Totowa, NJ: Rowman and Allanheld.

Lipton, Michael. 1989. *New Seeds, Poor People*. London: Unwin Hyman.

Lobao, Linda, and Katherine Meyer. 1992. "The Political Adaptations of Women to the Farm Crisis." Unpublished manuscript.

Long, N. 1984. *The Family and Work in Rural Societies: Perspectives on Non-Wage Labour*. London: Tavistock.

Lorde, Audre. 1982. *Zami, A New Spelling of My Name*. Trumansberg, NY: Crossing.

Lovett, Margot. 1990. "Gender Relations, Class Formation, and the Colonial State in Africa." Pp. 23–46 in *Women and the State in Africa*, edited by Jane L. Parpart and Kathleen A. Staudt. Boulder: Lynne Rienner.

Lucier, Richard. 1988. *The International Political Economy of Coffee*. New York: Praeger.

Lyson, Thomas, and Willam Falk. 1993. *Forgotten Places: Uneven Development in Rural America.* Lawrence: University Press of Kansas.

Maggard, Sally Ward. 1990. "Gender Contested: Women's Participation in the Brookside Coal Strike." Pp. 75–98 in *Women and Social Protest,* edited by Guida West and Rhoda Blumberg. New York: Oxford University Press.

Malaza, Millicent. 1994. "Food Security in Swaziland: Factors Influencing Dietary Patterns." Ph.D. diss., Penn State University.

Manchester, Alden C. 1983. *The Public Role in the Dairy Economy.* Boulder: Westview Press.

Mangelsdorf, Paul C. 1974. *Corn: Its Origin, Evolution, and Improvement.* Cambridge: Harvard University Press.

Mann, S. A. and J. M. Dickinson. 1978. "Obstacles to the Development of Capitalist Agriculture." *Journal of Peasant Studies* 5:466–481.

Marten, Gerald, and Daniel Saltman. 1986. "The Human Ecology Perspective." In *Traditional Agriculture in Southeast Asia.* Boulder: Westview Press.

Matsuda, Sonoko Kumagai. 1992. "Farm Mechanization and Women's Life Pattern: Changing Time Allocation." Paper presented at Eighth World Congress for Rural Sociology, State College, Pennsylvania, August 11–16.

McCay, Bonnie, and James Acheson. 1987. *The Question of the Commons.* Tuscon: University of Arizona Press.

McGlothlen, Michael E., Paul Goldsmith, and Charles Fox. 1986. "Undomesticated Animals and Plants." Pp. 222–238 in *Food in Sub-Saharan Africa,* edited by Art Hansen and Della E. McMillan. Boulder: Lynne Rienner.

McMillan, Della E., and Art Hansen. 1986. "Overview: Food in Sub-Saharan Africa." Pp. 1–10 in *Food in Sub-Saharan Africa,* edited by Art Hansen and Della E. McMillan. Boulder: Lynne Rienner.

Mellor, Mary. 1992. "Eco-feminism and Eco-Socialism: Dilemmas of Essentialism and Materialism." *Capitalism, Nature, Socialism* 3(2):43–62.

Mencher, Joan P. 1988. "Landless Women Agricultural Laborers in India: Some Observations from Tamil Nadu, Kerala and West Bengal." Pp. 351–371 in *Women in Rice Farming.* Los Banos, Philippines: International Rice Research Institute.

Merchant, Carolyn. 1980. *The Death of Nature: Women, Ecology, and the Scientific Revolution.* San Francisco: Harper and Row.

_____. 1989. *Ecological Revolutions: Nature, Gender, and Science in New England.* Chapel Hill: University of North Carolina Press.

_____. 1992. *Radical Ecology: The Search for a Livable World.* New York: Routledge.

Mies, Maria. 1986. *Patriarchy and Accumulation on a World Scale: Women in the International Division of Labour.* London: Zed Press.

Miller, James, and Herman Bluestone. 1988. "Prospects for Service Sector Employment Growth in Non-Metro America." *Review of Regional Studies* 18(Winter):28–41.

Miller, Lorna Clancy, and Mary Neth. 1988. "Farm Women in the Political Arena." Pp. 357–380 in *Women and Farming: Changing Roles, Changing Structures,* edited by Wava G. Haney and Jane B. Knowles. Boulder: Westview Press.

Mohanty, Chandra T. 1989–1990. "On Race and Voice: Challenges for Liberal Education in the 1990s." *Cultural Critique* 14:179–208.

_____. 1991. "Under Western Eyes: Feminist Scholarship and Colonial Discourses." Pp. 51–80 in *Third World Women and the Politics of Feminism*, edited by Chandra Mohanty, Ann Russo, and Lourdes Torres. Bloomington: Indiana University Press. First published in *Feminist Review* 30:61–88.

Momsen, Janet, and Janet Townsend. 1987. *Geography of Gender in the Third World*. Albany, NY: State University of New York Press.

Montagu, Ashley. 1969. *Man, His First Two Million Years: A Brief Introduction to Anthropology*. New York: Columbia University Press.

Moore, Keith. 1989. "Agrarian or Non-Agrarian Identities of Farm Spouses." *Rural Sociology* 54(1):74–82.

Moser, Caroline. 1989. "Gender Planning in the Third World: Meeting Practical and Strategic Gender Needs." *World Development* 17(11): 1799–1825.

Mullings, Leith. 1986. "Uneven Development: Class, Race, and Gender in the United States Before 1900." Pp. 41–57 in *Women's Work: Development and the Division of Labor by Gender*, edited by Eleanor Leacock and Helen I. Safa. South Hadley, MA: Bergin and Garvey.

Mumbengegwi, C. 1986. "Continuity and Change in Agricultural Policy." In *Zimbabwe: The Political Economy of Transition*, edited by I. Mandaza. London: Council for the Development of Economical and Social Research in Africa.

Muntemba, M. S. 1982. "Women as Food Producers and Suppliers in the Twentieth Century: The Case of Zambia." *Development Dialogue* 1(2):29–51.

Murindagomo, F. 1990. "CAMPFIRE Program (Dande Communal Lands)—Zimbabwe." Pp. 123–140 in *Living with Wildlife: Wildlife Resource Management with Local Participation in Africa*, edited by Agnes Kiss. Washington, DC: World Bank.

Myers, N. 1981. "A Farewell to Africa." *International Wildlife* 11(6):36–47.

Naples, Nancy. 1991–1992. "Rural Economic Development: What It Means for Women." *Prairie Journal* 2(4):8–9.

Nash, June. 1988. "The Mobilization of Women in the Bolivian Debt Crisis." Pp. 67–86 in *Women and Work* No.3, edited by Barbara Gutek, Ann Stromberg, and Laurie Larwood. Beverly Hills, CA: Sage Publications.

National Research Council. 1989. *Alternative Agriculture*. Washington, DC: National Academy Press.

Newbury, Catharine, and Brooke Grundfest. 1989. "State, Peasantry, and Agrarian Crisis in Zaire: Does Gender Make a Difference?" Pp. 91–110 in *Women and the State in Africa*, edited by Jane Parpart and Kathleen Staudt. Boulder: Lynne Rienner.

Ng, Cecilia, and Maznag Mohamed. 1988. "Primary but Subordinated: Changing Class and Gender Relations in Rural Malaysia." Pp. 52–82 in *Structures of Patriarchy: State, Community, and Household in Modernizing Asia*, edited by Bina Agarwal. London: Zed Books.

Obbo, Christine. 1990. "East African Women, Work, and the Articulation of Dominance." Pp. 210–222 in *Persistent Inequalities: Women and World Development*, edited by Irene Tinker. New York: Oxford University Press.

Okeyo, A. P. 1980. "Daughters of the Lakes and Rivers: Colonization and the Land Rights of Luo Women. In *Women and Colonization: Anthropological Perspectives*, edited by M. Etienne and E. Leacock. New York: Praeger.

Ong, Aihwa. 1987. *Spirits of Resistance and Capitalist Discipline. Factory Women in Malaysia.* Albany, NY: State University of New York Press.

Nwapa, Flora. 1986. *Cassava Song and Rice Song.* Lagos, Nigeria: Tana Press.

Padavic, Irene. 1993. "Agricultural Restructuring and the Spatial Dynamics of U.S. Women's Employment in the 1970s." *Rural Sociology* 58(2):210–232.

Pankhurst, D. 1989. "The Dynamics of the Social Relations of Production and Reproduction in a Communal Area of Zimbabwe." Ph.D. diss., University of Liverpool.

Papenek, Hanna. 1990. "To Each Less than She Needs, From Each More than She Can Do: Allocations, Entitlements, and Value." Pp. 162–181 in *Persistent Inequalities: Women and World Development,* edited by Irene Tinker. New York: Oxford University Press.

Parpart, Jane. 1993. "Who Is the 'Other'?: A Postmodern Feminist Critique of Women and Development Theory and Practice." *Development and Change* 24(3):439–464.

Parpart, Jane, and Kathleen Staudt. eds. 1989. *Women and the State in Africa.* Boulder: Lynne Rienner.

Pearse, Andrew. 1980. *Seed of Plenty, Seeds of Want: Social and Economic Implications of the Green Revolution.* New York: Oxford University Press.

Perfecto, I. 1992. "Pesticide Health Effects on People of Color." Paper presented at Diversity in Food, Agriculture, Nutrition and Environment conference, East Lansing, Michigan.

Perkins, John, and Nordica C. Holochuck. 1993. "Pesticides: Historical Changes Demand Ethical Choices." Pp. 390–417 in *The Pesticide Question,* edited by David Pimentel and Hugh Lehman. New York. Chapman and Hall.

Pfeffer, Max J. 1989. "The Feminization of Production on Part-Time Farms in the Federal Republic of Germany." *Rural Sociology* 54(1):60–73.

Piercy, Marge. 1991. "The Common Living Dirt." Pp. 340–342 in *Sisters of the Earth,* edited by Lorraine Anderson. New York: Vintage Books.

Pimentel, David, Lori McLaughlin, Andrew Zepp, Benyamin Lakitan, Tamara Kraus, Peter Kleinman, Fabius Vancini, W. John Roach, Ellen Graap, William S. Keeton, and Gabe Selig. 1991. "Environmental and Economic Impacts of Reducing U.S. Agricultural Pesticide Use." Pp. 679–718 in *Communications Research Center Handbook of Pest Management in Agriculture,* edited by David Pimentel. Boca Raton, FL: Communi-cations Research Center Press.

Plumwood, Val. 1991. "Nature, Self, and Gender: Feminism, Environmental Philosophy, and the Critique of Rationalism." *Hypatia* 6(1):3–27

Ponts, Susan V., Marianne Schmink, and Anita Spring, eds. 1988. *Gender Issues in Farming Systems Research and Extension.* Boulder: Westview Press.

Rao, Brinda. 1991. "Dominant Constructions of Women and Nature in Social Science Literature." *Capitalism, Nature, Socialism.* Pamphlet 2. Santa Cruz, CA.

Redclift, Michael. 1987. *Sustainable Development: Exploring the Contradictions.* New York: Metheun.

Redclift, Nanette, and Enzo Mingione. 1985. *Beyond Employment: Household, Gender, and Subsistence.* Oxford: Basil Blackwell.

Reimer, Bill. 1986. "Women as Farm Labor." *Rural Sociology* 5(2):143–155.

Rich, Adrienne. 1978. *The Dream of a Common Language.* New York: W. W. Norton.

Rocheleau, Diane. 1988. "Gender, Resource Management, and the Rural Landscape: Implications for Agroforestry and Farming Systems Research." Pp. 149–169 in *Gender Issues in Farming Systems Research and Extension*, edited by Susan V. Poats, Marianne Schmink, and Anita Spring. Boulder: Westview Press.

Rodda, Annabel. 1991. *Women and the Environment*. London: Zed Books.

Rogers, Barbara. 1980. *The Domestication of Women: Discrimination in Developing Societies*. London: St. Martin's Press.

Rose, Hilary. 1983. "Hand, Brain, and Heart: A Feminist Epistemology for the Natural Sciences." *Signs* 9(1):73–90.

Rosenfeld, Rachel. 1985. *Farm Women: Work, Farm, and Family in the United States*. Chapel Hill: University of North Carolina Press.

Rural Sociological Society Task Force on Persistent Rural Poverty. 1993. *Persistent Poverty in Rural America*. Boulder: Westview Press.

Sachs, Carolyn E. 1983. *The Invisible Farmers: Women in Agricultural Production*. Totowa, NJ: Rowman and Allenheld.

_____. 1988. "The Participation of Women and Girls in Market and Non-Market Activities on Pennsylvania Farms." Pp. 123–134 in *Women and Farming*, edited by Wava G. Haney and Jane B. Knowles. Boulder: Westview Press.

Salleh, Ariel K. 1984. "Deeper than Deep Ecology: The Ecofeminist Connection." *Environmental Ethics* 6:339–345.

Sargent, Frederick Leroy. 1899. *Corn Plants: Their Uses and Ways of Life*. Boston: Houghton, Mifflin and Company.

Schoepf, Brooke. 1986. "Food Crisis and Class Formation in Zaire: Political Ecology in Shaba." In *The World Recession and the Food Crisis in Africa*, edited by Peter Lawrence. London: James Currey.

Schrijvers, Joke. 1988. "Blueprint for Undernourishment: The Mahaweli Rice Development Scheme in Sri Lanka." Pp. 29–51 in *Structures of Patriarchy*, edited by Bina Agarwal. London: Zed Books.

Schwarzweller, Harry. 1991. "Division of Labor on Dairy Farms in Michigan and New South Wales." Paper presented at Rural Sociological Society Meetings, Columbus, Ohio, August.

Sen, Gita, and Caren Grown. 1987. *Development, Crises, and Alternative Visions: Third World Women's Perspectives*. New York: Monthly Review Press.

Shiva, Vandana. 1988. *Staying Alive: Women, Ecology, and Survival*. London: Zed Press.

Silverblatt, Irene. 1987. *Moon, Sun, and Witches: Gender Ideologies and Class in Inca and Colonial Peru*. Princeton: Princeton University Press.

Simpson, Ida Harper, John Wilson, and Kristina Young. 1988. "The Sexual Division of Farm Household Labor: A Replication and Extension." *Rural Sociology* 53(2):145–165.

Simpson, James R., and Robert E. McDowell. 1986. "Livestock in the Economies of Sub-Saharan Africa." Pp. 207–221 in *Food in Sub-Saharan Africa*, edited by Art Hansen and Della E. McMillan. Boulder: Lynne Rienner.

Smiley, Jane. 1991. *A Thousand Acres*. New York: Fawcett Columbine.

Smith, Dorothy. 1987. *The Everyday World as Problematic: A Feminist Sociology*. Boston: Northeastern University Press.

Smith, Michal. 1989. *Behind the Glitter: The Impact of Tourism on Rural Women in the Southeast*. Lexington, KY: Southeast Women's Employment Coalition.

Stamp, Patricia. 1990. *Technology, Gender, and Power in Africa*. Hartford, CT: Kumarian Press.

Stanley, A. 1982. "Daughters of Isis, Daughters of Demeter: When Women Sowed and Reaped." In *Women, Technology, and Innovation*, edited by J. Rothschild. New York: Pergamon.

Stanley, Liz. 1990. *Feminist Praxis: Research, Theory, and Epistemology in Feminist Sociology*. New York: Routledge.

Staudt, Kathleen. 1987. "Uncaptured or Unmotivated? Women and the Food Crisis in Africa." *Rural Sociology* 52(1):37–55.

Stolcke, Verena. 1988. *Coffee Planters, Workers, and Wives: Class Conflict and Gender Relations on Sao Paulo Plantations, 1850–1980*. New York: St. Martin's Press.

Stratton, Joanna L. 1981. *Pioneer Women: Voices from the Kansas Frontier*. New York: Simon and Schuster.

Summers, Gene. 1977. "Industrial Development in Rural America." *Journal of Community Development Society* 8:6–18.

Tallen, Betty. 1990. "How Inclusive Is Feminist Political Theory? Questions for Lesbians." Pp. 241–258 in *Lesbian Philosophies and Cultures*, edited by Jeffner Allen. Albany, NY: State University of New York Press.

Tallichet, Suzanne. 1991. "Moving Up Down in the Mine: Sex Segregation in Underground Coal Mining." Ph.D. diss., Pennsylvania State University, University Park, PA.

Thi, Le. 1993. "Women, Marriage, Family and Sex Equality." Paper presented at Family and the Condition of Women in Society, Institute of Social Sciences, Ho Chi Minh City, January.

Tickamyer, Ann, and Janet Bokemeier. 1988. "Sex Differences in Labor-Market Experiences." *Rural Sociology* 53(2):166–189.

Tien, Ha Thi Phuong. 1992. "On the Problem of Female Labourers' Health Protection." *Social Sciences* 4:51–64.

Tigges, Leann, and Deborah O'Toole. 1990. "Labor Supply, Labor Demand, and Men's Underemployment in Rural and Urban Labor Markets." *Rural Sociology* 5(3): 328–356.

Timberlake, Lloyd. 1985. *Africa in Crisis: The Causes, the Cures of Environ-mental Bankruptcy*. London: Earthscan.

Trenchard, Ellen. 1987. "Rural Women's Work in Sub-Saharan Africa and the Implications for Nutrition." Pp. 153–172 in *Geography of Gender in the Third World*, edited by Janet Momsen and J. Townsend. London: Hutchinson.

United States Bureau of the Census. 1950. *Census of Population*. Washington, DC: Government Printing Office.

_____. 1980. *Census of Population*. Washington, DC: Government Printing Office.

United States Bureau of Labor Statistics. 1982. *Labor Statistics*. Washington, DC: Government Printing Office:

United States Department of Agriculture. 1987. *Census of Agriculture*. Washington, DC: Government Printing Office.

_____. 1990. *Agricultural Statistics*. Washington, DC: Government Printing Office.

Unnevehr, L. J., and M. L. Stanford, 1985. "Technology and the Demand for Women's Labor in Asian Rice Farming." Pp. 1–20 in *Women in Rice Farming*. Manila, Philippines: International Rice Research Institute.

Visser, Margaret. 1986. *Much Depends on Dinner*. New York: Collier Books.

Walker, Alice. 1986. "Everyday Use." Pp. 1461–1469 in *The Norton Anthology of Short Fiction,* edited by R. V. Cassill. New York: W. W. Norton.

_____. 1991. "Why Did the Balinese Chicken Cross the Road?" Pp. 206–209 in *Sisters of the Earth,* edited by Lorraine Anderson. New York: Vintage Books.

Ward, Kathryn. 1990. *Women Workers and Global Restructuring.* Ithaca: Industrial and Labor Relations Press.

Warren, Kristin, Robert G. Lee, and Matthew S. Carroll. 1992. "Timber-Dependent Communities in Crisis: Assessing the Roles and Reactions of Rural Women." Paper presented at Rural Sociological Society Meeting, Columbus, Ohio, August 21.

Wasserstrom, Robert F., and Richard Wiles. 1985. *Field Duty: U.S. Farmworkers and Pesticide Safety.* Washington, D.C.: World Resources Institute.

Weatherwax, Paul. 1923. *The Story of the Maize Plant.* Chicago: University of Chicago Press.

Wenger, Morton G., and Pem Davidson Buck. 1988. "Farms, Families and Superexploitation: An Integrative Reappraisal." *Rural Sociology* 53(4):460–472.

Werlhof, Claudia von. 1988. "Women's Work: The Blind Spot in the Critique of Political Economy." In *Women: The Last Colony,* edited by M. Mies, V. Bennholdt-Thomsen, and C. von Werlhof. London: Zed.

Whatmore, Sarah. 1991. *Farming Women: Gender, Work, and Family Enterprise.* London: Macmillan.

_____. 1993. "On Doing Rural Research (or Breaking the Boundaries)." *Environment and Planning* 25(5):605–607.

Whitener, Leslie, and Janet Bokemeier. 1992. "Moonlighting in Rural America." *Rural Development Perspectives* 8(1): 27–31.

Wolf, Margery. 1985. *Revolution Postponed: Women in Contemporary China.* Stanford: Stanford University Press.

World Bank. 1990. *Vietnam Stabilization and Structural Reforms.* Washington, DC: World Bank.

Zita, Jacqueline. 1989. "The Feminist Question of the Science Question in Feminism." *Hypatia* 3(1):158–169.

_____. 1990. "Lesbian Body Journeys: Desire Making Differences." Pp. 327–345 in *Lesbian Philosophies and Cultures,* edited by Jeffner Allen. Albany: State University of New York Press.

About the Book and Author

Applying a feminist and environmentalist approach to her investigation of how the changing global economy affects rural women, Carolyn Sachs focuses on land ownership and use, cropping systems, and women's work with animals in highly industrialized as well as developing countries.

Viewing rural women's daily lives in a variety of circumstances, Sachs analyzes the rich multiplicity of their experiences in terms of their gender, class, and race. Drawing on historical and contemporary research, rural women's writings, and in-depth interviews, she shows how environmental degradation results from economic and development practices that disadvantage rural women. In addition, she explores the strategies women use for resistance and survival in the face of these trends.

Offering a range of examples from different countries, *Gendered Fields* will appeal to readers interested in commonalities and differences in women's knowledge of and interactions with the natural environment.

Carolyn E. Sachs is associate professor of rural sociology and women's studies at Pennsylvania State University. She is the author of *Invisible Farmers: Women in Agricultural Production*.

Index